A VOICE AT THE WORKPLACE

By the same author

THE POLITICS OF CHANGE

A VOICE AT THE WORKPLACE

Reflections on Colonialism and the Jamaican Worker

MICHAEL MANLEY

ANDRE DEUTSCH

First published 1975 by
André Deutsch Limited
105 Great Russell Street London WC1

Printed in Great Britain by
Tonbridge Printers Ltd
Peach Hall Works
Tonbridge Kent

ISBN 0 233 96719 2

To the workers of Jamaica

CONTENTS

INTRODUCTION

THIS book's most important quality is its authenticity. The author, Michael Manley, is totally at home with his subject and has chosen to be frank with his readers about the most controversial aspect of Jamaican public life – trade unionism. He has written an honest account of his twenty years in the trade union movement. Though the bulk of the story is told in a series of episodes, this book is by no means anecdotal. At every stage the episodes which Manley describes are placed in the context of his trade union philosophy. It is obvious that he thought a great deal about what he was doing while he was doing it. His exposure to every facet of Jamaican society has led him to recognise the uniqueness of our situation and to formulate in an original way the meaning of our experience. The result is that whatever one may think of Manley or his career, his book rings true.

One consequence of this honesty is that it may subject Manley's career to the criticism of those who have been neither as successful nor as honest. Those of us who have sat with him on the workers' side of the table know that it is a price he will be willing to pay. Every practitioner in the field of trade unionism can make use of this book. It is amazing how very little scholars or journalists know or have chosen to reveal about trade unionism in Jamaica. At the same time trade unionists have usually been far too busy to write themselves. Manley is to be congratulated for finding the time, while Prime Minister, to write the first comprehensive account of industrial relations in Jamaica.

If Michael Manley's book were a mere recounting of the basic facts of his career as a trade unionist in Jamaica, it would still be useful. We remember that when we started our careers as trade unionists there were virtually no printed sources to which to refer for even the most elementary facts about the history or structure of industrial relations in

Jamaica. Now the new union delegate or organiser will have at his disposal a book which will save him years of learning through practical experience. However, this book does more than narrate facts. Although ostensibly it is simply the story of Michael Manley's career as a trade unionist, in the course of telling this story Manley makes a serious contribution to the understanding of our recent past. As such it will inform the new generation of Jamaican workers who must build the kind of union movement capable of playing its full part in the now urgently needed transformation of our society. In so doing they will be well advised to understand our recent past and to build on the solid foundations that have been left by their predecessors.

What then does this book tell us of the achievements of the recent past? What are the foundations laid by our predecessors, on which we must build?

The National Workers Union insisted on democracy at the place of work as the cornerstone of organisation and, as a result, was able to modify the employer-employee relationship on a far wider range of issues than any authoritarian union could have achieved. Furthermore, at the intellectual level, the NWU led by Manley mounted a sustained attack on all those ideological assumptions of employers, largely inherited from colonialism and slavery, which made them regard workers as vastly inferior to themselves in every way. These assumptions tended to pervade the society as a whole and substantially undermined the self-confidence of the working class. But once these assumptions had been undermined, it became much more difficult for employers to treat workers like chattels rather than like human beings. For one thing, the employer's belief in his own superiority as a person was shaken. For another, the self-esteem which the worker acquired made him a far tougher combatant, far less deferential, far more capable of resisting the blandishments of paternal employers.

Manley tells us that Jamaica inherited an extremely vicious class system from the British through the agency of capitalism and its ally colonialism. Down to the nineteen fifties, despite the events of 1938 and after, worker resistance was unorganised, unsystematic and concerned only with the most glaring abuses of the employer's power. Manley understood that the arbitrary power of the employer could not be curbed by anything less than a coherent, persistent and sustained attack on his economic power and his ideological assumptions. The attack could only be coherent and sustained if it relied on careful, systematic and detailed organisation at the place of work. This level of organisation was only feasible if it relied on democratic decision-making at the place of work. Sporadic and spontaneous protest needed only the flamboyance of a Bustamante. But this kind of protest had achieved all it was going to achieve by the fifties. The authoritarianism in the union movement which had gone with the charisma of Bustamante would never sustain a worker's spirit over long periods or on any but the most outrageous of moral issues.

To the ideological attack and the democratic, systematic organisation the NWU, again under Manley's leadership as Island Supervisor, added a sophistication of technique in the mechanics of collective bargaining previously unknown in Jamaica. The use of cost of living indices, the careful study of company accounts, the introduction of welfare benefits into contracts, the careful planning and timing of strikes: all these were pioneered by the NWU. It is not a negligible part of Manley's achievement that other unions have now adopted these techniques.

By the nineteen seventies, at the end of Manley's career as a trade unionist, the Jamaican working class was represented in the economic market place by a trade union movement which was effective and viable within certain spheres. Conscious of his class and not simply a victim of his place in the class structure, the Jamaican worker was capable through his trade union, of increasing his income, protecting his job, securing certain social benefits and defending his dignity as a worker at the place of work. This achievement to which all the trade unions in Jamaica have contributed was the more remarkable because it was accomplished in the face of a consistently high level of unemployment. Michael Manley, whether as advocate, organiser, or charismatic leader, played the most important part in developing the movement as a whole. His account of the last twenty years of trade union history is an extremely well written, absorbing, and intellectually stimulating narrative enriched by ideas and quickened by the pace of unfolding events. It is a difficult book to put down.

Moreover, the book not only illuminates the past but lights the way to the future which the movement must now take. Michael Manley tells us that the trade union movement 'failed certainly up to 1972, to achieve an effective level of organisation concerned with the total life of the worker' as a citizen. This was the consequence he argues of an 'intense union rivalry which was endemic, dissipated energy, squandered scarce resources and led to an unhealthy preoccupation with the question: Which of the competing unions offered the best representation to the workers at the workplace? He suggests that 'union people tended to think that the worker's total life was not the union's concern because somehow the political party to which the union was affiliated would look after that broader aspect of things.

The lesson for the future is therefore clear. The advancement of the worker's total life interests cannot be achieved at the level of the workplace, though it must be firmly based upon that. Workers cannot take it for granted that political parties will take care of their interests, though unions must work through political parties. It is the task of the trade union movement of the future, therefore, to develop that form of organisation, with a broader base than the workplace, which can have the most fundamental effect on our political parties and other political institutions. Workers, through their unions, must become strong in relation to their numbers within political parties. Only in this way can they take their political future and their full development as citizens into their own hands.

No party but a socialist party will accommodate workers in this way. No party which does not base itself unambiguously on the working class can sustain a socialist faith, however deeply held. Only socialism can serve the broader interests of workers. It therefore follows that no union can advance these broader interests except through a socialist party. Unions which rival each other over representation at the place of work for the sake of rivalry and to the exclusion of any consideration of how they may serve the broader interests of workers, do not serve their members and do not advance socialism. Michael Manley as President of the People's National Party has renewed that Party's commitment to socialism. The trade union movement as a whole must take its cue from that.

Carlyle Dunkley
Leighton Holness

PREFACE

This book attempts to portray three things in particular: class attitudes in Jamaica; the struggle by Jamaican workers to achieve rights, status and ultimately responsible freedom at the workplace; and my own observation of the first and involvement in the second.

The interaction between class attitudes and the workers' movement within a colonial and immediate post-colonial framework is basic to the understanding of modern Jamaican, and probably Caribbean, development. Political, social and economic institutions have all been influenced by the, as yet, unresolved tensions of the class structures which were bequeathed to us by the kind of bastard capitalist system which was the peculiar creation of nineteenth and twentieth century colonialism.

Indeed, in the quest for a viable basis for nationhood, class is to the Caribbean what tribalism is to independent, black Africa: the equation of the past which must be resolved if we are to build the future upon reliable institutional foundations.

My hope is that this book may, in some small way, help Jamaicans to look at themselves, or perhaps more accurately, look within themselves, particularly where they meet each other at the workplace. In the process it may also be of use to others who feel themselves constrained by those invisible but terrible bars which form the prison of class within a society.

My thanks are due to Rex Nettleford, Carlyle Dunkley, Leighton Holness and Corina Meeks for much help with ideas and editing; to Barbara Mowatt, Betty Dufour, assisted by Carmen Gauntlett and Scherrie Gopie, from time to time, for typing; to all the officers, organisers, office staff, delegates and members of the National Workers Union of Jamaica for all their help, loyalty, support, solidarity, courage and, above all, comradeship during twenty great years, and since; and to my wife Beverley, who continues to encourage me to set down my thoughts and observations in an act of faith that goes beyond the call of duty.

M.M.
Jamaica, November 1974.

1
COMING EVENTS

In December of 1951 I returned to Jamaica. However, nothing in the purpose or circumstances of my return could have led anyone to believe that within a year I would be becoming more and more involved in the trade union movement. I had just finished a period of six years in England during which I had to explore the first approaches to adult commitment. I trod obvious paths which led to conventional achievements like a Bachelor of Science (Economics) degree at the London School of Economics majoring in government. But I had managed to tread them in an unconventional way. After a year of economics I had spent more time at the Royal Albert and Wigmore Halls listening to music, and at the National and Tate Galleries looking at art than with the pages of Mr Benham's exceptionally conservative introduction to the discipline of economics. I came to the conclusion that this was not for me and that my real calling lay in the arena of art criticism. It may have been a delusion, but I was sure that I was more comfortable with the late chamber music of Beethoven than with the theory of diminishing returns. Certainly, there was a period when I found cubist painting less mysterious than elasticity of demand. I was later to discover that the problem was not one of mystery so much as boredom. For a year, at least, I doubted whether mine would be a life style to which economic theory could contribute much, if anything. Even now, twenty-seven years later, I would not swear that I had found a confident answer.

So, after a year, which some would have dismissed as unconstructive but which I found vastly stimulating, I decided to switch to the faculty of arts. I discovered that this required Latin to Intermediate Bachelor of Arts standard which was a pity since mine had never got beyond 'amo, amas, amat'. I then spent an improbable six months in a remote Cornish village taking Latin to intermediate standard by correspondence course. Three results attended this effort. In order of importance they were: the birth of my first child, my daughter, Rachel; a credit in Latin; and a conviction on the part of the villagers that I was a spy from 'foreign parts'. This last was probably occasioned by my habit of going for long jogs at dusk in a black turtle-neck sweater past the deserted shafts of ancient tin mines. It did not occur to the villagers that St Agnes was hardly the scene of anything that a foreign power would seek to discover.

Having got my Latin and my acceptance at another college in the University of London complex, I promptly changed my mind and decided that the economics and government degree was relevant after all. I think a big factor in this reversal, which was not actually as arbitrary and whimsical as it must have seemed at the time, was my involvement in the West Indian Students Union which was then an infant organisation bringing together students from the English-speaking Caribbean in an environment that was certainly alien though not yet hostile. Throughout my youth there had been a certain duality of interest between the world of politics, as it began to unfold in a colonial territory with a growing appetite for freedom, and the world of the arts to which I had been exposed from infancy. My first recollection of my mother, for example, is of the smell and feel and sight of mahogany chips from her sculpture. Equally, one of my early recollections of my father relates to the long night conferences which he used to hold when he was planning the launching of Jamaica Welfare Limited, the first major attempt at organised social welfare in rural Jamaica in the 1930s. The social, economic and political explosion of 1938 took place when I was thirteen and intensely aware of a father who helped to negotiate the wage settlements for Kingston dockers while my mother, along with other great women like Aggie Bernard, organised the feeding of the strikers. Before my fourteenth birthday the People's National Party was formed by my father at a time when people like Sir Alexander Bustamante were to be found amongst the early members. By then some of the fundamental commitments of my life had begun to emerge. First amongst these is a completely instinctive attachment to the notion of equality. From as far back as I can remember,

I have challenged the view that any person is inherently superior to any other person. From a very early age I was able to make the philosophical distinction between inherent worth and natural talent and to conclude that any advantage enjoyed by one person over another should never exist in spite of or at the expense of the worth and rights of another, but should only reflect legitimate differences in talent and application as they emerge in a context of equal opportunity. Equally, from very early I tended to passionate commitment. I was never able to accept the easy distinction between commitment and behaviour which is the hallmark of the relaxed soul who saunters through life undisturbed by the contradictions that surround us all.

These personality traits and the tendency to strong conviction were allied to a somewhat intemperate spirit. This had led by the age of eighteen to a regrettable but perhaps prophetic contretemps. In my last year at school, Jamaica College, a new headmaster had arrived, bursting with intentions which I am sure upon reflection must have been good. Unfortunately, the new arrival had a completely different value system than that to which I had grown accustomed. Worse yet, he was only twenty-eight and as strong-willed as I. Within a month, confrontation, which was as inevitable as the clash between freedom and imperialism, had taken place. He was a sincere, dedicated young Englishman representing at that time probably the finest and, as it turned out, last stage in the evolution of those who bore 'the white man's burden' around the world. Although the quarrel was not articulated in these terms, it was implied throughout. I did not regard myself as any man's burden. In any case, we could not agree upon the fundamental question of rights. It is true that the rights involved were really very trivial, turning around questions like whether prefects should be allowed certain privileges and whether the Junior Boarding School should be allowed to visit the neighbouring Hope Botanical Gardens every Sunday afternoon. But to both of us they seemed terribly important and so one thing led to another until the final clash when I forestalled his obvious intention to expel me by leaving of my own free will. I packed my bags and left the school the same afternoon and my departure sparked an immediate explosion in which the whole school went on strike in protest for a fortnight. Since then, I have been quite wrongly credited with anticipating my later career by organising the strike. I fear that no such credit is due as the strike was a genuinely spontaneous affair which reflected the fact that the new headmaster and I, in an entirely unarticulated way, were symbols of the new tension which was impelling Jamaica towards freedom.

The events at Jamaica College in the early part of 1943 clearly foreshadowed and anticipated much of my later life. The truth is that I have always been an activist. In fact, someone once remarked of me that I was one of those people with whom 'to think is to act'. By 1947 when I had hurdled the obstacle of Latin, West Indians at London University, Oxford, Cambridge and other seats of learning were all increasingly caught up in the tide of nationalism that was sweeping the colonial world. In those days, the commitment to justice expressed itself in the thrust for freedom. Obviously, there could be no ultimate justice for men in the colonial situation. Equally, students from the many Caribbean Islands and Belize (British Honduras as it then was) and Guyana (British Guiana as it then was) were discovering their common ties. These expressed themselves in a very real cultural affinity, and a shared history of displacement, of populations that had come from Africa, India, China, the Middle East and of course the British Isles. We were beginning to explore an intellectual middle ground that could connect ancient sources with the contemporary reality of a common cricket team. The West Indian Students Union was the activist forum within which all this could come together; it provided for each of us a means of mutual defence in a strange land together with a preparation for the immediate struggle for freedom and the later task of re-making colonial society.

The decision to revert to economics was really an inner, unspoken response to a call to arms. The truth is that the activist egalitarian of strong conviction and impatient ways could not be contained for a life time by the analysis, however fascinating, of the factors that led Picasso and Braque to go their separate ways.

As fate would have it, my period as an executive member

of the West Indian Students Union was marked by another strike. This time I did play an active part and was, in fact, one of the principal organisers. This was the strike at the Hans Crescent Students Hostel, a hostel provided by the Colonial Office of the British Government for West Indian students. The conditions were deplorable. We made many protests. These were ignored. And so we struck. The formula is less than unique. The result was predictable. The then Secretary of State for the Colonies met a deputation, concessions were made on both sides and a certain measure of improvement could be detected when the smoke of battle had blown away. I was intensely involved in the dispute even though I did not then, nor after, live at Hans Crescent myself. This also may have been a pointer in the wind. At the time, however, it had for me no particular significance beyond being a situation about which I felt intensely because it seemed that people's rights were being ignored.

In due course, I collected my degree, did a year's post-graduate work looking at comparative forms of government in the Caribbean but decided that research was not for me.

At this point I decided to become a political journalist. I say 'political' deliberately. I had no doubt in my mind that the main focus of interest for me was politics: not in the sense of the partisan quest for power so much as in the sense of a commitment to certain ideas about society coupled with a desire to play a part in the general assault upon those things which I felt stood between people and elementary social justice. Many people have assumed that all this was the probable product of my association with my father and my experience as a student of Harold Laski. Unquestionably these were very powerful influences. But I have always been a fiercely independent person with a stubborn determination to travel my own route to my own conclusions. Perhaps one day I will explore the psychology of the relationship between a son and an overwhelmingly gifted father in a small community. For now, suffice it to say that all my youth was dominated by a total loyalty to and love of my parents coupled with a fierce, unending quest for independence. By the end of the triumphant West Indian cricket tour of 1950, during which time I must have seen half the matches, shared in full measure the nationalist exultation in the result, and made three lasting friendships, with those great cricketers Allan Rae, Alf Valentine, and Everton Weeks, which I continue to cherish, I was reluctant to go home. I launched out on a moderately successful career as a freelance journalist with the BBC doing all sorts of odd things ranging from discussion which I imagined to be learned about the prospects of Federation for the West Indies, to descriptions which I strove to make vivid of Olympic runner, Arthur Wint, scoring triumph after triumph at the White City Stadium.

At no stage did it even cross my mind that I might spend the next twenty years of my life as a trade unionist. In fact, I was extremely shy and had never made any kind of speech either on a public or social occasion in my life. It may well be that I thought of journalism as a way of expressing my instinct for political activism, because it seemed to side-step the problem of having to speak in public which, by the time I was twenty-seven had become an almost obsessive fear. When an offer came from the distinguished, progressive weekly newspaper, *Public Opinion*, to join their staff as an associate editor, I jumped at it. It was towards this occupation that I headed on the *Queen Mary* in early December of 1951. Needless to say, it is, somehow not a part of my life style or experience to have had an uneventful crossing. We ran into the worst Atlantic storm in a decade and were forced by mountainous seas to crawl for most of the journey. We arrived in New York four days late, but in one piece, and in due course I was having my first Christmas at home since I had left to join the Canadian Air Force in 1943.

Public Opinion had been formed in 1937 by O. T. Fairclough and H. P. Jacobs. A weekly paper, it set out to be nationalist, progressive and anti-Establishment. Within a year of its birth, though not on account of this event, modern Jamaica was to be born in the great labour upheavals which swept the island, and most of the Caribbean in 1938. By 1952 the paper, though still financially insecure, had become a major institution of the progressive movement.

Bright and early on the first working Monday of January of that year, I reported to work. It was a very exciting time so far as the paper was concerned. The editor, Fred Wilmot, was Canadian born of a famous Jamaican family from the parish of St Ann. He was a creative journalist, a hard worker and a very sincere editor who really wanted the paper to become both good in a journalistic sense and hard hitting and constructive in a political sense. His wife, Cynthia, was a very talented columnist with strong radical commitments and a sharp eye for hypocrisy in general and political humbug in particular. They were a very exciting pair to work with. At the same time the publisher of the newspaper who was also the general manager, was that very remarkable and unusual Jamaican, O. T. Fairclough. He was a man of deep, nationalist commitment but something in an early exposure to Haiti together with a probably unconscious bourgeois caution made him uneasy in the presence of radical innovation. A man of enormous energy and dedication, Fairclough had kept this improbable, radical weekly alive since 1937. Its survival was a financial miracle and its future always uncertain. My salary was twelve pounds a week. There were no allowances. My duties were varied. I wrote one or two editorials each week, covered stories, worked on features, handled lay-out and generally managed the sports and features pages. And I wrote a column, 'The Root of the Matter', in which I commented upon just about every aspect of Jamaican life. Inevitably, however, politics provided the main focus for the column.

By a curious historical coincidence, the very first column that I ever wrote in that same January, 1952, was called 'High Wind in South Africa' and was devoted to an examination of apartheid and called for a Jamaican and world attitude of repudiation and action. It predicted that apartheid would lead Africa inevitably to bloodshed. Twenty-one years after writing that article I was privileged to make a speech at a Third World Summit Conference in Algiers in which I renewed the summons to activist concern and offered to organise Jamaican volunteers for the struggle in Southern Africa, if it were felt that they could help.

In 1952, local politics held the greatest part of my attention. The modern Jamaican scene has been dominated since 1942 by the fact that there are two major and entrenched political parties. At the time of the labour uprisings in 1938,

Jamaica was a Crown Colony. There was a legislative council to which fourteen members were elected from each of the parishes of the island. However, this election was held on the basis of a severely limited franchise. One had to be a property owner paying taxes of a certain value to have a vote. As a consequence only some 69,000 persons had a vote in 1938 by comparison with an adult population of some 1,160,000. In any event, the state of the franchise hardly mattered since the legislative council had no real power in the crucial matter of policy formulation, being more or less advisory in function. The real power was exercised by the British Government through a governor chosen in Whitehall and appointed by the British monarch. The island's economy at the time was dominated by the sugar industry and a smaller but growing banana industry. There was a large rural peasantry which was confined mainly to the mountainous hinterland to which freed slaves had fled in 1838. Each year tens of thousands of these people would descend from the mountains and hills to take seasonal jobs cutting and loading cane on the great sugar estates which occupied all the best flat lands on the plains. There was little indigenous industry and most of the rest of the island's economic activity consisted of a commercial superstructure which imported nearly everything that the island consumed. This pattern of one or two major agricultural exports dominating production and paying for a wide range of imports from an industrialised 'mother country' was the common effect of the colonial system. Indeed, it had become the very badge of colonialism.

Before 1938 there was no trade union movement and no effective political organisation. The mass of the people were poor and virtually without hope. Agricultural wages were low and peasant farming, condemned as it was to poor hillside land and bereft of organised credit, marketing or transportation facilities, unprofitable. The merchant and sugar estate owning classes were comfortable if not spectacularly rich. A small but well defined, professional middle class existed secure in economic terms but socially divided from and uneasy with the masses, on the one hand, and excluded on the other, from the society of the merchants and the big landowners. It was only a matter of time before this situation was bound to blow up. The explosion came in late 1938 when trouble flared on the Kingston waterfront and quickly spread to the sugar estates. In no time there was a general state of civil disorder and a number of deaths as the police began shooting in the attempt to restore order. By the end of that year, when the dust of civil commotion had settled for the time being, two institutions which were to shape modern Jamaica between them had been born. Firstly, the labour unrest had given birth to a trade union movement which was, in due course, to make Jamaica one of the most highly unionised of all the young countries which were later to form the membership of the Third World. The main organisation of the new trade union movement was the Bustamante Industrial Trade Union. This had been formed and named after the main hero of the national uprising, William Alexander Bustamante.

Secondly, in the political field, the People's National Party emerged as the island's first formal political institution and was dedicated to the attainment of independence and nationhood for Jamaica. The PNP was also committed to work for the social and economic reconstruction of the island. To this end, it had by the early 1940s, formally adopted democratic socialism as its political philosophy. Its founder was my father, Norman Washington Manley. These two men, Bustamante and Manley, were to dominate Jamaica public life for the next thirty years.

During the years 1937, 1938 and 1939, a number of small unions were formed representing special worker groups. But the BITU, which started out as a blanket organisation catering for all worker groups, was comparatively dominant on the labour scene. In 1938 it won a settlement for dock workers in Kingston and by 1939 was spoiling for a more general fight. In the meantime, the PNP was organising groups all over the island. Bustamante joined the PNP and the PNP supported the unions in general and the BITU in particular. All seemed well set for a massive popular movement on the political and union fronts. Then suddenly in 1939 everything was changed.

After a nearly disastrous general strike which was attempted by the BITU in that year, a trade union advisory council was formed in an attempt to bring some measure of order and unity to trade union development. Soon after, however, Bustamante pulled the BITU out of the Trade Union Advisory Council, resigned from the People's National Party and embarked upon a general programme of denunciation of everything and everybody. All the other unions that had formed the Trade Union Advisory Council became affiliated to the People's National Party and so was born the historic split in the trade union movement of Jamaica in which one part allied itself to an ideologically conservative movement headed by Bustamante and the other half allied itself to an ideologically progressive movement headed by Manley. In due course, the Trade Union Advisory Council was consolidated in the Trades Union Congress which was later (in 1948) to be transformed into a blanket union on structural lines not unlike the BITU. In 1943, Bustamante was to form a political party, the Jamaica Labour Party. The Jamaica Labour Party was based primarily on the union in organisational terms. Ideologically conservative Bustamante was bitterly opposed to socialism. Paradoxically, Jamaican politics became polarised around a political party based on a union, the Jamaica Labour Party, which was conservative; and a Nationalist Party, the People's National Party, which was radical progressive and was also to become union based.

Soon after this, Jamaica was to get a new constitution based on adult suffrage and providing a measure of responsible government. A first election in 1944 was swept by Bustamante's newly formed Jamaica Labour Party. In 1949 a second election was narrowly won by Bustamante with a minority of the popular vote. By that time the BITU had become a sprawling giant and the other unions had merged into a major, rival blanket organisation of their own, the Trades Union Congress, affiliated to the People's National Party.

At the time of my start with *Public Opinion* in 1952, Bustamante's JLP was half way through its second term of office, controlling the House of Representatives 18–14. However, although the People's National Party was in opposition, it was dominating the island's political news at that time. This happened because the attention of the whole island was focused upon a struggle that was going on inside the People's National Party led by my late father who was then

Leader of the Opposition. A tremendous internal struggle of considerable complexity had been fluctuating, now threatening, now dormant for years. This struggle was partly ideological arising from the conflict between the Marxist convictions of a small group led by Richard Hart, the radical-activist, and the somewhat less than Marxist outlook of a trade union faction led by the brothers Ken and Frank Hill, and the more moderate views of certain elements of both the political party and the trade union movement which were led respectively by Wills O. Isaacs and Florizel Glasspole. As is often the case, it is difficult to distinguish between ideological differences, activist styles and the personality conflicts that arise in a political movement. Sometimes these problems can be traced to the relationship between personality and power, where the true nature of the quarrel is masked by ideological differences which are more imagined than real. Sometimes, on the other hand, potential leaders dislike each other because they cannot bring themselves to respect each other's views. I was not in Jamaica during all the years in which the difficulties between the Hart group, the Hill group and the Isaacs/Glasspole group were simmering. I arrived in Jamaica at the moment when everything came to the boil. Hence, it is hard for me to judge how much of the difficulty stemmed from problems of personality, how much can be attributed to differences of style, and how much reflected genuine ideological conflicts. In the fullness of time the historians will deal with that.

Unquestionably, the PNP which had always proclaimed itself to be socialist, was suffering to some extent, from the problems of definition that sometimes attach to that commitment. Richard Hart interpreted socialism along Marxist lines and made no bones about it. Ken Hill, who was the President of the Trades Union Congress, and, by 1951, the Mayor of Kingston, made common cause with Hart although not publicly proclaiming himself a Marxist. Wills Isaacs was the Opposition member of Parliament for Central Kingston, the seat which I now hold, and proclaimed himself opposed to Marxist socialism and, therefore, opposed to Hart and Hill. Florizel Glasspole was the General Secretary of the TUC and made common cause with Wills Isaacs. In due course this led to a series of power struggles within the party with one or the other side in the ascendancy from year to year until the whole thing came to a head shortly before my return to Jamaica in 1951. I arrived to find the party engaged in a formal investigation into charges brought by the so-called right wing against the so-called left wing. Night after night, discussions would take place at my father's home between the three enquirers who were Noel Nethersole, the First Vice-President of the party and Member of Parliament for Central St Andrew, Vernon Arnett, the General Secretary of the party and himself. Many hours of hearings were conducted at the Party Leader's Duke Street law office. In due course in a wrenching, traumatic scene at the Ward Theatre in downtown Kingston, the party voted to confirm a finding and recommendation of the Tribunal of Enquiry that Ken Hill, Frank Hill, Richard Hart and their associate, Arthur Henry, be expelled for activities contrary to the constitution and purpose of the party and that the Trade Union Congress be disaffiliated. The party voted to uphold this decision and so a new phase of Jamaica's political development commenced.

The PNP had always regarded trade union work as an integral part of the movement. The traditional union arm, the TUC, was now lost since it was dominated by the Hills.

Therefore, in April 1952, it was decided to launch the National Workers Union. Nethersole was the provisional President, AGS 'Father' Coombs, Member of Parliament for North St James and a labour leader of pre-'38 days, was named Vice-President, Florizel Glasspole, the Member of Parliament for Eastern Kingston, and the former General Secretary of the TUC, was named the General Secretary, and Ken Sterling, the All Island Organiser of the People's National Party, was named the Island Supervisor.

This was a rough time for the People's National Party. The TUC forces, led by Ken Hill, moved quickly to form a political party of their own, the National Labour Party. A significant attempt was made to run the PNP off the streets of Kingston. The party had been badly hurt because Ken Hill had become a symbol of the hope for change with the masses of Kingston and the ideological problems which were the proximate cause of the difficulty were not easy for the masses to understand.

This was a time, therefore, that called for action if the PNP were to be held together and the fledgeling NWU built into a viable Union organisation. The whole party machine went into action. My father characteristically challenged the Kingston threat head-on, helped by brilliant organisational work by Arnett and many stirring speeches by Wills Isaacs. He led the party back to complete control of the Kingston streets, though not before some anxious moments had been endured and survived.

The new National Workers Union with Glasspole and Sterling as its active leaders, began to make headway beginning with a gas station in Cross Roads but soon moving on to significant conquests as they captured places like Cable and Wireless Ltd., the Bybrook Milk Condensery, the mental hospital at Bellevue, the Customs Department and other government groups, and so on, from the TUC. Some of these successes were due to the natural political loyalty of the groups concerned, some were due to the fact that sections of the old TUC had been serviced by Glasspole and so naturally crossed over to join him in the new organisation; and some were due to brilliant organisational work particularly by Sterling in his new role as Island Supervisor.

In all this, I felt that the contribution that I could make, aged twenty-eight, and totally new to the scene, was to offer my services as a speaker at group functions throughout vital areas of Kingston and St Andrew. The capital city was vital to the survival of the People's National Party. It was always the heart-land of PNP strength but had also been the scene of Ken Hill's greatest popularity. This was a peculiarly agonising decision for me because of my personal difficulties about speaking. However, when my first invitation came to address a group in Eastern Kingston, I realised that I was at a crossroads in my life, took a deep breath and accepted the invitation. That was in late January 1952. The invitation came from the Patriot Group in Eastern Kingston and it was a very challenging first occasion because they were in a very uneasy relationship with their Member of Parliament, Florizel Glasspole. The majority of the group were Ken Hill supporters caught in a problem of institutional loyalty since they were a part of the Eastern Kingston Party machine. It was into this complex situation that I was thrown, having discovered the facts after I had accepted the invitation. Characteristically this aspect of the matter worried me far less than the sheer fact that I was going to make my first speech. I very nearly never made it. In the end, having eaten nothing since the night before, and bolstered by a half tumbler of neat rum I arrived at the Patriot Group at around 8.30 p.m. in a state that bordered upon abject terror. My speech was distinguished mainly for the fact that it had not occurred to me that you have to work out an ending. After I had said all the things for which I had elaborately prepared myself for at least two weeks, I suddenly realised that I did not know how to bring it all to a close.

I remember stumbling through a series of sentences each more desperately disconnected from the main theme than the one before, as I searched for a climax. None came and in the end I astonished my audience by sitting down in the middle of a sentence which didn't seem to begin in any particular place and was certainly proceeding in no discernible direction. The applause that followed sometime later stemmed, I suspect, more from sympathy than admiration.

However, once launched it seemed there was no turning back. In the course of that first year, I addressed over a hundred meetings and was duly elected to the National Executive and the Central Executive Committee of the party. There may be some who feel that I owed this success to my relationship with my father. Doubtless this played its part. But I think that I also earned my place by sheer hard work. In addition to speaking as often as three and four times a week, I had formed a new group of the party in Barbican, my father's constituency, and was running quite a tight little political ship with all of twenty-three members.

During this period the fledgeling NWU quite early asked me to come to one of their branch meetings to give a lecture. The section was the Mental Hospital Workers and I duly made my speech in a school hall near the hospital. Although I was extremely nervous of speaking, I had gained a little confidence and had certainly learnt to work out in advance how to bring a speech to a close. I remember finding it a fascinating challenge to think of a speech for a trade union group for the first time in my life. Up to then I had been an egalitarian concerned with political categories such as social justice, independence, democracy and the like. I had never specifically addressed my mind to the question of how all these imperatives related to the worker in his working situation and in relation to his employer. There is no record of what I said and I must confess that I don't really remember. However, it must have gone reasonably well because the invitations began to come steadily after that.

Later in that first year, perhaps around October, an invitation came to address a group of workers in Spanish Town, the capital of the parish of St Catherine, who were employed in a new textile mill which is still the only one of its kind on the island. The company, called the Ariguanabo Textile Mills employed about five or six hundred workers and was owned by a Cuban group of American extraction headed by a Mr James Hedges. The Hedges family were friends and supporters of Colonel Batista and his regime and ran a major textile operation in Cuba. They had set up this mill in Jamaica and the workers had been organised by the TUC while it was still affiliated to the PNP. It had become the scene of a critical extension of the power struggle between the Hills and Glasspole. The new NWU was anxious to capture it and the BITU, sensing its opportunity in this new division, was beginning to organise. The Hills had done such a thorough job of propaganda on Glasspole that it was imprudent to introduce him into the equation. Ken Sterling was too busy trying to establish a new union in the bauxite industry to spare more than occasional attention to this struggle and so Wills Isaacs, although not really a trade unionist, had taken on the job of leading the battle. I do not know through what prescient alchemy he was led to invite me to join the team that was seeking to organise the Ariguanabo Textile Mills. He is an intuitive man with a keen political instinct and perhaps this explains the invitation. However, whatever his reasoning, he did invite me and I accepted. I then became involved in a fascinating struggle in which evening after evening I would go down after finishing my work at *Public Opinion* to address meetings of the Ariguanabo textile workers in Spanish Town. In due course a plant election was in the offing. Then a boiler burst and the plant had to shut down. For a number of weeks there could be no election because there was nobody at work. However, in due course, the boiler was fixed and the workers went back to work and the election was held. The NWU routed both the TUC and the BITU in a success that had a bearing on the future of Jamaica beyond the significance of the immediate contest.

Having won the poll, the union was now responsible to bargain for the workers. The new contract was due to be negotiated but the circumstances were less than encouraging since the mill had already served notice of its future habits by losing money in the first years of its operations. After the poll I had gone back to a more complete concentration on my duties at *Public Opinion* and had resumed addressing PNP groups at nights. I still had not thought of trade unionism as a full-time career although I had found myself intensely involved in the problems of the Ariguanabo workers as an issue entirely separate and apart from the question of who would win the right to try to do something about those problems. All of a sudden one day the phone rang. It was Wills Isaacs. He told me that they had just worked out a claim for wage increases and other fringe benefits for the Ariguanabo workers and were due to hold a first meeting with the management at the Ministry of Labour and would I like to come along. Naturally, I was fascinated at the prospect of sitting in on a trade union negotiation for the first time.

I extricated myself from my journalistic duties for the morning and presented myself at ten o'clock sharp on a morning in March of 1953 at the Ministry of Labour. The management was out in full force under the leadership of Mr Hedges. The union was out in even greater force under the leadership of Mr Wills Isaacs who put me to sit on his left hand. Mr C. Greaves Hill who later became Permanent Secretary of the Ministry of Labour and then became Industrial Relations Manager of the Sugar Manufacturers' Association, presided. Isaacs, with characteristic charm, made an utterly disarming speech about the desire of the union for good relations with the management and how anxious all were that there should now be a period of peace, tranquillity and production. There was, he assured the meeting, a small matter of claims for wage increases and fringe benefits to be dealt with but he was quite confident that between men of eminent sense and infinite good will, these wishes of the workers could be accommodated in no time. However, said Mr Isaacs, he had a rather urgent meeting that he had to attend in Port Antonio, the capital of the parish of Portland. There, a great figure of Jamaican politics, Sir Harold Allan, the Minister of Finance in the Jamaica Labour Party Government, had died. A by-election was about to take place and the Opposition PNP had to choose their candidate. He was due to preside over this operation and so could not spare any more time at the Ministry of Labour. However, said Mr Isaacs, without batting an eye, there was a young man sitting at his left who had been associated with the campaign which had led to the presence of the National Workers Union at the bargaining table. This young man would carry on from there. Thereupon affecting not to notice the stunned silence which had followed this announcement, he excused himself with a broad smile and proceeded to Port Antonio.

To say that I was aghast is to do a disservice to the occasion. I had never seen the claim. I had no idea how to negotiate a claim nor even any idea as to what should happen next. Reaching into some inner reserve of cunning and hoping that nobody would notice the rate of my heart beat, I called for an adjournment. I think Mr Greaves Hill, bless his heart, realised that I had been taken by surprise, and acceded to my request without calling on me to explain why I should need an adjournment at the very beginning of a negotiation. My first task was to read through the claim so that I should have some idea of what it was I was supposed to represent. So I called the delegates outside and hastily read through it. This done, we returned to the table and commenced a negotiation which lasted for several weeks but which resulted in substantial concessions in the field of wage increases and fringe benefits in spite of the heavy losses which the company demonstrated that it had suffered. By the time it was over I knew that this was the arena which suited my egalitarianism, my commitment to social justice and my instinct for activism.

Within a month I was fully involved in the first great strike of the National Workers Union at Alcan Jamaica Ltd., and had discovered something of my physical stamina. I made an agreement with Fairclough and Wilmot which allowed me to undertake part-time trade union and political duties. For many months my schedule went something like this: I would finish my newspaper duties by lunch time, travel to the Alcan strike in the afternoon which involved some fifty miles to Williamsfield in the parish of Manchester. In the late afternoon I would travel back to Kingston and then travel sixty miles in the other direction to the constituency of East Portland where I would speak for the party's candidate, Adrian Gray, at night. We kept this up for several weeks until the strike was settled by the institution of arbitration proceedings and the by-election was settled by a PNP victory.

Shortly after, I was asked to become the Sugar Supervisor of the National Workers Union with the task of organising the NWU in the sugar industry which was, and still is, the largest employer of labour in the Island. This was a particularly fascinating challenge because the Island's sugar workers were among the worst treated and worst paid members of the labour force. They were part of an economic entity that could be traced directly back to slavery and worked in a situation which was still scarred by attitudes which derived from that earlier spiritual and moral desert. As an added inducement, this was a labour scene that had been totally dominated by the BITU since 1938 although the TUC had made a minor incursion in 1951 when they had captured two small estates out of some twenty sugar estates which were then employing upwards of 50,000 workers during reaping time. After the excitement of addressing worker education sessions, the Ariguanabo battle and the epic strike at Alcan, I had no hesitation in accepting the offer. I resigned from *Public Opinion* and although I continued to write my column 'Root of the Matter' for at least another year, I joined the National Workers Union as Sugar Supervisor in August 1953, with a salary of eight pounds a week plus a Hillman Minx car with a loudspeaker system attached to the roof and a travelling and subsistence allowance of seven pounds a week.

2
THE UNION MOVEMENT

AND what of this union movement to which I had committed myself? By the time of my return home in 1951, the movement had become a large and vigorous institution in Jamaican life. Indeed, the records show that on 31 March, 1952 the Bustamante Industrial Trade Union had 64,679 members of which 44,118 were men, 20,561 were women and of which 33,339 were paying members and 31,340 were non-paying members. The same records show that the Trade Union Congress of Jamaica had 26,560 members of which 17,534 were men, 9,026 were women and out of which 10,628 were paying members and 15,932 were non-paying members. The same records would show that there were eight other registered but extremely small or even extinct workers' organisations in Jamaica at that time with a registered membership of 1,306.

The BITU had been formed in 1938 and was the product of the labour uprising of that year and the subsequent era of worker unrest. In every sense of the term this organisation was the creature of its founder, William Alexander Bustamante. By 1938 Bustamante had had an interesting but somewhat erratic career. Born in Hanover, he had spent a period when he was poised between youth and early manhood at the St Catherine farm, Belmont, of his cousins, the Manleys. Thereafter he had had a series of overseas adventures which took him to the police force of Cuba, a short-lived marriage to a Panamanian widow with a period in Panama and thence to the United States and Canada and a second marriage to a Canadian nurse. It is a matter of record that as of 1938 he had not crossed the Atlantic and certainly had never been to Spain; this last being of some interest in the light of an entirely apocryphal story to the effect that he was either of Spanish origin or had been to Spain. In fact, he was born Clarke and took the name Bustamante at some point during his Latin American period. The middle 1930s found him back home and a figure of increasing controversy as an inveterate writer of 'Letters to the Editor' and controversial commentator upon the local scene. By 1938 he was fifty-four years of age and a man of great energy and self-assurance – a potentially charismatic figure. In every sense he was a man in search of a cause and in need of an occasion.

1938 was the year when one hundred years of oppression under the mantle of legal freedom produced its inevitable harvest of rebellion. Emancipation had come to the Jamaican slaves, finally, in 1838. One hundred years later, the legal question apart, it was a moot question as to who was better off, in material terms: the slave of 1838 or the worker of 1938. Throughout the island, labour in the sugar industry was paid an average of a shilling a day; dockers received three shillings and eight pence for an eleven hour work day. The men and women of the banana industry, the thousands in domestic service, in road gangs, indeed workers throughout the economy were no better off. The few attempts which had been made to form trade unions in the early twentieth century had all proved abortive and there seemed no end to the physical and spiritual misery of the working man and woman. As happens so often in history a moment came when the people had had enough. There were riots at Frome, one of the two huge Tate and Lyle estates, situated at the western end of the island.* There was trouble in Kingston and elsewhere, and most importantly, the dockers of the Kingston waterfront went on strike for higher wages. This was Bustamante's chance. He put himself at the head of the uprising and became, at once, its symbol and the channel through which it proclaimed its grievances. Helped by his cousin, Norman Manley, a wage increase was negotiated. Bustamante's career was launched and the BITU was formed. Thousands of workers flocked to the Union which immediately became a vital, symbolic focus for the simple aspirations of a people, brutalised by history and beleaguered by circumstance.

The early years were marked by expectation and turmoil.

*The two Tate and Lyle estates, Frome in the west and Monymusk in the south, were controlled by a subsidiary, the West Indies Sugar Company.

Having regard to Bustamante's temperament and the people's inexperience, it is not surprising that serious organisation was strikingly absent. In 1939 a highly personal incident in Montego Bay* precipitated a Bustamante rage and was followed by an abortive attempt at a general strike. A state of emergency was averted when Manley intervened and persuaded the then Governor, Sir Arthur Richards, to stay his hand provided the Trade Union Advisory Council were formed with the BITU as a member. Bustamante agreed, the Council was formed, the state of emergency averted and a comparative state of normalcy restored. Shortly after, however, Bustamante pulled his union out of the Trade Union Advisory Council and denounced the other emerging trade union leaders. In the meantime he resigned from the People's National Party which had been formed by Manley the previous year and launched a savage, personal attack upon him.

The next couple of years saw a steady growth in the membership of the BITU but very little effective organisation or real achievement. Then came a fateful moment in Jamaica history. Bustamante made a speech in which he attacked the colonial authority. Britain was at war and, as was the way with colonial powers who were at war, a little impatient of criticism. As a result of a drastic misreading of Bustamante's character, the colonial authorities detained him. This was quite remarkable because Bustamante was and is the most conservative of men, passionately loyal to the British monarch, and a stout-hearted defender of the free enterprise system which Britain had bequeathed to its Empire. There was no fundamental respect in which the Bustamante of 1941 posed a threat to the British raj. He was, at that time, a threat to the local vested interests insofar as oppressive treatment of their workers was concerned. However, even at this level, he had shown a greater talent for agitation than for change and certainly had led thousands of sugar workers for upwards of two years without settling down to the hard business of negotiating a wage increase and a first labour contract.

*While visiting the Montego Bay waterfront Bustamante is believed to have been abused by a dock worker. A demand that the worker be disciplined was refused and thereafter one thing led to another as the dispute escalated.

Be all that as it may, the British locked him up and added to the heroic status which he had earned for himself in 1938, a martyrdom which was to stand him in good stead in his later career.

Bustamante's detention on 7 September 1940, triggered a widespread and continuing agitation for his release. On 8 February 1942 this happened. Manley, submerging his own hurt at Bustamante's intemperance and seeming betrayal in 1939, campaigned vigorously for his release. He clearly continued to hope for a unified front between the political and trade union forces aimed at national independence and social justice. While he and others campaigned for Bustamante's release he poured the whole resources of the newly formed People's National Party into the business of keeping the Bustamante Industrial Trade Union alive. There is no doubt that they helped to bring a measure of organisation to the union and in due course, decided that it was time to face up to the issue of a contract for the Island's sugar workers. This led to the great sugar strike in St Thomas in March 1941 and the first negotiated, sugar workers' contract in Jamaica's history. This provided for a general wage increase of approximately 10 per cent and created the original document from which all subsequent action on the labour front of the sugar industry was to flow.

Although this was, when seen in historical perspective, a tremendous achievement, it was characteristic of Bustamante that he should denounce it upon his release in 1943. Thereafter, and for the nine years until my innocent, unheralded and essentially irrelevant arrival on the scene in 1952, the BITU went from strength to strength. The organisation of the sugar workers was completed and many subsequent wage increases and new agreements negotiated. Waterfront workers throughout the Island became members as did those of other agricultural industries and even some of the Island's urban workers. By 1952, the union was firmly established amongst what we might loosely categorise as the agricultural proletariat and unskilled labour in the urban centres. The BITU also commanded considerable allegiance among the women in that huge but amorphous industry which we loosely describe as domestic service. All authority was centralised. No decision could be taken without Bustamante's personal approval. The separate identity of the various groups and types of workers was expressed in the most rudimentary form. If you were a worker at a particular sugar estate you would be on the books as a member of branch number so and so of such and such an estate and your number would be 'X'. This would be duly reflected in your membership card and you would probably have an organiser whose services you shared with a number of other sections and would certainly have a delegate to call your own. But there was no real attempt at that time to create a separate branch structure with clear democratic procedures through which the independent will of the branch could be expressed and the separate needs of the group identified. Rather, the identification was with a large mass of persons who would be sure to get a wage increase in due course and who could probably expect some kind of defence if they were dismissed. By 1952, these workers were undoubtedly very conscious of the existence of a political party, the Jamaica Labour Party, which was headed by their Union President General, Mr Bustamante and knew that they would be expected to vote for him in the next election. There were many voices to jog their memories with the constant reminder that their leader had come forth in defence of their class in 1938 and been to prison in 1940. They had only to listen to him to know that he was a dramatic personality with a completely unconventional platform style and a genius for the articulation of things that seemed to have been drawn from their own innermost thoughts and frustrations. However, they were unlikely to be challenged, individually or collectively, to examine whether there is a purpose to life; nor even to consider whether the union movement should be concerned with wider issues than questions of money and job protection. Inevitably, where goals are so limited, problems are inevitable. If money is one leg of the two-legged creature of progress, then more and more money must be produced if credibility is to survive. Equally, where job security is the only other leg, allegiance will begin to evaporate when a man's job is not threatened and will disappear instantly if the job is lost and not restored. Thus, by 1952, the BITU had come to a critical point in its history. It had grown from strength to strength quantitatively for fourteen years. Now, however, it was beginning to suffer from the internal contradictions which arise when material gain becomes the sole purpose of effort and where there is no wider philosophical purpose to bring consolation should material advance be deferred.

By contrast the Trades Union Congress and hence all that section of the Labour movement which became closely linked with the nationalist and democratic socialist forces of the People's National Party had a completely different genesis. The BITU began as an emotionally appealing but philosophically incoherent protest movement. It came reluctantly to even the most rudimentary recognition of the role of organisation. On the other hand, the TUC began as a series of particular, tightly organised responses by small and easily identified sections of the working classes to their problems in the workplace. In 1937, a year before the great uprisings, the Jamaica Clerks' Association was formed with one Ethelred Erasmus Adolphus Campbell as its titular head and Florizel Augustus Glasspole as its General Secretary and driving force. Later, Campbell was to achieve no particular distinction in the emergent politics of the island but Glasspole was to become the General Secretary of the TUC in 1939, the Member of Parliament for Eastern Kingston in December 1944, the General Secretary of the National Workers Union on 2 April, 1952, the minister of Labour and Leader of the House of Representatives in 1955, the Minister of Education in 1957, the Minister of Education and Leader of the House again in 1972 and the Governor-General of Jamaica on 24 May, 1973.

By 1939 a number of small unions, structurally similar to the Jamaica Clerks' Association had begun to emerge. These included a union for railway workers, for water commission workers and a number of others. It is these bodies which had come together with the BITU in 1939 to form the Trade Union Advisory Council. When Bustamante pulled the BITU out of the advisory council shortly after, the other groups remained as members of the council and were generally orientated towards the People's National Party which was striving to build a national consciousness and to organise the movement behind the idea of self-government and social change in a generally democratic, socialist direction.

It soon became apparent, however, that the BITU was seeking to dominate the trade union field at the expense of any other union operating in the country. This led inevitably to a struggle for survival on the part of the smaller unions of the Trade Union Advisory Council who were in any event bitter about Bustamante's decision to pull out of the council and declare a sort of generalised war against the nationalist movement. There was an interregnum in this war while Bustamante was interned and the Manley forces ran the BITU for him; but upon Bustamante's release in 1943, the BITU's onslaught was resumed and was now taking on almost messianic tones as a consequence of Bustamante's internment. Not long after on 8 July 1943, the Jamaica Labour Party was formed as a political outcropping of the BITU. This added a final political dimension to the BITU crusade for trade union hegemony.

While this power struggle in the union movement was raging with events running very much in favour of the BITU, a parallel political exercise was unfolding under the leadership of the People's National Party and directed towards representative government as the first step on the road to independence. The constitution which provided for universal adult suffrage and a fully elected lower house was promulgated in 1943. The new constitution was the result of Manley's work and organisational pressure both on a personal level and through the growing strength of the People's National Party. But in one of those ironies in which history abounds, Manley was not to be the political beneficiary of the universal adult suffrage for which he fought and in which he so passionately believed. In the first elections of 1944, it was the Jamaica Labour Party which carried the day with twenty-three seats to the PNP's four. Five Independents made up the complement of thirty-two in the House of Representatives. The truth is that Bustamante's union together with his own charismatic personality and capacity to articulate the simple, proximate needs of the mass of the people had carried the day. The union groups of the Trade Union Advisory Council paid the price and entered a period of renewed pressure now that the BITU had the backing of a government of sorts which was the creature of the union's power with the voters.

This was a testing time for the PNP and the Trade Union

Advisory Council groups alike. Manley, Nethersole, Ken and Frank Hill, Glasspole, Dick Hart, Arthur Henry, A. G. S. Coombs, Ivan Lloyd and F. L. B. Evans, Ken Sterling, V. Bancroft Edwards, Osmond Dyce and many others were the heroes of the struggle to survive. Some were operating at the political, and some at the union level, but, more and more, all were involved in a struggle in which normal union and political boundaries were obliterated by the JLP/BITU onslaught. Great strikes were launched and won at the mental asylum, the Gleaner Company (which produced the island's only daily newspaper) the Kingston Bus Company and so on. In due course, as an inevitable response to the logic of events, it occurred to the leaders of the Opposition political party and trade union that there was little to gain and much to lose as a consequence of the form of organisation of the Trade Union Advisory Council union groups. They were in the main clinging to small, separate organisational forms with separate identities. Faced with the problems of duplicated overheads and in a situation where their very survival depended upon the capacity to organise every sympathetic element into a single activisit force, the various PNP orientated unions of the Trade Union Advisory Council decided to amalgamate in a single, mass union which they named the Trade Union Congress. This body adopted a blanket union form which was similar in a number of respects to the BITU in structural terms. However, this group was as politically focused and articulate as the BITU was incoherent. The BITU was, in every sense of the term, an extension of Bustamante and therefore committed to support him regardless of such things as his passionate support of British royalty and the free enterprise system which were coupled with a notable lack of interest in the nationalist call. The TUC, by contrast, declared itself in favour of independence, democratic socialism and the People's National Party as the champion of these causes. In other words the TUC declared its support for a policy and a philosophy and allied itself to a political party that shared these aims. The BITU was loyal to the man who was its Life President, and who happened, incidentally, to be an extremely conservative politician.

Throughout 1950 and 1951, the new TUC began to counter-attack. Substantial gains were made at the expense of the BITU, including small but enormously significant victories in union elections on the two small sugar estates of Worthy Park in the parish of St Catherine and Barnett in the parish of St James. For the first time the hitherto total grip of Bustamante on agricultural labour had been successfully challenged even if it was on a narrow front. Simultaneously, the TUC had begun to build up a formidable presence amongst government workers, at Reynolds Jamaica Mines which was the first bauxite company to go into production, and throughout the ranks of artisans and industrial workers generally. The TUC had also become the dominant force amongst the workers of the light manufacturing industrial sector and the public utilities. Indeed it has been contended that the disposition of union strength as of April 1952 closely paralleled the social structure of the support of the two political parties. Certainly, by 1952, the TUC, though smaller in numbers than the BITU was more articulate, better organised, reflected a more clearly defined role and was becoming almost as much of a felt presence in the society. It is as a consequence of this history that the union could claim on 31 March, 1952 to have 10,628 paying members.

A lot has been said throughout history about the relative merits of the crafts union, the industrial union and the blanket union. The truth is that each represents a response by people to a particular problem at a particular time in a particular situation and having regard to a particular set of ambitions. Crafts unions emerged largely in the nineteenth century as the response of skilled persons to the question of adequate recognition for themselves as specialists in a field. Hence, carpenters and plumbers and metal workers of varying skills have formed unions in different countries at different times as an expression of their practical need for adequate economic reward and, more profoundly, because they needed a sense of pride and identification as plumbers or carpenters or metal workers. In addition, they probably chose this form because they were incapable of expressing a group need in a wider context than could be provided by the familiarity of the immediate occupational group. Perhaps this may be amplified by pointing out that the need for more money in a money economy is a consequence of the pressure of poverty, on the one hand, and the comparative affluence of your neighbour on the other. The desire for more, therefore, is internally driven by need and externally induced by example. Even more directly, this may be expressed as the positive response to basic needs, like hunger, together with the induced appetite for more, such as the bigger refrigerator which your neighbour's wife has just installed. These internal and external factors will create the conditions within which men will seek an institutional means through which they can hope to satisfy both appetites. However, the perception of means involves a far more complex intellectual exercise than the recognition of need. The simplest form of institutional response to the problem is that of the crafts union. This is so because carpenters most easily identify with other carpenters and can conceive of a body of carpenters demanding freedom from hunger on the one hand, and the neighbour's refrigerator on the other, without any particular strain on their understanding of society as a whole. Hence, at a time when the notion of class interest and in particular working-class interest was novel, it is understandable that workers should respond to their inner needs with that simplest of all working-class responses, the crafts union.

In due course, the movement was to discover that this inevitably produced a fragmentary response to a general problem. To what general avail should a group of carpenters come together to demand more if the claims of masons and steel erectors and even unskilled labourers were to be ignored? In due course, it began to dawn on people that the same moral factors which created for one group of craftsmen a right to a better standard of living, applied in equal measure to all people within an economic system. Hence, a time came, particularly in the United States of America, when the form or organisation known as the craft union began to give way to a more general aggregation in the industrial unions.

An industrial union was firstly a response to modern economic organisation which created the mass industries such as automobile assembly and steel. These were so palpably of a piece as economic entities as to invite a single organisational response from the workers. More fundamentally, however, the workers' movement itself was becoming more conscious of the class struggle and more responsive to the moral imperatives of a progress that is shared by all. This led to the formation of the great industrial unions such as the United Automobile Workers of America and the United Steelworkers of America. Whereas the crafts union was a European creation exported to North America, the industrial union was a North American institution exported, in turn, to Europe.

The blanket union, however, is something else again. Perhaps the most famous trade union of this type is the Transport and General Workers Union of Great Britain. This body organises within its scope any and every kind of worker in need of representation in the workplace. All the groups are held together by the single idea of justice for all workers within the economy. It is this last kind of trade union organisation which had emerged in a dominant but highly competitive form in Jamaica by 1952.

There are many reasons why the blanket union was a natural form for the Jamaican trade union movement today. First amongst these is the fact that the Jamaican union movement did not arise primarily as the response of small, particular worker groups to the problem of poverty and oppression. Rather, the movement was born out of a generalised class explosion in a colonial situation which could be traced back to the phenomenon of slavery. The reason why the Bustamante Industrial Trade Union was so successful in spite of its lack of organisation, lack of philosophy and lack of organisational method in the early years, was because Bustamante himself symbolised the right of the workers to express their discontent and to action on their own behalf, regardless of the nature of the discontent, the articulation of the protest or the possible form of a solution. Jamaican workers were originally slaves. The fact of Emancipation in 1838 had not effected a general release of the person and the spirit into the atmosphere of freedom. The more subtle form of slavery which was colonialism had ensured that the state power continued to maintain the unquestioned supremacy of the employer and the cringing inferiority of the employed. Hence, in a very real sense the men who flocked to the trade union movement after 1938 were not free men, regarding themselves as free, but who suffered from a particular discontent and particular needs; rather they were men who felt spiritually enslaved and were first of all in search of a sense of personal freedom as workers within their society. This is not an industrial response. It is not essentially a trade union response. Rather, it is a political response happening to express itself in trade union terms. The instinct of the Jamaican worker was to make common cause with all those who identified themselves as workers in a general movement born as a response to a general discontent.

In addition to the natural social and psychological forces tending to a general rather than a particular form of union organisation, is to be added the realities of size. In a small country, the number of workers in any one industry is commensurately small. But unions like any other form of enterprise have inescapable overheads. Offices have to be rented, stationery acquired, staff engaged and telegrams sent. No union can be so small as to escape certain fundamental obligations and the costs that arise from them. In a small country, therefore, it becomes prohibitively expensive to have a number of union organisations; all economic logic compels union organisation to seek the economies of scale. These are best obtained in a blanket union where one general secretary services many sections embracing many industries and where one headquarters building spreads the rental burden across a number of participating union groups. Hence, there has always been a natural centrifugal force creating centralised administration in the union movement as the price of economic survival.

Finally, the Jamaican situation has lent itself to the blanket union because of the intensity of the political rivalry that resulted from the artificial split of the movement between those who tended to Bustamante's flamboyant conservatism on the one hand, and those who sought the fulfilment of their dreams in the articulate ideology and more radical purpose of the PNP orientated union movement. The very fact of this political confrontation drove both unions to the discovery and perpetuation of the advantage of the centrally directed, blanket union.

As a consequence, 1952 saw an established BITU which was

totally centralised in its leadership, organisation, inspiration and administration. The BITU had been at this time under significant attack by the TUC which had become an equally centralised institution. Now, the TUC had been disaffiliated from the PNP for purely political reasons and the National Workers Union had been launched as the legitimate union partner of the nationalist and democratic socialist sector of the Jamaican polity. But the NWU had also, in response to the social, economic and political realities of Jamaica been launched as a centrally directed, blanket union.

In all three organisations, a central corps of leaders tended to formulate the policies, advance the claims and negotiate the settlements for all categories of workers whether this involved dockers in Kingston, banana plantation field hands in St Mary, cane cutters in Frome, public utility workers in Kingston, bauxite miners in St Ann or Public Works Department bulldozer operators throughout the Island. Particular groups of workers found satisfaction at two levels: there were the wage increases that were secured; and there was the general sense of belonging to a family grouping in search of legitimate progress. Union agreements ranged from the crudest of documents to the verbal gentleman's agreement. The movement was too young to have established sophisticated guidelines for union settlements, and it may have been short on sophisticated technique. It was not, however, short on energy and a sense of urgency among the workers, of the need for better conditions in the workplace, more self-expression as a group and a greater material base for happiness in the home. For the truth is that after fourteen years of activity there was still a long way to go before the workers could feel a sense of equality and personal worth in their jobs.

To understand the psychology of the labour struggle one has to go back to the institution of slavery. Slaves had no freedom and possessed no rights. Up to 1838, when slavery was abolished, the slaves enjoyed neither wages nor fringe benefits. It is true that they were fed and received rudimentary medical attention but this was not because it was felt that the humanity of a slave entitled him to these things. Rather, this was the grudging price that was paid to ensure a minimum economic capability. A hundred years later when the Jamaican revolution began, descendants of those freed slaves continued to enjoy legal freedom. However, neither they nor their employers had accepted the fact that freedom without rights is a myth. It is true that in 1938 wages were paid and there may even have been some workers who enjoyed small periods of vacation leave. Not all workers were being constantly dismissed, so it might be argued that in practice workers did enjoy some measure of job security. However, none of these things happened as a matter of right. All of these things were seen as examples of the employers' generosity. The employers had no doubt whatsoever of their generosity and totally repudiated the notion that a worker could have rights. On the other hand the workers may have disputed the idea that their employers were generous but had not yet successfully formulated in their own minds the notion of 'rights'.

Even as late as 1938 it would be true to say of the Jamaican society that the employer groups felt that the workers were lucky to have emerged from slavery through emancipation to a state that was described as freedom. At the same time it seems clear that the workers still had little idea concerning the uses to which their freedom might be put. It is in this attitudinal state that the country came to the explosion of 1938. I can well remember as a boy of fourteen, the shock-waves of disbelief that ran through the establishment. The employers were incredulous. The country was never to be the same again, because for the first time the idea was rife in the society that all men are entitled to articulate for themselves certain rights which they consider to be essential to their well-being. Hitherto the establishment, consisting of the plantocracy, the merchants, the professionals and that vital technical apparatus which served them which we call the 'middle class', had been able to order their lives on the basis that they were entitled to certain things as of right. Hence, this group did not have to actively seek its rights in society because each member of the group was able to grow up safe in the knowledge that his rights were a part of the natural order. On the other hand, the workers, in the sense of cane cutters, grass weeders, banana carriers, dock workers, factory hands, artisans, shop assistants and the like having been deprived in practice had little or no sense of their economic rights. It is true that the law protected them from arbitrary loss of property and *habeas corpus* applied. But there the law stopped. Insofar as all of that vast range of relationships which flow from the economic nexus was concerned, they had no rights whatsoever. Rather, they existed at the whim and pleasure of the employer in a system which was founded upon the notion that the employers' rights are absolute in the economy.

By 1951 when I returned to Jamaica, it would be true to say that two fundamental changes had occurred. In the political arena it had come to be accepted that all adults were entitled to an equal voice in the political process through the ballot box and universal adult suffrage. Here, for the first time, the freedom of 1838 was leading to a concept of rights for the mass of the people and a method for securing those rights through the political system. This had been Norman Manley's task and was peculiarly his accomplishment. Simultaneously, in the workplace, the notion that the freedom of 1838 implied rights for workers in their relationship with their employers had become accepted. This had been the task of Bustamante and was peculiarly his accomplishment.

Hence, by 1952 thousands of workers in Jamaica drew their wages, vacation leave and other fringe benefits and enjoyed their first taste of job security as of right rather than at the will and pleasure of their employers. These rights were secured in contracts negotiated on their behalf by the unions with their employers. Understandably, the contracts were still rudimentary, providing for little more than minimum wages for various categories, the entitlement to annual vacation leave, annual sick leave, overtime rates for work beyond a certain number of hours per week and minimal job security. However, the degree, extent and sophistication of the rights which had been secured for the average worker by 1952 is not what is important. What is important is that the society had undergone a critical transformation for the first time since 1838. For a hundred years the freedom of 1838 was seen as the final discharge of all moral responsibility towards the slaves by their former slave masters. In this view the question of rights was held to be irrelevant since the slaves were deemed to be lucky to have got their freedom in the first place. Now, by contrast, we had a situation in which the workers had asserted their humanity, their intrinsic equality and, hence, their entitlement to formulate, articulate and secure rights for themselves. It is impossible to overestimate for Jamaica or for any other society, the significance of this massive step forward in the long historical process by which modern man seeks to redefine society in terms of the moral imperative of equality.

In 1952 the laws that governed the relationship between employers and employees in Jamaica were rudimentary and mostly favoured the interests of the employer. For example, the basic statute under which trade unions had their right to existence, did not make it obligatory for an employer to recognise a trade union and to treat with it where a majority of the workers wanted this situation. Employers were entitled to defy the wishes of their workers in this regard. The same law placed severe restrictions on the capacity of a trade union to picket a strikebound plant effectively. The sanctions against effective picketing would, of course, be completely reasonable if the law compelled employers to take reasonable steps to discover whether their workers wanted a trade union, and provided that they did, required the employer to recognise that union and deal with it. Hence, the same law, by implication, permitted an employer to defy the legitimate wish of its workers to be represented by a union while denying to the worker the right to take effective action against the employer who might act in this way. Of course, those in favour of the law pointed out that all it sought to achieve was peaceful picketing and to this end it gave the police the power to determine how many pickets could appear at a factory gate and made it clear that pickets were not allowed to do more than speak to any person seeking to enter the plant. On the face of it this seemed entirely reasonable. However, those who know the inner workings of the employer/employee relationship know that it is common for employers to hire strike breakers who can then enter a factory with impunity because the picket can only speak to them as they pass by on their way into the factory. Clearly, the principle of peaceful picketing can only have relevance in a context of laws that secure the fundamental rights of workers and their trade unions. The Jamaican Law did not make this connection.

Simultaneously, there was a law named the Public Utility Undertakings and Arbitrations Law, Chapter 325, which was commonly but not affectionately, known as the Essential Services Law. Under the statute certain services like light and power, water, fire services, communications, public transport, health and the like were scheduled as essential. This meant that the workers in these services were not allowed to strike in the first instance in support of claims for higher wages or for the correction of grievances. Instead, they were required to report their complaints to the appropriate authority which was set up as an arbitration tribunal to hear the case. However, these tribunals became increasingly irrelevant as the years passed, since they were inhibited from working effectively by the very statute that created them. A substantial part of my later career as a trade unionist was to be devoted to the struggle first to explain to Jamaica why this law was an inadequate instrument and secondly to have it changed.

By 1952 wages had risen quite considerably as compared with those of 1938. For example, the sugar workers day minimum rate for men had ranged between eight shillings and three pence to nine shillings and six pence a day for men, and for women six shillings to seven shillings a day. The Sugar Contract at that time provided for nine days vacation leave in the case of daily paid workers and one week annual vacation leave for crop period services, similar periods of sick leave, overtime rates of time and a half for work done in excess of forty-eight hours a week or in excess of eight hours a day. There was a grievance procedure of sorts under which a worker was entitled to have his problems heard and adjudicated upon. And all of this was subject to an over-riding arbitration clause which entitled the worker to an impartial tribunal to declare his wages annually or his grievances from time to time. The parties were required to choose mutually acceptable arbitrators, and it was understood that any awards that were made were final and binding without right of appeal, save on grounds of impropriety or illegality.

On the surface, therefore, it was clear that much progress

had been made. The majority of employers accepted the rights of workers to join trade unions and were willing to deal with those unions. The existence of contracts indicated that the employers of the country, however, reluctantly, had accepted the notion of workers' rights. However, the degree of this acceptance was sharply limited. Equally, the attitudes of employers at the level of their personal relationship with workers had changed little, if at all. For example, in the matter of the right of the employer to dismiss the worker, employers had gone so far as to accept the idea that the worker had a right to question his employer's judgment of his guilt or innocence. This was, of course, an important break-through because prior to 1938, the employer was accepted as the sole judge of the guilt or innocence of his employee. This is a fantastic fact which is hard to grasp, but is nonetheless true. To understand this phenomenon, one has to understand what is involved. In society at large each man is faced with a number of laws which he must obey. If he is felt to have broken any of these laws, two processes are instantly invoked. The first is the attempt to determine whether he broke the law or not. The second is to determine what punishment should arise on the assumption that he did break the law. It is vital to understand that the process is critically separated into the question of determining guilt or innocence on the one hand, and the further question of punishment which only arises if guilt is reasonably established. The relationship between workers and employers however was remarkably different. The employer was accepted as having not only the right unilaterally to punish a guilty worker but similarly, to determine whether that worker was guilty or innocent. This was implicit in the employer/employee relationship, because the notions of justice which society accepted as governing all of its members in relation to the law did not extend to the relationship between some members who were workers in their dealings with other members who were employers. By 1952 this had been changed to the extent that employers were beginning to recognise that they could not be the sole determinants of guilt or innocence. Hence, they would agree in most cases to have this question determined by third parties who were not involved in the dispute in the form of arbitrators. However, employers continued to arrogate to themselves the right to punish workers by dismissal, even where they had been held to be innocent by impartial arbitration tribunals. A substantial part of my subsequent career was to be devoted to the struggle against this survival no less than to the right of workers to be represented by unions.

At a more personal level, relationships at the workplace were ugly. I say ugly because most employers still had those hectoring, domineering, rude attitudes which are the unconscious expression of the notion of employer superiority. As late as 1952 I can remember employers who thought they were entitled to abuse their workers in the most shameful way. Indeed, I can even remember one employer who had to deal with nearly two thousand workers who used to command everyone, regardless of age or skill, to remove their caps while speaking to him. This order was usually preceded by the word: 'Boy!' I was to spend much of my career trying to educate employers to a different view of their personal relationships with their workers. Indeed, I came to be known, in certain employer circles, as a communist because I unswervingly asserted the proposition that employer and worker are essentially equal though with different functions to perform. So deep were the class attitudes in Jamaica that this unoriginal and ideologically pedestrian notion was enough to stamp me as at best a dangerous radical and at worst, and more probably, as an out and out communist.

As the years passed, the mutual ambivalence of the employer/employee relationship in Jamaica and of the smouldering tensions which resulted was to engage more and more of my attention. But this was to come. In 1952 I could only observe the stubborn arrogance of the employer group and the lingering uncertainty of the workers.

3

CLASS AND THE WORKPLACE

In any country one will tend to find that the workplace is a microcosm of class attitudes in the society at large. In highly class-stratified societies with little social mobility and a tradition of hereditary power, this will be particularly true and will involve troublesome consequences for the nation at large. Much in the relationship between workers and employers in Jamaica has to be considered in the light of this central fact. The Jamaica of 1952 represented a confluence of three great forces which were all inter-dependent though each occupied its separate place in our history. Colonialism, slavery and capitalism comprised the dominant political and economic experience and, therefore, profoundly shaped the social patterns of the country. It is worthwhile pausing to consider what each category contributed to the total experience. Colonialism acted to create a society with a privileged class. The British colonisers came for the purpose of exploiting such wealth as could be wrested from the soil and to ensure that the control of that wealth was passed to the generations that sprung directly from their loins. This was both a logical corollary of the colonising process and a natural extension of the class system which was so sharply defined and powerfully entrenched in British life. It is true that the British exported the notion of parliamentary democracy and the importance of an incorruptible civil service but they also exported the most durable class system of modern history.

Slavery was introduced to provide the manpower through which colonialism could achieve its economic purpose. By enforcing, through military power, a legal system which denied the elementary humanity of all those who supplied the manual content of the total social work output, colonialism achieved the final expression of the class system and gave it the sanction of the rule of law. A more subtle, dangerous and enduring association of ideas was established, however, and that was the notion that manual labour bears the stigma of slavery.

Capitalism was, by coincidence, the dominant form of economic organisation at the time when the institution of slavery finally outlived its economic usefulness. The capitalism of the nineteenth century was associated with the notion that he who had money to invest was the most important figure in the society. Hence, the employer of labour was regarded as the central figure in the economic process and, hence, entitled to all the privileges and power which had hitherto been the exclusive preserve of the landed aristocracy. The position of this new elite was sanctified by the philosophies of the day and so a 'new aristocracy' of ownership evolved. This encompassed the original plantocracy which was now expanded to include any kind of sizeable employer of labour.

Because of the nature of British society, of slavery and of capitalism each would be capable of creating a class society by itself. With all three forces present in Jamaican history, the result was one of the most sharply class-stratified and class-conscious societies in modern history.

The consequences of this social experience can be measured by the attitude of the Jamaican middle and upper classes, so-called, towards everyone else, but in particular those who lived by manual labour of one sort or another. It is no exaggeration to say that until quite recently in our history, the working classes did not exist as human beings for the privileged. So total was the cumulative effect of history that the average members of the privileged groups were incapable of perceiving the common humanity which made the worker a part of the same total experience as themselves. In fact, the great novelist and painter, Roger Mais, occupies a unique place in our history because his first novel, *The Hills Were Joyful Together* was probably the first in which a Jamaican writer broke out of the myopia of class to tell the story of working people as human beings. Prior to Mais' time and his particular insight the working class remained an opaque phenomenon to the privileged. Mais' achievement and that of the poets, sculptors and painters of his time was remarkable because only a member of the privileged classes could hope to possess the basic education with which to be capable of a viable novel. Of middle-class origin himself, he was one of those definitive figures who transcend the limitations of their time and attempt to explore the truth of the human condition.

The workplace in the factories, offices and fields, as I came to know it in 1952 was the point at which the privileged came into unavoidable contact with large numbers of the under-privileged. In the home this situation was essentially duplicated between housewife and household help. The treatment of the latter by the former beggared description. Whole generations of women, and of young men, working in the beautiful gardens, were brutalised by the treatment that they received at the hands of their employers. It may take the rest of this century to heal the wounds and learn to live with the scars inflicted upon Jamaican society by this experience. I will not dwell upon it here, however, because our purpose is to examine the arena in which collective action by workers made possible the transformation of the relationship between employer and employee. The isolated vulnerability of the household helps made them incapable as a group of strong concerted action. Accordingly, progress here was to follow after achievements in the trade union and political fields. This group lacked the power to be principal agents in the processes of change.

The industrial or agricultural workplace, however, was another matter. On the one hand, there were the old style employers of the family businesses with their managerial and supervisory retainers. These were all part of the privileged classes because the political and educational systems operated to ensure that only the offspring of the privileged had the education and training to occupy top positions. Having occupied all the top positions in a business there never seemed to be any room for bright persons of zeal and application to work their way up from the lower ranks of an enterprise to the higher. Later, another dimension was added to the equation in the shape of the early shareholders in corporate enterprise. Since only the privileged had money to invest, it was inevitable that all shareholders sprung from this group. Therefore, it was literally the case that all those in positions of authority brought to the economic relationship the class attitudes which had been created by history.

These attitudes are themselves important to dissect. To

the members of the privileged the working classes were essentially lazy, naturally violent and congenitally stupid and untrustworthy. They were seen as a species of animal life that only responds to harsh discipline and punishment. It was assumed that they were neither capable of understanding the higher issues of economic organisation nor entitled to share in the mystery. Fundamentally, therefore, the system bred alienation which it sought to contain with discipline.

Inevitably, where people are treated in this way they react in kind. A person who has no sense of recognition and who is made to feel worthless reacts accordingly. This reaction is then interpreted as confirmation of the original hypothesis and so the attitudes of oppression are self-perpetuating for the oppressor provokes an echo which he interprets as confirmation. Thus, the workplace which begins as a microcosm of class attitudes ends up by reinforcing the very attitudes that created its original atmosphere.

Throughout the nineteenth and twentieth centuries the basic concepts of the rule of law developed and acquired a general currency in British political thought. The rule of law rests upon the notion that all men are equal in the eyes of the law, equally entitled to due process, fair trial and the prerogative of presumed innocence. Simultaneously, however, capitalism was creating a legal system within a legal system. Men might be equal before the law in the society at large, but they were by no means equal in the economic relationship. Surrounding the employer/employee relationship with a mystique of its own, nineteenth century Britain was brainwashed into believing that crime and punishment took on a completely different aspect and character in the workplace as distinct from the outside world. A person who committed an offence in the outside world would at least have the consoling knowledge that the great questions of innocence, guilt and possible punishment would be handled with impartiality. In the workplace, on the other hand, justice was summary and the notion that each worker was entitled to a fair trial dismissed as irrelevant. No one seemed to have stopped to consider the fact that a worker dismissed from a job was suffering penalties as severe in terms of his domestic economy as a citizen sentenced to six months for stealing. For both the loss of income was total. And though it may be true that a grave stigma would attach to the citizen who went to prison, at least he would be fed. In the case of the dismissed worker, the stigma would be less acute, but the loss of earnings would be just as complete. In the case of the convicted felon, the state would at least ensure a full stomach. In the case of dismissed workers, hunger was their own private concern.

Even as late as 1952, I was horrified by the way in which disciplinary cases were handled. When a supervisor made a charge against a worker it was almost universally accepted by employers that the supervisor must be right. It was common to have a charge levelled against a worker and without the slightest consideration of whether the charge reflected private prejudice, it would be treated as sacrosanct. Workers who tried to defend themselves were often denied the right to question their accusers on the grounds that this would undermine authority and discipline. We had here, therefore, the assertion that authority rests not upon justice but upon the capacity to inflict punishment. One well recognises the importance of authority and discipline in life in general and the economic process in particular. Indeed, much of the challenge to social ingenuity in the modern world is how to reconcile the need for discipline as a guarantee of efficiency with the principle of equality which is necessary to justice. The employing classes of Jamaica as late as 1952 resolved this dilemma entirely in favour of discipline and authority because they neither accepted the equality of those who receive orders nor their right to justice.

Of course, none of this must be misunderstood as suggesting that the members of the privileged groups were as individuals bad people. Many were persons of the greatest intellectual distinction, good family men and capable of great personal generosity. But collectively they were the products of an historical process and were imprisoned within the attitudes which that process made inevitable. Naturally, as often happens throughout the history of the world in strongly authoritarian class systems, the natural generosity of the individual found an outlet in 'paternalism'. As late as 1952, many employers were capable of great individual kindness towards their workers. It was common to find situations in which considerable sums of money had been lent to help individual workers with family difficulties. Of course, it did not seem to occur to anyone that a simpler solution might be to pay adequate wages so that the worker did not get into these difficulties.

The effects of paternalism on both sides of the fence were fascinating. It became the focus for all the ambivalence that is inherent in the employer/employee relationship. On the employer's side it was at the same time an expression of generosity, a salve to conscience and a confirmation of his own superiority, to be able to lend. On the worker's side, it was seen as the sole confirmation in an otherwise bleak landscape that the employer cared for them as individuals. Simultaneously, it confirmed the worker's sense of inferiority in his own concept of himself. And so the love/hate cycle was completed. For both persons, paternalism acted to confuse and distort reality. Faced with a wage claim, the employer rationalised his natural objection to the pressure by a petulant recitation, to himself and anyone else who would listen, of his many acts of kindness. Workers reacted with equal irrationality. A wage claim would be served, pressed and increases secured. By this act the workers had declared their independence and asserted their rights. However, they would continue to expect loans and Christmas bonuses and be bitterly hurt if these were rejected despite the obvious contradiction between the new kind of relationship in which one asserts one's rights and a former relationship in which one is the casual object of kindness.

Of particular interest were the attitudes to work, justice and co-operation as I found them among workers in my twenty years as a trade unionist. Naturally, none of the attitudes which I shall describe were universal. There were exceptions – and notable and interesting ones at that. But the general tendencies and patterns of behaviour which could be observed give vital clues to the effect upon the nature and development of Jamaican society of slavery, colonialism and the capitalist system.

I recall *work attitudes* first. Granted the historical experience, it was not surprising that workers tended to approach the whole question with little sense of urgency. In this they were of a piece with their employers who, in the main had also mastered the technique of the minimum effort. Truly hard-working employers could be found, but they were few and far between. Lunch periods commonly ran to two hours or more. It is not altogether surprising therefore that workers took a somewhat elastic view of rest periods although it was my experience that the worker was far more tolerant of the employer's lapses than he was of theirs. In fact, it used to amaze me sometimes to hear an employer berating a worker for overstaying his lunch hour by ten minutes when it was common knowledge that an hour and a half was the normal time span of his own meal. On the other hand, I was constantly surprised by the stamina and endurance of the Jamaican worker and by his capacity to face crisis with heroic effort. When there is a major breakdown in a plant, he is capable of an enthusiastic and total response. It is as if the centuries of hardship have honed an appreciation of crisis which transcends other tensions and disincentives to effort. One reads with admiration of the Stakhanovite tradition which was celebrated in Stalinist Russia. Without any 'orders of Lenin' or other form of recognition, I have seen this sort of transcendental effort over and over from groups of Jamaican workers confronted by crisis. When faced with a challenge that is understood because of its stark simplicity, I have seen workers perform for thirty-six hours on a stretch without complaint and without any noticeable loss of concentration or skill. I suppose that this happens because the crisis of a broken machine lifts everyone out of the web of inter-personal relationships in which they are normally entangled and joins everyone in the common concern for survival. It is on occasions such as these that one observes locally, qualities of energy, zeal and application which the Jamaican worker so commonly displays when he migrates out of the social tensions of his homeland into the concrete challenge of 'making it big' as a migrant in America, Canada or the United Kingdom.

The other thing that I observed over the years was the non-involvement in the creative process which was the lot of the average worker. In the main this led to a mute indifference to the whole question of intelligent organisation, efficiency and productivity. Can a person care when no one cares whether they care? Can people contribute when their superiors assume that they have nothing to say? It came as no surprise to observe how bitter and frustrated the brighter and more imaginative workers became. It was a commonplace to hear a worker comment upon some managerial shortcoming and then cap it with a bitter: 'But they don't care what we think!' Very often, one would just have come from an office in which employers would be complaining about the fact that none of their workers think. Here was the ultimate irony of groups that could not help each other because they could not communicate. And they could not communicate because history had condemned each to an allotted place in a macabre minuet wherein each proceeded around the sides of a pre-determined square, conscious of each other but incapable of the embrace of understanding that both needed.

Equally fascinating was the *attitude to justice*. The employer was certain that a divine equation existed between justice and his own interests. In predictable response the worker repudiated the notion of justice as irrelevant to his circumstances. Certain that justice could never be depended upon, workers tended to see every disciplinary issue as a matter for circumvention. Brer Anancy is the supreme symbol of the means by which the slave survived. The slave survived by outwitting the slave master. The proletariat of the post-slavery era survived by the same means because working men had no rights. Where men have no rights justice is not so much a travesty as a non-phenomenon. The notion of justice cannot exist in the mind of a man who is not conscious of any rights. In this context, the conventional notions of morality, obedience, discipline and truth do not command allegiance. It is not so much that they are ignored as that they are outside the institutional grasp of the man who has no rights. In this situation Brer Anancy is a symbol and Anancyism is a methodology. Symbolism and methodology alike are concerned with survival. Hence, when it came to justice in relation to disciplinary matters, the spirit of Anancy reigned supreme in the Jamaican workplace. Anancy was the worker's answer to the employer's divine right over crime and punishment. The employer who would take the word of his supervisor unquestioningly was faced with a worker body who would often invent any story to save a guilty colleague. The truth is that the system had created an atmosphere in which truth became irrelevant. However, it was remarkable to observe that the employer had neither insight nor humour in relation to his own preposterous position. He was completely solemn about the larger need that justified his every peccadillo. The workers on the other hand, with a person whom they trusted, would be both shamefaced and amused about the fact that they had conspired to lie to save a colleague from dismissal. Where the employer had surrendered to philosophical arrogance, the workers had a more modest appreciation of their sins and could even laugh, like Anancy. More often than not the employer would compound the offence of arrogance with pomposity.

Attitudes towards truth were, accordingly, a response to discipline. If a person is precluded from any sense of sharing in responsibility they are not likely to accept discipline gracefully. I was always struck, and often horrified, by the extent to which workers viewed discipline not as the pre-condition of efficiency and success or as an extension of each man's responsibility to the society, but rather as the arbitrary, whimsical and unnecessary imposition of the employer. It was common to hear workers describe disciplinary requirements as 'the wishes of the slave master'! And what a volume was spoken in that phrase – 'the wishes of the slave master'. If I heard this once, I heard it a thousand times. It meant that the society had not moved one inch towards a world of shared responsibility. Jamaica was still, in the economic sphere, the arena in which the tyranny of the employer reigned supreme. This is not to suggest that society can run without order, or industry without discipline. Rather, it is to point out that free men must understand in order to obey freely. No society fashioned in the name and the image of freedom can intelligently organise itself on the basis of blind obedience. To do this is to ensnare itself in a contradiction of terms, of ideas and of purposes. The Jamaica that I found in 1952 upon my return was thus ensnared.

A fascinating example of worker attitudes towards discipline was to be found in the case of the cane cutters of a certain sugar estate in the parish of St Catherine. The sugar industry depends for its profits on the reaping and grinding of cane in the shortest possible period of time before and after those few weeks in a year when the sucrose content of the cane is at its peak. We need not detain ourselves with the agricultural chemistry and the economic logistics that are involved. Suffice it to say that once a crop starts in the sugar industry, it is a matter of real urgency that it proceeds quickly and smoothly to its conclusion. Every worker in the sugar industry knows this and an entire fabric of discipline has been built up to support the importance of this course of events each year. However, on this particular estate, a number of the cane cutters came from another parish where they lived as small farmers. Each year to supplement their meagre farm earnings, they would migrate to this estate in St Catherine, pick up a nice bit of cash for twenty-six weeks cane cutting and repair to the small farm holdings which their wives and families had kept going in the meanwhile. However, there was one difficulty. Planting time in St Thomas occurs early in March. These cane cutters were mainly the heads of their families, the strongest and most efficient farm workers in their group and, in any event, responsible for the success of their holdings. Hence they all felt the need each year to go home for the first fortnight of March to plant out their plots and generally make sure that their private agricultural endeavours were well set for the season. How then to reconcile the problem of the duty of obedience to the sugar estate for which they cut cane each year with their responsibility to their own holdings? The solution which they devised and enacted each year was remarkable for its ingenuity and its innocent indifference to the normal canons of truth and discipline. Each year this formidable group of men would create a labour dispute and religiously by the start of March they would foment it into a strike. The minute the strike began they would dash across to St Thomas for a fortnight, plant out their holdings and satisfy themselves that all was well on the home farming front. After two weeks, they would reappear at the scene of the strike and in one way or another, find themselves able to accept whatever was the latest offer by the management in settlement of the dispute. This went on year after year and several times occasioned me considerable agony as a trade unionist, filled with the normal sense of the fitness of things and with a considerable passion for order and logic. Then one day a wise old man who liked me and realised that my loyalty to the cane cutters was being strained to the limit by what seemed like an annual exercise in madness, took me into his confidence, told me the inner truth and taught me a whole new chapter, perhaps a whole new book about the nature of the Jamaican society. In a flash I could see that in the minds of those cane cutters, the 'slave master's' system could not weigh in the scales of right and morality beside their own system which was predominantly concerned with survival. What was equally remarkable was that all the other cane cutters who came from the neighbouring districts of St Catherine and who did not have plots of land to cultivate, were willing collaborators. They joined enthusiastically in the masquerade because this was their way of expressing class solidarity. And this expression of solidarity leads me to my third observation which was to do with the *spirit of co-operation within the working classes*.

Much has been written about 'share-pot'. 'Share-pot' is that remarkable Jamaican and Caribbean institution in which the poor create their own social security system. The family whose breadwinner has no job literally shares the pot of the family whose breadwinner is temporarily less fortunate. Many have speculated as to whether this accounts for the absence of revolutionary violence in those societies of the English speaking Caribbean that are so distorted by maldistribution of wealth and massive unemployment. However, the example that I just gave of the landless St Catherine cane cutter supporting the St Thomas small farmer in his manufactured strike is a classic example of a class attitude which leads to 'share-pot' in a tenement yard and to unquestioning support for a strike from which one cannot benefit but which another group feels to be in its own interests. And here I must make it clear that this was not a consequence of union discipline. We were not witnessing the studied intellectual response to the *equations* of group action where one is thinking of tomorrow as well as today. Very often the unions concerned were trying manfully to get a resumption of work during this annual exercise in St Catherine. What we were watching was a response in today's arena of action to yesterday's shared experience. The landless St Catherine cane cutter was expressing his own unarticulated instinctive class solidarity in the face of a system that he deemed to be hostile.

Another graphic illustration of this attitude could be found in worker attitudes towards disciplinary action such as suspension. It was common to find workers making voluntary contributions to a suspended worker for the period when he was off the job. In fact, I have known cases where a worker on two weeks suspension would take home as much in voluntary contributions from his fellows at the workplace as his combined straight time and overtime earnings in the period before he got into difficulties. Here again one was witnessing the instinctive group response. Here again was a group action that had nothing to do with union organisation or discipline. Very often, the worker might have been guilty of quite a serious offence and the union might have felt that he was lucky to get away with a suspension. With one part of their minds the workers would accept and understand all this but another and deeper instinct would produce a drawing together, a closing of the ranks against the common historical enemy. The money would be contributed not only because of a human recognition of the suffering that is occasioned by loss of earnings. I believe that more deeply it reflected a group defiance of an employer's finally separated law which had not yet been from the memory of the slave master's injustice.

The workplace that I found in 1952 was, in many ways, like a primitive cave. Spiritually and psychologically, the employer group ranging from superintendent to managing director occupied an upper ground of power and authority. They glared across barricades but were without sight. The workers were drawn up in tight defensive ranks on a lower ground of disadvantage and servility. They too glared but saw through the falsity of the employer position all too clearly. Their problem was that they could not understand the economic process of which they were a part because they could not see past the immediate enemy.

It is interesting how little dent fourteen years of mass

politics had made upon this equation. In the meantime it was obvious that the real casualty was the larger society and its hopes for the future.

4

ASPIRATIONS

PRESUMABLY every person finds that professional life involves an interaction between the disciplines and attitudes that are traditional in the job which they attempt and their own personal philosophy of life. As a result, some people acquire great skills and demonstrate enormous discipline within their occupation but never try to change its rules and objectives. Others constantly question everything including values and objectives. I tend to be a questioner. Hence, I found that in my twenty years as a trade unionist two parallel developments were constant. Part of me was always trying to improve and perfect my grasp of the traditional techniques of unionism while at the same time I tried to re-examine the relevance of those disciplines and to keep the normally accepted objectives of the movement under constant review. This was not an obsessive preoccupation. Too much critical energy expended on the re-examination of objectives can lead to a paralysis of action and, if nothing else, I have always tended to be an activist. But as the years passed, a process of re-assessment proved to have been taking place because from time to time I would find myself in the midst of a crisis of attitude which always ended in some adjustment of objectives and priorities for the movement, however marginal.

One can best analyse this process which was my principal source of creative tension, by contrasting the view of society which held unconscious sway throughout the first half of the twentieth century in Jamaica with my own philosophy of social organisation. Like all highly class-stratified societies, Jamaica entered the twentieth century with a deeply rooted acceptance of the principle of hierarchy and of the legitimacy of the hereditary transference of privilege and power. It was accepted that the sons of the rich were entitled to be rich themselves and that the children of the powerful should at least occupy important positions in society. Equally, it was accepted that the offspring of the poor should continue in the disadvantaged status of their parents. These fundamental attitudes in the society at large were duplicated in the employer/employee relationship. Within the economic process it was assumed that the higher positions of authority conferred upon their holders more than an authority of function. Authority was invested with a mystique in which the holder of high office was accepted as a superior human being by virtue of that fact. Equally, the holder of the lower position was deemed to be an inferior human being within the relationship. The understanding of this equation is fundamental to one's ability to grasp the nature of the working relationship. It was fascinating to observe how this view led to all sorts of conscious and unconscious consequences. For example, it is this attitude that led to both the assertion and the acceptance of the right of the employer to dismiss a worker regardless of guilt or innocence. It was this atmosphere that led to the often unconscious arrogance and rudeness of the employer and the continuing acceptance of this type of behaviour by the worker. Whatever tensions of guilt in the minds of the employers or resentment in the minds of the workers this may have created, neither fundamentally challenged the propriety of the relationship nor the behaviour that it seemed to justify.

The events between 1938 and 1952 had led to momentous changes in the sense that the society had been forced to accept the right of the worker to assert his claim to a share of the wealth that is created by labour. I do not for a moment belittle this change nor the first expressions of resistance to the notion of the employers' unchallenged right to discipline. What I do assert is that by 1952 the challenge was expressing itself within the framework of a continuing acceptance of the system and its fundamental relationships. The union movement was not, as such, advancing its challenge against the fundamental employer/employee relationships but only against the more obviously unjust consequences of the relationship. It is interesting to observe that the Master and Servants Law which had been enacted in the 1830s was still the fundamental statute governing the relationship between worker and boss. The very name of the law 'Master and Servant' expresses the true nature of the relationship and the fact that no one had thought to repeal it seemed to me to reflect the unconscious acceptance by society of that relationship.

Because of my own egalitarianism I have always rejected systems that are based on hereditary hierarchies insofar as social structures go and notions of inherent superiority and inferiority as they touch on personal relationships. For this reason, I have always been unable intellectually and emotionally to accept the institution of monarchy or any form of aristocracy, whether formalised with titles or merely institutionalised through the passing of power and privilege by birth. As a realist, I understand the need for differing rewards for differing tasks within society. Equally, I recognise and accept the need for authority and command in society at large and within the economic process. In the last analysis, whatever the decision-making process, someone must possess the authority to give orders and to see that they are carried out. However, to me the fact that one person is chosen to give the orders and another to carry them out, does not create a difference in the inherent worth of either. What is really involved is a difference in function rather than a difference in worth. Hence, I have always commenced my approach to economic relationships in terms of the human rather than the structural equation. Let me illustrate. Whether the economic structure is based on capitalism or state ownership, the problem of the relationship between worker and manager, between those who receive orders and those who give them, will remain. A state-owned enterprise can be built upon a totally authoritarian notion of the relationship between the giver and the receiver of orders. Management can be just as arrogant and imbued with a sense of innate superiority in a system of state ownership as it can in the free enterprise system. Equally, either system is capable of producing relationships that are founded on the notion of equality and where the differences between persons are genuine differences of function rather than of status. Therefore, within a very short time of becoming an active trade unionist, I was conscious of this fundamental difference in attitude between the majority of society as I found it and myself. The commonly accepted view of the employer/employee relationship was authoritarian and rooted in the notion of the inherent superiority of the employers and by extension of the manager's position. The union-management dialogue consisted in the main of a continuing examination of the question: How far could this natural and inevitable superiority-inferiority relationship be modified in the interest of the worker? My fundamental view was exactly the reverse. I began with the assumption of the equality of all the people who were involved both as individuals and in terms of their rights and asked myself the question: How far should the principle of equality be modified in the interests of efficiency and in response to the need of the manager to exercise control? My career as a trade unionist often reflected this fundamental difference in attitude.

I was not, by any manner of means, the first person to question basic relationships. The establishment of the right to protest and of the claim for a larger share of the wealth of the economy, already represented a substantial revolution. Insofar as the Bustamante Industrial Trade Union was concerned, this can fairly be said to represent the extent of its fundamental contribution to the society's problems by 1952. The Trade Union Congress with its democratic, socialist leadership and political affiliations went further in challenging the notion that the free enterprise system existed by divine right as part of the natural order of things. By 1952 the People's National Party and, along with it, the thinking leadership of the TUC had entered a meaningful political *caveat* against these traditional economic notions. To that extent they were challenging the philosophical foundations of the capitalist system. However, they had not, up to that time, challenged the deeper inner equation involving the relationship between those who manage and those who obey within the economic process itself. In 1952 when I entered the union movement I had not articulated that challenge myself because my own analysis of society had been inhibited by the socialist doctrine which I had unquestioningly accepted up to that point. In this view of socialism, the fundamental problem is seen in terms of the relationship between those who own the means of production and those who work in the productive process. It was only as I tested my trade union experience against my egalitarian socialism that I found myself examining the deeper question which involves the relationship between those who manage, and of necessity give orders, and the rest. There is a sense, therefore, in which my trade unionist experience contributed to the evolution of my particular brand of socialist belief and gave it, in the end, a humanist and individualistic focus concerned with the human equation within society as distinct from a more general and structural focus concerned with the ownership of the means of production.

By 1952 it would be true to say that the average socialist in Jamaica would have contended that to nationalise some major industry would achieve two clear advantages: firstly, the wealth, in terms of the profits created by the particular activity, would benefit society as a whole rather than a handful of shareholders; and secondly, the workers, in contributing to the creation of that wealth, would be contributing to the whole of the society of which they themselves were a part, and not a small section from which they were themselves excluded. So far as it goes, this argument was and is valid provided you can ensure optimum levels of efficiency both in terms of current operations and in preparation for the needs of the future. However, the mere change in the pattern of ownership would not necessarily alter the individual experience of the worker. Indeed, it is probable that it would not alter fundamental relationships. In a class-conscious society such as Jamaica's, the probability is that the management of a state-owned industry would be drawn of necessity from the same social and economic group as would the management of a privately-owned industry. One would probably have found, therefore, that management attitudes, insofar as the worker was concerned, would be the same in both situations and that the worker would be subject to the same form of authoritarianism, and even arrogance, in either case. I will confess that this had not occurred to me in 1952. After a few years in the trade union movement, however, I was concerned with this deeper question involving the actual experience of the worker at the workplace. Here, one is concerned with the worker as a total human being: Does the worker have access to due process when he is charged with an offence? Is the worker treated with courtesy and respect? Is the worker given a chance to understand the total industrial process and, hence, the reason for the rules and regulations and the need for the orders that are given from time to time? Is the worker invited to apply his own critical intelligence to the process and to make suggestions in the knowledge that someone will pay attention? Is the management-worker relationship evolving towards a point where there is general participation in the decision-making process? Can the workers feel that everyone accepts their right to a share in the wealth of the process? All these are considerations that are fundamental to the workers' well being. None of these are matters that are dealt with by the mere fact of changing the pattern of ownership.

My trade union career might be summarised as the process by which I discovered these deeper problems that must be answered if egalitarianism is to translate into a relevant philosophy of action.

However, as I say, I began with far less understanding of the workers' problems than I was later to acquire. In 1952 I was concerned with four main things. Firstly and most importantly, that the workers should be organised in a genuinely democratic organisation within which they had access to the decision-making process, over which they had effective democratic control and through which they would become the agents of their own progress in life; moreover, through the discipline of collective action, workers would come to understand and master the democratic process itself. Secondly, I was concerned and, necessarily so, with the sheer question of earning power. At a shilling and one shilling and sixpence an hour even in 1952, no one could approach a decent existence. Such wages could not provide an adequate life for a single individual much less for a whole family. Thirdly, I was concerned with the workers' rights in relation to disciplinary matters. In the jargon of the trade this is called the question of 'job security'. The phrase is a good description of the objective that is involved. More fundamentally, I was concerned with the concept of due process through which the worker would have the same right to the fair and impartial consideration of evidence in relation to alleged offences as was the right of the citizen in society under the rule of law. And fourthly, I was concerned with something that is harder to define but which can loosely be described as the dignity of the individual in the workplace. This last expressed itself initially in a concern for manners and mutual respect. It represented, however, the first stirring of an awareness that modern industry was dehumanising and that mankind was condemned to spend upwards of a half of its waking life in a situation which denied any outlet for creativity and self expression. Later this first, perhaps primitive expression of a humanist concern was to articulate itself in the assertion that the economic process must be reorganised to include the worker as a responsible partner in the decision-making process.

In contrast to the Bustamante Industrial Trade Union, the Trades Union Congress and later the National Workers Union were both organised on democratic lines. All of the officers of the NWU were elected by an annual conference at which all sections of the union were represented in accordance with their membership. In addition there was an executive and the constitution provided that the number of paid organisers who could be elected to the executive was limited. This ensured that actual workers in the fields and the factories had access to the union's final decision-making body. This was a very important constitutional foundation for a democratic union. However, I always felt that the union's democratisation should not be allowed to stop there. Accordingly, in the years in which I was Island Supervisor and First Vice President responsible for the union's industrial relations, I made it a constant objective to secure a working union democracy in each plant and worker group. We used to insist on the annual election of stewards who would represent each identifiable separate section of an undertaking. These would, in turn, elect a central group of delegates who would represent the workers in all labour negotiations. At least in theory each section of the union was supposed to elect its own chairman, secretary and executive who were responsible for the affairs of the group throughout the year.

At some levels we failed to live up to these lofty democratic objectives. I could not honestly claim that we were able to maintain one hundred per cent performance at the level of union sections electing presidents, secretaries and executive. In some sections we did well and had a perfect record; in other sections we failed either because the staff officer of the union failed to understand the importance of these things or because worker groups themselves lacked the organisation or mental stamina to sustain the democratic effort that was needed. On the other hand, we had a remarkably good record in terms of the maintenance of a system of shop stewards and delegates responsible for workers' grievances and contract negotiations. At this level the union was dealing specifically with immediate concerns like job security together with the scope of the labour management contract and the extent of the next wage increase. However, a worker's life consists of more than problems at the workplace. Many things will determine the quality of that life ranging from job security through savings to the ability to purchase a house. A union section ought to be concerned with the whole spectrum of interests involved in the worker's life. Shop stewards and delegates, on the other hand, are concerned specifically with the workers' interests at the workplace. With some interesting exceptions, the National Workers Union failed during my time to achieve a viable democratic life at the wider level but achieved a remarkable degree of worker participation within a democratic frame at the level of the workplace itself.

One of the reasons why the Jamaican Union Movement had failed, certainly up to 1972, to achieve an effective level of organisation concerned with the total life of the worker, is because the intense union rivalry which was endemic dissipated energy, squandered scarce resources of leadership and led to an unhealthy preoccupation with the question: which of the competing unions offered the best representation to the workers at the workplace? This led to duplication of union offices and staff where unions were competing for the attention of the same workers. This in turn led to the waste of resources which could have been better employed in worker education and the organisation of the worker as a total citizen rather than as a factor in production. It may also be that the relationship between union and politics which was so fundamental and pervasive has led union people to feel that the worker's total life was not the union's concern, because, somehow, the political party to which the union was affiliated would look after that broader aspect of things. Finally, this phenomenon may have reflected the difficulty which the society as a whole experienced in conceiving of the worker as a complete and equal human being. It may well be that all those concerned with leadership were themselves the unwilling victims of the prevailing blindness in the society which obscured from everyone's view the essential humanity of the individual members of the working class. Be that as it may, even the NWU which was socialist in ideology and with a leadership of sincere motivation failed at this level.

On the other hand, the NWU did not fail at the level of worker participation in the decision-making processes of the union. Having ensured that our shop stewards and delegates were properly elected and representative of the majority wishes of each section of the plant, farm or economic unit as a whole, we used to ensure worker participation at every stage of a contract negotiation, disciplinary dispute or interpretative wrangle under a contract. In the case of the claims for a new contract, we had elaborate mechanisms by which every single section was called upon to make known its feelings about wages and working conditions. Shop stewards and delegate committees used to sit down with the relevant union staff man and hammer all these proposals out so that a single claim would be served. This document was then submitted to a general meeting of the workers to be amended and finally ratified as the total claim of the whole body. In the later stages this would sometimes result in a document embodying more than one hundred claims ranging from general wages to obscure but passionately felt questions affecting the working conditions of some small group in the remotest corner of a factory.

Upon the date appointed we would then settle down to negotiate with the management with a full complement of delegates present. The bargaining sessions would cover hours, days and weeks until that point was reached when the negotiating group felt that the time had come for a general report to the membership. The latest offers and counter proposals were then reported and fresh mandates sought from the workers. So we would continue until the negotiations had brought us close to the moment of truth. This was when the management had made its 'final' offer but probably had a little in reserve. On the other hand, the negotiating team would have indicated its own rubicon, though the union might also hope that the workers would permit it the freedom of keeping a little bargaining manoeuvre in reserve. At this stage one would find that an employer might have offered 12 per cent on wages and four significant advances in fringe benefits. The union's mandate, however, might be 20 per cent in wages and six significant advances in fringe benefits. And there we would be stuck. Our technique then would be to put the whole position frankly to the workers and point out that they had the right to strike for the 8 per cent in wages and the two fringe benefits that were still in question. Sometimes we would find that the workers would volunteer a further point of final settlement which might involve a trade-off on the outstanding two fringe benefits giving both sides one along with an 'absolutely final' position of 18 per cent on wages. This would leave the parties only 6 per cent apart instead of 8 per cent. We would then return to the table, secure the missing fringe benefit and get a 'super final' employer offer of 15 per cent on wages. This would necessitate yet another general meeting of the membership which would probably accept this offer with a minority grumbling about the missing 3 per cent in wages. However, the majority would point out that the 3 per cent was not worth fighting about because in the course of a two-year contract the whole of the additional earnings represented by 3 per cent of wages would be exhausted in a three week strike. And so the commonsense of the majority would prevail because it had been, at all stages, involved in the decision-making process; had been at all times responsible for the decision to carry on or to stop, with all the consequences in human suffering that the latter decision could involve.

These exercises in worker participation were fundamental and infinitely rewarding because workers were being invited at all stages to be full, responsible participants in a number of activities that helped to determine their own well being.

When I began my union career, and this remained true throughout, we brought a sort of passion beyond professional skill to the question of raising wages. This was justified on so many grounds. It was justified because the wages that we found were so low and because no matter how quickly we drove up the earnings of the worker, it seemed that the wealth of the establishment grew even faster. And finally it was justified because the Jamaican economy and, indeed, Jamaican society operated without guidelines or any rational frame of discipline. In this situation, it seemed that pressure for higher wages for any particular group was supported by the clear moral justification that every other section of society was pressing equally hard. It is only later that one became conscious of a contradiction between egalitarianism and the wage thrust which was creating an ever widening gap between organised labour, on the one hand, and unorganised labour and the unemployed on the other. Even when assailed by these doubts, however, one could but shrug and remark: 'It is the system.' The truth is that the union movement cannot supply the answer to this problem; that must be sought and organised in the political arena.

Throughout my career I think that we can truly claim that the NWU pioneered the development of the modern labour contract. When we began we saw the contract as the means through which one could develop elementary protection for the worker at the level of job security and fringe benefits. We began to fight for grievance procedures which would guarantee the worker the right to be heard in his own defence if charged with an offence and, additionally, we sought for the right of an aggrieved worker to initiate his own complaint. In the area of fringe benefits all the unions were fighting for the usual vacations with pay, sick leave with pay, overtime rates for work beyond normal hours and so on. In due course, however, the struggles about the contract became more and more political in the sense that we sought to underwrite concepts of social justice through this instrument. As the years passed, grievance procedures were not only concerned to provide 'due process' but also became the instruments through which one sought to redefine the relationship between 'master and servant' and to establish a new relationship founded in the notion of economic egalitarianism. The battles about fringe benefits went beyond the simplicities of fatigue and sickness and sought to underwrite the elements of social security in a worker's life through the labour contract. Much of what we sought to do was occasioned by the failure of Jamaican society and its political system to transfer the abstract notions of social justice which were accepted outside the workplace to the workplace where they might govern the relations between management and worker. As the years passed I used increasingly to vow to write into the union contracts which I negotiated, the principles of social justice which the political system was failing to provide. Throughout this period the concern for human dignity, in simplistic terms, was translating itself into a new dimension in trade union activity where we were consciously using the power of the union to demand a new system of human relationships.

That early hero of the American union movement, Samuel Gompers, once summarised the objectives of the trade union movement with more pith than vision when he said that the movement was about 'more'! The movement that absorbed my attention could take the need for 'more' for granted but had to be concerned with more than that! More wages for a worker who was treated little better than an animal in the workplace is not widely separated in my mind from the slave who is better rather than less well fed. The difference in degree may be great but I am not sure that any difference in kind is discernible. There is no real freedom until the individual is conscious of the opportunity to influence the environment within which he must seek to survive.

Of course, all these objectives in relation to wages, the contract, job security and fringe benefits within the context of a given style of union organisation, must be achieved by a bargaining technique. I confess that I devoted a lot of time, energy and thought to the development of technique across the table: across the bargaining tables at which I sat for so much of the twenty years from 1952 to 1972. If I had to summarise my own concept of technique I think I would have to distinguish two separate but important elements. On the one hand, I believed in knowledge, preparation, the careful exposition of one's case. One had to be absolutely clear-headed and single-minded about the important objectives of a particular negotiation and to deploy other issues as bait. To arrive at a settlement which maximised the welfare, progress and satisfaction of the membership without damaging an industry beyond repair and still leaving the employer with his dignity and sense of fellowship intact, required considerable skills. To the identification of priority, one had to add intuitive timing skill in the capacity to stage the graceful surrender of those claims that were expendable. Above all it was my belief that a cause persuasively argued was more likely to secure agreement than the crude assertion of a demand. I never thought that any claim that could not be eloquently argued belonged at the bargaining table. Equally, it was my conviction that the first purpose of negotiating technique was to set aside human pride as irrelevant. Hence it seemed to me that blustering and the crude assertion 'I want' were unhelpful because they brought personal tension to an already difficult situation and aggravated that imponderable ingredient, the contestant's pride. Hence, the technique rested upon the search for skilful advocacy in a context of good manners.

In the early days of a movement which was angry and understandably sought relief from frustration through rudeness, polite bargaining techniques could easily be suspect. In fact, people used to ask me whether I pounded the table and shouted as was the custom of the time. I very rarely did, however, nor did I ever experience a want of confidence from my worker colleagues as a consequence. The truth is that where a union has come to the bargaining table on the basis of the most careful democratic involvement of the members who are concerned, bad manners quickly become irrelevant because all of the union team at the bargaining table are concerned with a higher reality. On the other hand, a union which duplicates within its own relationships the authoritarian patterns of the general society will find that it brings a sullen team to the table: a team which has not begun to experience that release from frustration which flows from involvement in the decision-making process. Many union leaders shout at the table because they can think of no other means of gaining the confidence of their members. A union leader who has evolved a worker claim in discussion with the membership and who has worked out the bargaining strategy in dialogue with the delegates who are the workers' elect, does not need to impress his team. Such a negotiator can concentrate on the real adversary across the table.

It is impossible to discuss the objectives that one brought to trade unionism without looking at that peculiarly Jamaican situation in which two major unions were each associated with an opposing political party. To this day (1974) the public life of Jamaica is largely dominated by the forces of the PNP/NWU and those of the JLP/BITU. By 1953 I had to face this issue as a fledgeling unionist. What was one's proper duty as a unionist towards the political party which represented the cause of democratic socialism and to which one's allegiance was accordingly owed? I never had any doubt about the fundamental support which the NWU owed to the PNP. This was a partly personal response because although I had no conscious political ambitions at the time I loved my father and admired him as the man I did not doubt to be the greatest living Jamaican. The NWU commitment to the PNP was a rational one for the latter stood for the democratic socialism to which I was ideologically impelled. Finally, I always recognised that the worker cannot hope to secure the 'Jerusalem' of his hopes through union action alone. Unions cannot make new societies; they can only modify old ones. It is only political movements that can organise fundamental change. There was no time in adult life when I failed to grasp this reality.

Much as I believed in the fundamental importance of the NWU/PNP relationship, I doubted whether it was healthy for this relationship to be too close and was jealous lest the union ever become the tool of the party. We felt strongly that there was need for a trade union movement in Jamaica which distinguished clearly and sharply between the workers' problems and interests at the workplace and the larger question of social and economic organisation. There are some who may contend that the distinction is unreal and that the person who imagines the distinction is naïve. Be that as it may, I felt then and feel now that the distinction is real because systems of social and economic organisation tend to be pre-occupied with macro relationships such as those concerned with the ownership of production. Economic and political theoreticians cannot be relied upon to remember the simpler but more profound human equations that deal with the individual worker's experience. A trade union properly understanding its duty can be relied upon to remind all those who wield authority that the worker who must obey is also a human being. Therefore, regardless of whether the economic context is capitalist, socialist or mixed, I held and now hold to the view that the union movement must have a clear element of autonomy and freedom. From this posture it can keep alive the needs of the worker as an individual even while it subscribes to and lends support for the political movements that seeks more just societies. Throughout my union career and now that I am, for the time being, a politician, I was conscious of these twin needs for autonomy, on the one hand, and political commitment on the other. I find that the balance which I sought then is not noticeably different from that which I now accept.

5

THE SUGAR STORY

By the middle of 1953 I suppose I could claim to have begun to win my spurs as a trade unionist on account of the Ariguanabo victory and the lesser though not unimportant part that I had played in the Alcan strike and the early bauxite negotiations. I used to get a travelling allowance of three pounds a week which was ample for the little Standard 8 that I used to drive in those days. I was allowed to sit on the union's executive and, generally speaking, was beginning to regard myself as being as much a trade unionist as a journalist. The union was beginning to establish itself as a significant influence and was making an impact with its aggressive wage concepts and its comparatively sophisticated approach to labour negotiations and labour contracts.

In June of 1953, Vernon Arnett who was the General Secretary of the People's National Party (later to be Minister of Finance from 1959 to 1962) and Treasurer of the National Workers Union, formally offered me a full-time job with the union. It was felt that the time had come to begin a major drive in the sugar industry which at that time was controlled by the BITU with the exception of two small estates, Worthy Park in St Catherine and Barnett just outside of Montego Bay, which were represented by the TUC. It can be argued that the motive behind an organisational drive in the sugar industry was partly political. This was true but not significant since all trade union activity in Jamaican history since 1938 has been partly political in its motivation. Indeed, there is nowhere in the world where economic institutions such as trade unions and employers' groups operate outside of political considerations. In the first place it would be impossible to do so since all politics is concerned with the creation, ownership and distribution of wealth. The economic system reflects the actual means by which people create and distribute wealth. Inevitably, therefore, politics and economics are inseparable as are the political and economic institutions that they work through.

Quite apart, however, from the obvious interest of the People's National Party in the success of the National Workers Union, the latter had itself an organisational duty to expand. By 1953 Jamaican workers had become accustomed to a tradition of aggregate strength. Workers were attracted to unions not only in their occupational capacities, seeking for narrow institutional protection, but equally as members of a class seeking the security of a wider brotherhood. From a purely organisational point of view the comparative smallness of Jamaica as a nation makes it difficult to build a viable trade union on the basis of a single occupation or union. All organisational logic drove the movement to seek to construct a national working-class alliance which would provide the economies of scale while answering the psychological need for class solidarity. Later, I will attempt to examine this in greater depth in considering the past and future relationship between the union movement and the political system in Jamaica. For now, suffice it to say, that the concern of the NWU for expansion rather than consolidation was a response conditioned by the nature of the trade union environment, which has incidentally changed little between then and now. Thus in June, 1953, the NWU was in search of an organiser to tackle the mighty BITU in the sugar industry. At the peak of a sugar crop, in those days, the industry employed between fifty and fifty-five thousand workers. Even during the six months of planting, 'the dull' season as it was called, when no cane was cut and the great mills were still save for the somewhat leisurely activities of the repair and maintenance crews, some twenty-five thousand workers would draw weekly pay cheques. To illustrate the importance of this group both politically and in relation to the strict equations of trade union economics, one has only to look at the employment figures in the bauxite industry. In 1953 the entire union work force of the three bauxite and alumina companies was less than two thousand.

I remember the terms of employment that I was offered vividly. Arnett offered me a salary of eight pounds a week along with a Hillman Minx car which the union would provide and maintain and a petrol, travelling and general subsistence allowance of seven pounds a week. The offer was made with a courteous but unembarrassed apology for the level of the salary. They knew that I knew the state of the union's finances. My salary at *Public Opinion* had been an equally apologetic but unabashed twelve pounds a week. I had not sought to bargain then and saw no reason why I should now since on both occasions the challenge and the opportunity seemed to be of over-riding importance. However, I told Arnett that I needed time to think because the step out of journalism and into full-time trade unionism was a major one involving a complete break with the concept of my life I had evolved in the last year before returning home. I knew enough of unionism to realise that it would be a tough and relentlessly demanding life. The opportunities for the creative use of leisure would have largely to be given up. It did not seem to me a step that one should take lightly. But the truth is that I always knew that I would say 'yes' and suspect that the delay, short as it was, was a formality to which I subjected myself so that the final decision would be cloaked with the respectability of proper reflection.

I took a short holiday with my family in August and reported for work at the beginning of September with the sonorous title of 'Sugar Supervisor of the National Workers Union'. At that moment it was all title and no substance since there was no sugar worker known to be a member of the organisation. However, there had been a promising development. Will Isaacs who had landed me with the responsibility for the Ariguanabo negotiations, had with his inimitable sense of occasion, used the occasion of a public meeting to announce that I was coming to organise the Island's sugar workers. This took place in Spanish Town which is the capital city of the parish of St Catherine, and almost surrounded by three large sugar estates. It seemed that news of the Ariguanabo negotiations had spread by word of mouth in the town where many of the textile factory workers had friends in the big sugar factory at Bernard Lodge Estate which was owned by the United Fruit Company. An enterprising gentleman named Mr Clayton Dunkley who was a scale clerk (responsible for one of the scales that weighed the canes coming in either from the fields of the estate or from neighbouring cane farms) led a deputation of Bernard Lodge factory workers to the union's office in Kingston. Their purpose was to make a formal request that I come to Bernard Lodge to organise the workers who numbered over four thousand during crop on that estate at that time. Shortly after, groups visited me from Caymanas and Bybrook Estates in St Catherine, and from New Yarmouth Estate in the heart of the Vere plain in the southern part of the parish of Clarendon. Caymanas and Bybrook had crop time work forces of around two thousand and New Yarmouth had approximately three thousand.

In 1953, the sugar industry in terms of employment practices represented a state of barely organised chaos. There was little, if any, standardisation of wage practices as between one sugar estate and another. No one has ever completed a count of the number of different work operations commanding different levels and types of remuneration in existence at the time. Each estate had, literally, hundreds of separate operations differently renumerated. No two estates had the identical range of operations and cases of equal pay for equal work occurred by pure coincidence. More often than not the genesis of a particular wage contract in relation to a particular task was lost in antiquity. As a consequence, any rate paid for a particular job at a given moment of time was as likely to be wrong as to be right. This was the case because formal wage negotiations had first commenced in 1941 and were then and subsequently expressed as percentage increases on a body of wages presumed to be in existence at the time of the first agreement in 1941. Therefore, to be certain that any given wage was contractually correct one had to be sure of the rate paid for the particular task by the particular estate in 1941, and this involved records. Assuming that the records existed which was doubtful, one had to be sure that there had been no mistakes in a series of complicated and progressive calculations involving escalating percentages over the intervening years. On the other hand, the task in question might not have existed in 1941 but come into being since then. In that case it was necessary to discover whether there had been some formal agreement struck between workers and management at the time. The existence of such a record was equally uncertain so all wage increases negotiated subsequently would relate to an uncertain premise. When one considers that there were literally thousands of tasks and rates throughout the industry one may begin to get a glimmering of the size of the problem involved in the determination of proper and equitable rates of pay.

The history of union representation in the industry was also interesting. Following the explosion of 1938, sugar workers had flocked to the BITU in thousands. Frome Estate which was owned by the West Indies Sugar Company, a subsidiary of the British sugar firm, Tate and Lyle, had been the scene of one of the most significant and dramatic events of 1938. Workers had been shot and killed in the course of a protest march and this outpost of the economy in the extreme West of the Island had become, along with the waterfront workers of Kingston, a major symbol of the new working class mood. During 1939 and 1940 the newly formed BITU had signed up members by the thousands on the sugar estates. In 1941 Bustamante was interned, and curiously enough, up to that time had never made a wage settlement involving general increases for the sugar workers. Following the internment, the PNP and TUC forces made a decision of historic importance. Deciding to bury the grievances occasioned by Bustamante's walk-out from the Trade Union Advisory Council in 1940, they decided to do everything in their power to keep the BITU alive while they campaigned for Bustamante's release and until this effort succeeded. It is a matter of record that the PNP and the TUC along with citizens' groups concerned with civil liberties and led by young lawyers and businessmen like Leslie Ashenheim, campaigned with unrelenting vigour for Bustamante's release. These efforts were crowned by success in February 1942. In the meantime, some of the TUC leaders, under the guidance of Manley and Nethersole, began to collaborate with the senior BITU organiser of the time, H. M. Shirley, to consolidate the BITU position. The initial big task that they undertook was that of a first general wage increase for the Island's sugar workers. Claims were served. Following the breakdown of negotiations, a strike was called at Duckenfield and Serge Island Estates in the parish of St Thomas. After a long and bitter struggle, the sugar manufacturers gave in and agreed to the first general increase in the history of the industry of $8\frac{1}{3}$ per cent. That first agreement established the tradition of relating wage increases to 'pennies in the shilling'. One penny in the shilling was equal to $8\frac{1}{3}$ per cent. A penny half-penny in the shilling was $12\frac{1}{2}$ per cent, a two-pence in the shilling, $16\frac{2}{3}$ per cent and so on. Since these thousands of rates were paid as so many shillings a day or so many shillings for a chain of trench dug or ton of cane cut, this was a simple, practical and logical way of expressing wage increases in a manner that the workers could understand and the clerical staff calculate.

Later, in a most incredible act of ingratitude or misunderstanding, depending upon your point of view, Bustamante was to denounce this wage settlement along with the people who helped to keep his union alive. He did this at the Kingston Race Course immediately after the release from detention which the same PNP and TUC leaders had campaigned for with such sincerity. By this act he created a deep and seemingly irrevocable schism in the working-class movement. He persuaded his own followers that the PNP was comprised of wicked, scheming men. Simultaneously, he confirmed the followers of the PNP in the belief that he was an unscrupulous and ungrateful self-seeker. Whatever the rights, wrongs, misunderstandings and calculated misrepresentations of the situation, I merely record for the time being the consequences of the action.

From 1943 to 1950 the BITU held absolute sway throughout the sugar industry. A number of wage settlements followed the first effort of 1941, all of them employing the same formula which Bustamante so casually and conveniently denounced at the time. As the war raged on, the sugar market which had teetered on the brink of disaster throughout the 1930s, recovered and grew relatively strong. Britain, plagued by wartime shortage was happy to pay more for Caribbean cane sugar and as the price improved, the BITU secured quite significant general advances in wages. However, they did little or nothing to rationalise the wage structure or set up the kind of contract that could cater for the general needs of the workers. In 1950 the TUC began a sustained bid for representation in the industry and after a long, brutal and sometimes bloody strike at Worthy Park Estate, in a beautiful valley in the hills above Linstead in the parish of St Catherine, they won the right to poll throughout the industry. They were successful at Worthy Park and Barnett Estate but took a terrible beating throughout the twenty or so estates that made up the rest of the industry. However, a very ingenious formula was worked out in which the TUC had formal majority bargaining rights on the two estates which it won but was also accorded minority bargaining rights at all of the estates on which it was defeated along with joint bargaining rights with the BITU insofar as general, industry-wide wage and contract negotiations were concerned. In effect, this meant that the two unions would henceforth share the responsibility of bargaining for the industry as a whole. However, each union would have the primary responsibility for servicing the contract and looking after members' grievances on the particular estates where it was certified as the majority bargaining agent. However, this did not preclude the minority union from having the right to represent grievances of its members on a particular estate. This was an extremely intelligent response to the pragmatic reality of the situation. Bustamante was shrewd enough to realise that the sugar industry was a huge, sprawling empire. Having failed to keep the TUC out he was quick to sense that only chaos would ensue if they were restricted to bargaining for the two estates which they won. If they were not brought in on the responsibility for general bargaining, all that they would have to do was to wait for him to reach a settlement for the major part of the industry which was the responsibility of the BITU and then denounce whatever settlement was made, demand more for the small section of the industry which was their responsibility while at the same time asserting that they would do much better than the BITU if the larger responsibility were theirs. No one was in a better position to understand how effective this kind of propaganda could be since that was the very technique Bustamante had employed at the expense of Manley and his PNP team when they had made the first agreement in 1941 at a time when Bustamante's detention had conveniently removed him from all responsibility for the outcome. Always a shrewd tactician, Bustamante decided that the best way to avoid being hoist with his own petard of

1941, ten years later, was to lock the TUC into a shared responsibility for the general fortunes of the workers in the industry. Thus was born the system of *joint bargaining* rights which has become a remarkable feature of the Jamaican labour scene since 1951. In fact, this was the method that had been employed on the Kingston waterfront when the United Portworkers Union eventually broke the BITU hegemony on the docks in the course of another grim strike in 1949.

This then was the task that faced us. Naturally, the first thing that we had to do was to settle the broad questions of strategy and tactics. Strategically, we had committed ourselves to the view that Jamaica needed a trade union movement that was politically affiliated but not subservient, professional in union terms and therefore never to be used as a political tool. Looking at the sugar industry it seemed to us that two considerations stood out. Firstly, the industry was literally crying out for tough, single-minded, efficient, professional representation. The wages were low, the fringe benefits negligible and worker-management relations deplorable. They were deplorable in human terms because of the unabashed class prejudice which poisoned all inter-personal relationships; and they were deplorable because the wages were in such a state of chaos and confusion that hardly any worker in the industry really believed that he was being paid correctly and in accordance with his contractual rights. By 1953 the general atmosphere, because of the confluence of all these factors was quite paranoid. At the same time, it was perfectly obvious that Bustamante was still a figure of immense, symbolic importance to sugar workers. The fact is that he had played an apparently heroic part from 1938 through his detention and into the time of his first election to power in December 1944. As a result his presence in the industry was an interesting compound of gratitude and heroic recollection. In short, all the ingredients of myth were present. It seemed, therefore, that since we were involved in a strategy aimed at the establishment of an effective, democratic and thoroughly professional trade union organisation we did not need to be concerned with a political analysis of the Bustamante myth. That could be properly left to the politicians. Once this was understood, we were released from any obligation to seek a confrontation with either Bustamante's person or his memory. Our task was to point to the inadequacies, deficiencies and even miseries of the worker's lot and to summon everyone from grass weeder to electrician to a democratic involvement in building an organisation which answered both the practical and the psychological needs of the worker. Wages had to be raised and job security guaranteed. At the same time employers had to be made to recognise the dignity of the workers and made to respect them as people. Most importantly, the workers had to learn confidence in themselves. We devised, accordingly, an organising strategy in terms of this analysis and towards these objectives. I did not myself attack nor allow anyone else to attack Bustamante personally. In fact, we did not attack anybody in this way since it has always seemed to me that personal vilification is counter-productive as it distracts attention from the message that you are trying to get across; and it is destructive because it introduces into public dialogue an irrelevant irritant that can poison the atmosphere of a political system and in the end overwhelm a people's capacity for achievement. What we planned to concentrate upon were those practical grievances which consumed the sugar worker's life at the time while suggesting that an organisation controlled by the workers themselves would be capable of the kind of sustained assault upon the worker's problems which general conditions seemed to demand.

The other important, practical decision that we had to make involved the question of whether to attempt to organise the industry as a whole, or whether to proceed selectively. As with the decision about Bustamante, I had no hesitation. We decided to work with the four estates which had a nucleus of workers who had made a positive approach. This means that we could operate with a carefully chosen and trained staff and within the confines of a manageable situation. And so the battle was joined.

The campaign proceeded at four distinct but interlocking levels. In the first place we had to build up a professional nucleus of full-time organisers, on the basis of at least one for each estate. The team was assembled from amongst sugar workers themselves in the main. There was Clayton Dunkley of Bernard Lodge, Wellesley Hay and Ben Beal of New Yarmouth, Fred Clarke who actually came from Kingston but had contacts in Caymanas Estate and Charles Bissick at Bybrook. Hedley Allman, an Ariguanabo delegate at the time was a great help throughout this period and later went on to become a senior officer of the union with a fine record. There were others who gave voluntary assistance of value like Mervin Harris who later became a parish councillor in May Pen. From the outset, Caswell Rodney who is now an assistant island supervisor of the union, was a tower of strength. A former BITU and JLP organiser, he had become thoroughly disillusioned and offered his services in the NWU campaign. A tough and resourceful man, he was a colourful and distinctive member of a team that showed remarkable dedication and courage in the months that were to lie ahead.

Then there was the delegate structure that had to be built from amongst the workers themselves. This was a careful operation that had to be carried out with considerable discretion. There were members of management who were not above dismissing a worker if he were suspected of activist tendencies in the cause of a new organisation, hence delegates had to be chosen with an eye to their excellence as workers as well as their desire for change. A bad worker is a weak link in the delegate chain because a management can easily fire him for non-performance even if this is not the real cause. A good worker is a powerful force for union organisation because a hostile management can only touch such a person at the risk of the clear exposure of victimisation. All these factors therefore, had to be borne carefully in mind as we built the delegate team.

The third element in the campaign involved my own activity. I determined from the outset to get to know the workers personally and to become familiar with their working conditions. For months I walked up and down the estates getting to know the field gangs, the cane cutters, the cane loaders, the grass weeders, the tractor drivers and sidemen, the trench men and, indeed, all this gallant company of men and women who were the heirs to and sufferers of the plantation system. It was harder to get to know the factory workers on the job because this group worked inside a fenced compound which was out of bounds to all unionists save the official agents of the organisations with bargaining rights. Instead, I used to talk to these groups through the fence and during their lunch breaks and outside the factory compound at the shift change-overs. This was an invaluable experience for me because it provided the living evidence of conditions which cannot be fully grasped from any written account, however vivid. My own experience had been limited to the observation of the workings of poverty in the home environment. Political work had brought me close to slum life in Kingston with its grim and endlessly repeated tragedy of poor housing, children and parents crowded into single rooms, and whole families undermined if not shattered by unemployment and the general conditions of shanty town life. I had not up to then had personal experience of the impact of the plantation system and the seasonal sugar crop upon rural life. For six months at a time thousands of rural families were disrupted while the men migrated to the sugar estates to earn the greater part of the year's income cutting or loading cane. During the crop period, these workers would bunk down, literally shoulder to shoulder, in large and mainly dilapidated barracks. If the barracks were full they would have to pay an exorbitant rent for a back room in a hovel that passed for a house in one of the sugar towns like Central Village, Spanish Town, Lionel Town, May Pen, Gimme-me-bit or Hayes.

In those days there was still a tendency to feel that a person with a job, any job, was lucky by comparison with those who had none. Society at large, under the prodding of the union movement, was only just beginning to accept that a job does not by itself discharge the national obligation under the social contract which is implied between each individual and the state to which he belongs. I owe to the sugar workers of Jamaica more than to any other group the development of my own understanding that a job is not an end but a beginning of that contract. It was in the course of my observation of the sugar workers' lives that I experienced the deepening of my own social awareness to the point where I understood that the theoretical equations of the socialist analysis of justice must be pursued to their logical conclusion in terms of the total human experience. Since at least a quarter of the average person's life span is actually spent at work, it is not enough to see that slice of time as providing the income with which to support the good life in the other seventy-five per cent. In any event, between a quarter and a third of the total span is spent asleep so that it is fair to say that people spend about an equal amount of their waking time between work and leisure. Hence, if human happiness is the aim of social organisation then a person's experience on the job is an indispensable element in the organisation of the pursuit of that happiness.

As the campaign proceeded in the latter part of 1953 and early 1954, I was increasingly shocked by the lack of any sense of responsible participation by management in the lives of the workers. Management and supervisory attitudes tended to range from a sort of lofty indifference through callousness to extremes of outright hostility. Very few estates bothered with simple expressions of concern like providing tents for shade and clean drinking water for thirsty field gangs still slogging it out under the merciless midday sun after a pre-dawn start. The workers shared the universal conviction that the managements were the unrepentant heirs of the slave masters of 120 years before. There was a general conviction that the rates were wrong and that the workers were the general victims of a conspiracy to defraud by means of chronically low wages. All this had combined to produce a group of workers who were fiercely loyal to each other. This was a group who saw themselves pitted against the larger society and surviving by their own group solidarity. Their collective experience of suffering and exploitation had made them into a strange and wonderful kind of elite amongst the sufferers of the land. Their elitism sprang from their capacity to identify with each other and to forge a group that was held together by the common bond of their resolve to fight back. Although I have never been privileged to know the miners of Wales as a group, I imagine from what I have read that there are strong similarities between the Welsh miner and the Jamaican sugar worker. This is particularly true at the level of a sense of group identity and a special perception of the relationship between the group and the rest of society.

During this period I think we gave sugar workers a new

sense of how progress might be achieved. Hitherto, union experience had tended to be authoritarian revolving around the notion of a group of workers in need of a Messiah. The element of self-reliance in the processes of progress was minimal; dependence upon outside leadership was the dominant theme. We tried to draw the sugar worker to the procedures and occasions of self-reliance. Naturally, one cannot claim total success because new ideas of this sort have to fight against powerful forces of habit and attitudinal inertia. Slavery and colonialism do not combine to produce the self-reliant man. That human being has to be forged in a new experience. Such a man has to evolve in the face of new challenges and a new process of group education. At least, however, we made a beginning and in the process, the larger education was to take place in my own mind and in the development of my own perceptions. Another benefit that I gained from the experience was the discovery of the rare degree of kindness, humour, loyalty and plain courage of the sugar workers as a group. It is a stimulating and rewarding experience to spend a morning with the field gangs on their cane farms. The conversation reflects a fascinating mixture of worldly wisdom, durable personal philosophy and sometimes incredible prejudice. And ever present is that quality of wit with which the genuine sufferer defends himself against adversity and lightens the spiritual burden of poverty.

The meetings which we used to hold as often as five nights a week were the fourth element in our campaign. To get to speak to sugar workers in Jamaica requires an enormous investment in time in that it means meetings in little villages all over the countryside. I had my car equipped with a loudspeaker bolted to the roof with an amplifier, microphone, and most importantly, a turntable for records. Having always believed that life need not be dreary, I personally chose all the calypsoes, rock-and-roll numbers, the 'yank' tunes and the other popular music which were in vogue at the time. We did not have tapes in those days so I used to park the car first, and start playing records. When a crowd had gathered and the young boys and girls established their presence and identity by quite dazzling displays of dancing, we would settle down to the serious business of speech making. I used to be able to speak with some authority about the sugar worker's plight because I was getting to know the nuts and bolts of his situation through daily contact with it. I avoided rhetoric, philosophy and the subject of 'Bustamante'. At most, the last would be subjected to a little light banter. Always the message was the same: 'Here are the problems, here is a chance to tackle them yourselves through democratic organisation.'

Those were great days. I used to feel that a really significant dialogue was developing between the sugar workers and our new team out of which we were all learning something. All my life I have had a tendency to attract nick-names. In school this occasioned me quite unnecessary grief because I firmly believed at that time that a nick-name was intended to express contempt. Curiously enough, it was the sugar worker who taught me that it is just as likely to be an expression of affection, or can even be a repository of popular hope. In no time I was dubbed – 'young boy'! In fact, the name spread so far and fast and stuck so hard that I used to have visions of myself in my later years being pushed to a sugar workers meeting in a wheelchair, shaking with palsy to the chant of 'young boy, young boy'! The fact that I was then approaching thirty didn't seem to deter anyone and the stage was eventually reached when organisers, delegates and everyone, even in ordinary conversation would address me that way. Indeed, I can remember hearing a delegate say to the manager of an estate during a negotiation: 'Mr Manager, what "young boy" is trying to tell you, is so and so.' I suspect that the name symbolised to those who used it the idea of a new start with a young leader.

Under the rules which were then and still are in existence for determining representational rights (between rival unions) at a workplace, a claimant union was required to furnish either a certificate of dues-paying membership in the establishment where bargaining rights were claimed or, in some cases, a signed petition was an acceptable alternative. Although we were building up a sizeable membership, we decided to instruct our members not to cancel their dues to the BITU which were paid by payroll deduction on the basis of a signed check-off form. On the one hand, we were afraid of having our members victimised by a management that would realise the significance of a cancellation of dues to the BITU; and, on the other, we had no desire to alert the BITU to the extent of the disaffection which was actually taking place. Therefore, we opted for the petition. Early in 1954 we began collecting signatures and at the end of about a month had gathered several thousand names; although I no longer remember the exact number. What mattered was that the petitions were sufficiently massive and authentic to persuade the Ministry of Labour that we represented a significant force. In due course the Ministry officials persuaded the manufacturers that the wisest course of action was to take polls on the four estates that we had claimed. I think that by then the manufacturers had realised that we had the capacity to shut down at least three of the four estates if they refused. Having already learnt their lesson from the bitter experience of the Worthy Park strike, the manufacturers were ready to co-operate rather than risk a repetition. In due course, on 31 March 1954, a poll agreement was signed involving the Sugar Manufacturers Association, the BITU and the NWU. The TUC were not directly involved as they had only a minority position on the particular estates. However, they raised no objection to the procedure. It was agreed that the polls would be conducted on a rolling basis on successive days starting at Caymanas and ending at New Yarmouth. However, all ballot boxes were to be sealed until the day after the final polling so that the later polls would not be affected by results at the earlier ones.

Once the agreement was reached to hold the polls, things took on something of the quality of a general election. After careful analysis we decided not to permit the People's National Party leadership into the battle in any significant way because we were dealing, in the main, with people who, still politically loyal to the JLP and to Bustamante, might react badly to a major PNP political presence. In any case, we did not wish a politically induced victory, even if one were possible, because this would have run entirely counter to our fundamental strategy of building up a union that was essentially independent and worker oriented with a firm political affiliation as a separate and differently motivated phenomenon. As a consequence, it was only in the last couple of nights that we introduced Manley himself and figures like 'Father' Coombs into the campaign. Up to the date of the poll agreement I had been the only major voice in the campaign backed up by the sugar team that we had created for the operation. After the poll agreement we brought into the battle trade union figures like Ken Sterling and Florizel Glasspole, to be followed at the very end by one or two of the political 'big guns'. On the other hand, the BITU, which was effectively led by its island supervisor, Mr Hugh Shearer, introduced Bustamante and the other JLP leaders and government ministers from the outset. The BITU strategy revolved around Bustamante's personality as the 'Messiah', who had been to prison for the sugar workers, and around Shearer, as the architect of the recent monetary benefits and the existing labour contract.

The result was a massive victory for the NWU which swept the polls at Caymanas and Bybrook in St Catherine, and most significantly crushed the BITU at New Yarmouth Estate which was the heart of Southern Clarendon, Bustamante's own constituency. The BITU salvaged its honour with a very narrow victory at Bernard Lodge estate; but the defeat at New Yarmouth was a critical blow since this occurred in the heartland of territory that was supposedly impregnable.

This victory, by its sheer size and drama, triggered a great surge of support for the NWU. By the end of 1954 we had become a major force at Frome estate and were making real progress at Hampden and Long Pond in the parish of Trelawny, Appleton in St Elizabeth, Monymusk in Clarendon, Gray's Inn in St Mary and Serge Island in St Thomas. Within a couple of years we were able to challenge the TUC at Worthy Park and at Barnett and by beating them handily in both places, established ourselves as the only other union in the sugar industry.

Our first task was, of course, to survey the scene, become familiar with the contract and negotiating procedures of the industry and to settle upon a strategy to achieve a new phase of progress for the workers. The contract that we inherited was not without merit. It provided for a grievance procedure through which the workers could seek redress for individual complaints; it provided a first approach to fringe benefits by establishing a forty-eight hour work week, an eight hour work day with premium rates for overtime work and work done on holidays. It also provided for paid vacation and sick leave on the basis of one day's paid vacation and sick leave for each twenty-three days worked provided that not less than two hundred days had been worked in the particular year. The estates were divided into three grades: A1, A and B with different minimum rates for men and women for each category. The larger estates such as Tate and Lyle's Frome and Monymusk, United Fruit Company's Bernard Lodge, and the English owned Duckenfield and Caymanas were grouped in the top grade. Roughly speaking, the medium sized estates such as Bybrook, which we had just captured, Gray's Inn and Appleton, were in the middle group. And the little estates, like Richmond Llandovery in St Ann and Holland in St Elizabeth, were in the bottom grade. The actual minimum rates were for men A1 9s 8d per day, A 9s a day, and B 8s 4d a day. For women the rates were slightly lower.

As I remarked earlier, the rest of the wage contract could only be deduced by working through the maze of early records as modified by agreed percentages of increase over the years. The startling feature of the agreement however, was to be found like a sting in its tail. As was perfectly natural, the contract provided that any dispute arising out of the interpretation of the agreement or from a worker's complaint about his rights under the agreement could be dealt with under the grievance procedure but was to be subject to compulsory arbitration in the event that no agreement could be reached. Under this clause, strikes were forbidden on the basis that grievances could be settled by arbitration. So far, so good. The contract went on to provide that there could be annual negotiations for improvements in wages, fringe benefits and other changes in other basic provisions of the contract. However, we discovered, to our horror, that negotiations of this annual sort and dealing with basic matters such as wages were themselves subject to a no strike clause and compulsory arbitration. What is more, this prohibition applied in perpetuity since the contract had no term. The parties to the agreement of 1951 had signed away the worker's right to strike in perpetuity. There was no pretence that the sugar industry was an essential service, there was merely a bald agreement that the worker's interests were subject to compulsory arbitration for the rest of time. We had never previously been able to get hold of the official agreement and this feature of it had been kept comparatively quiet. It certainly took us by surprise.

In due course we settled on five major objectives. The first of these was to change the agreement which made annual negotiations about the interest of the workers subject to compulsory arbitration. Understandably enough, we made this a cardinal point of policy. Next we determined to press for a codification and rationalisation of rates in the industry so that workers could both know and enjoy their rights. Thirdly, we set ourselves to achieve the standardisation of wages so that there could be equal pay for equal work. Then we determined to press for a normal range of fringe benefits such as severance pay, shift premiums and the like. Finally, we decided that it was important to seek ways of promoting stability in the industry, having regard to the dangers inherent in a situation of chronic union rivalry. Some of these objectives, such as the thrust for standardisation and restoration of the right to strike, were new. The cause of stability found ready support from the BITU. The desire to codify, standardise and press for fringe benefits were eminently sensible proposals which obviously commended themselves to our new partners. However, much of this proved to be easier in the formulation than the performance.

From the outset we made a habit of bringing a number of delegates from our estates to conferences so that the workers could have representatives from their midst as witnesses to the discussion and advisers to the main negotiators. Thus, surrounded by a corps of estate delegates, we entered our first official negotiation right after the polls and found the sugar manufacturers in the midst of an offer of a half penny in the shilling bonus to be paid on crop wages earned in the 1954 crop period. This matched what had been done the year before. Our very first time out we called for the manufacturers' accounts. What we got were figures of the most rudimentary sort, but deficient as they were, they were enough to prove that the manufacturers could do more. In the end the offer was increased from $4\frac{1}{6}$ per cent to $8\frac{1}{3}$ per cent (one penny in the shilling), the bargain was struck at that level and the NWU emerged as the hero of the piece. Whether we deserved all the credit is not for me to say. However, deserving or not, we had arrived with a bang. This was in 1954.

The years that followed were a mixture of accomplishment and frustration. It proved incredibly difficult to make any major breakthrough which would lead to the rationalisation and modernisation of worker conditions in the industry. I sometimes felt that we were bogged down in some vast, complex morass. It seemed that there were so many sources of resistance to change that nothing really effective could be accomplished. It was as though the processes of change were themselves caught like a great ram whose horns have become entangled in the undergrowth of a jungle.

It was not until the early 1960s, for example, that we were able to negotiate comprehensive new labour agreements with the industry which could be the basis of proper booklets issued to each worker. In due course we hammered out a new agreement which restored the right of the worker to strike if negotiations for a new contract broke down; and in time we won an important, indeed historic, severance pay agreement which provided that any worker who became redundant through technological change or rationalisation would be entitled to a sum of money to compensate for the loss of job and having regard to accumulated service. In fact, the severance pay formula was well ahead of anything then obtaining in either England or the United States, and provided that any worker who became redundant and who had more than three years of service would receive one week's current wages for each of the first three years of service; a further one and a half weeks' wages for each of the fourth and fifth years of service; and two weeks' wages for each year of service from the sixth year onwards. Although the qualifying period was three years, once this was met the formula applied to the start of service. Naturally, there was another formula for arriving at a week's wages in the case of workers who did not work on a year round basis which also covered task workers who had no weekly wage as such. During this period sick and vacation leave were improved somewhat and shift premium payments were introduced for the first time. There were also first and rather limited attempts to rationalise the wage structure of the industry.

One very significant change took place in fringe benefits. Throughout the history of the labour movement the question of union dues has been a constant source of wrangling between management and labour. Unions have contended that no worker should be able to enjoy the benefits of negotiated increases without paying 'tithe' to the union which secures those increases. In fact some unions have gone so far as to insist, sometimes successfully, that no worker can obtain employment in an industry except through membership of the union. On the other hand, employers have argued with equal fervour that no worker should be compelled to join a union contrary to the dictates of individual conscience. If the argument is conceived in logical – moral terms it is incapable of solution. Depending upon the premises from which you begin it is possible to construct an unassailable argument. As a consequence, neither side has ever persuaded the other. On the other hand, it is doubtful whether either side to the dispute has been too concerned about the moral issue. As so often in life, institutional self-interest and considerations of power create the real framework within which man acts. Having decided upon a course of action we summon up our intellectual ingenuity to justify the actions which we have determined to pursue and upon which we are already embarked. Obviously, you can argue a perfect case to justify the right of the majority to impose its will upon a minority which is a part of a total group of workers. Equally, one can justify the right of the individual to oppose a course of action which is inconsistent with individual conscience and to retain a job notwithstanding. Of course, we used to point out that democracy operates on the basis of majority rule. Majorities impose systems of taxation upon minorities. Minorities do not have the right to refuse to pay taxes. Therefore, I would argue why should a minority of workers have the right to refuse to pay dues? In its own context, the contention is unassailable. Ironically, the employers would reply that this principle was valid where it was a question of the state imposing this will upon everyone but not valid when it was merely a majority of workers imposing their will upon a minority of their fellows. This was particularly amusing because the employers who invested the state with a mystical personality through which all decisions are validated regardless of the nature of the decision, would be the first in another context to protest against the power of that same state. It did not occur to them that it is the process by which the state makes its decisions which validates those decisions and not some mystical authority that attaches to states as such. In the case of our society taxation is validated by the fact that a majority elects the government which imposes the tax. Equally, therefore, the necessity to pay union dues is validated to the extent that a majority elects a union to represent their interests and to make rules on their behalf. The philosophical similarity between taxes and dues where governments and unions are democratically elected consistently escaped the attention and the understanding of employers. Instead, they preferred to advance the interests of the individual against the majority in the case of payment of dues in an intellectual formulation which would have come more appropriately from anarchists than from men who were quick to assert the right of the employer to give orders and to demand that the state punish all who transgress against the rights of property.

The truth is that no one ever wins arguments of that sort. Nevertheless, we were able to back the sugar manufacturers into a corner from which they could not logically escape. The fact that they made fundamental concessions, however, is perhaps due less to the success of our arguments than to their own perception of self-interest. In due course, it occurred to the sugar employers that the unions had come to stay and that the union leaders were not wild men bent upon the destruction of the industry. Instead, it became clear that these were rational people seeking to maximise the workers' share of the proceeds of a successful industry. Doubtless with this in mind, they eventually worked out a very interesting formula with the two unions; it was decided that all workers in the industry must elect either to pay dues to the DITU or the NWU or, in the event that they objected absolutely to paying dues to either as a matter of conscience, they were permitted to elect that their dues be handed over to a charity to be designated jointly by the unions.

The truth is that this clause providing an alternative was a sensible and pragmatic solution. Originally the employers had wanted to resist the compulsory payment of dues in the hope of keeping alive a potential anti-union, strike-breaking force against times of trouble. The unions, for their part, could not tolerate a group of people who enjoyed all the benefits of union negotiation but contemptuously refused to pay dues, usually through indifference or 'bad-mindedness'. At the same time, we were aware of the fact that there are a few individuals who belong to religions that refuse to permit membership of organisations such as trade unions and political parties. I myself have come across cases where people were trapped in a genuine crisis of conscience because they wanted to support a trade union but had been threatened with expulsion from their Church. It was this experience which had led me to conceive of the idea of the 'charity option'. From the employers' point of view the 'charity option' was a useful device because it enabled them to keep faith with the principle of individual liberty which they had championed. The extent to which the devotion to individual liberty reflected a genuine moral passion as distinct from a tactical position is neither here nor there. What really matters is that the 'charity option' proved to be the pragmatic device which laid the foundation for a historic breakthrough in the sugar industry in which the agreements provided for the compulsory payment of dues by payroll deduction to the unions which had been democratically chosen by the workers.

On the wage front progress was equally slow. The year following our full-scale (or NWU's) entry into the industry, negotiations proved as difficult as ever. In the end, we were unable to secure any agreement about the 1955 crop and the matter was referred to arbitration under an English professor of Economics, C. G. Beasley. A tribunal of which he was chairman and whose other members were Mr W. L. Hay, Managing Director of Jamaica Milk Products Ltd., the wholly owned Nestle subsidiary in Jamaica, and Mr W. J. Masterton, the Manager and owner of Masterton's Ltd., an engineering firm. On May 6, 1955 the BITU, NWU and TUC had signed a memorandum of agreement with the Sugar Manufacturers' Association setting out the terms of reference for an arbitration. The arbitrators were asked to decide, firstly whether the SMA should pay a basic permanent wage increase for the 1955 crop; and if so, how much? Secondly, whether the SMA should pay a crop bonus for the 1955 crop; and if so, how much? The unanimous findings, handed down on the June 7, were that the SMA should not pay a permanent wage increase but should pay a crop bonus of 12½ per cent (1½d in the shilling) on all earnings during the crop period.

In 1957 the world price of sugar sky-rocketed and we were able to secure a basic wage increase of 12½ per cent and in addition to that a crop bonus of 1¾d in the shilling (just under 15 per cent). New minimum rates were established as well as further minor increases in fringe benefits. However, the real showdown on wages was to come in 1959.

The spectacular movement of the world price of sugar in 1957 had led to the first major breakthrough in wages since 1952 when the Commonwealth Sugar Agreement opened up a new era for the sugar industry. However, I had always been deeply suspicious of the methods by which the Sugar Manufacturers' Association reported their profits to us, and indeed, of the earnings which they admitted. Although I had no particular training in accounting techniques, it seemed to me that the annual exercise was crude and casual. In 1959 we decided to try to put the whole question to the test. The artificially high price of sugar on the world market had receded and we were once again dealing with an industry with what one might term a normal market in terms of average prices. As usual, we put in a claim for wage increases and other fringe benefits. The 1957 agreement had raised minimum day labour rates to the princely sum of eleven shillings (11s) a day for men and eight shillings and six pence (8s 6d) a day for women on the A1 Estates and nine shillings and four pence (9s 4d) a day for men and seven shillings (7s) a day for women on the bottom B grade estates. The negotiations took the usual form with the manufacturers assuring us that nothing could be done other than some minor crop bonus adjustment. Certainly, they recoiled in horror at the thought of another basic increase in wages.

I decided that the time for action had come and began threatening to organise strikes in the industry. Bustamante's first reaction was characteristic. The thought of somebody else calling a strike in the industry which he regarded as his own did not appeal to him and he issued a statement denouncing those who were seeking to foment 'trouble'. This obviously meant me. He had clearly under-rated the extent of my own influence and of the NWU's 'presence' in the industry. We went ahead with our plans and in due course Shearer realised that the BITU was not so much being out-manoeuvred, as out-manoeuvring itself as a consequence of Bustamante's resistance to the idea of a strike. In due course, he made overtures and a meeting was arranged at Bustamante's Tucker Avenue residence to be attended by Shearer and me. The meeting was noteworthy for two things: the fact that Sir Alexander served an extremely pleasant champagne at ten in the morning; and the bargain which was struck to call strikes at Monymusk, New Yarmouth and Frome Estates. This was a remarkable reversal on the part of the BITU but Sir Alexander always was a practical man and, doubtless, Shearer had advised him of the trouble that they were heading into by opposing my wish to put the SMA to the wall with a strike.

At the height of the 1959 crop in one of those rare moments when a new dimension emerges in the historical process, the first joint strike between the unions in the sugar industry was called. For the first time a joint trade union meeting was scheduled in Lionel Town in the heart of Southern Clarendon and to this were invited all of the maybe 6,000 workers at Tate and Lyle's Monymusk Estate. I will never forget it. There were, literally, thousands of workers gathered in the town square. This is a dusty space bounded on two adjoining sides by shops, with mainly open land punctuated by the odd shack to the north and entered from a dirt road, flanked by some houses, from the east. The square was bursting. The atmosphere had that electricity which is present when history is to be made and the people know it because they know that the event itself is historic. The BITU and the NWU, with all that that implied, were about to launch a joint strike. I cannot recall the preliminary speeches but in due course, Shearer was on. He made, as always, a clever, tough, hard-hitting speech full of sarcasm and where advocacy was well reinforced by the skilful selection of facts and figures. He got a great and well-deserved reception. Then it was my turn. I was extremely nervous and tense. But then, I always am, although no one seems to believe this. I was introduced and came forward to the microphone conscious of the history of the occasion and the emotion that it had generated. For a long moment I stood silent surrounded by that magnetic force a crowd exerts when it is tense with expectation. I heard a voice that sounded like mine but seemed to come from someone else going through the preliminaries 'Mr Chairman, Mr Island Supervisor of the BITU, officers and delegates of the BITU and NWU . . .' and then I paused feeling for that inspiration which if it comes, will express the inner essence of the moment. Suddenly, I said: 'Brothers and Sisters of the BITU; Brothers and Sisters of the NWU, we have a common struggle. We have been divided . . . but now, we are joined . . . and the word is love!' Never before or since have I experienced anything like what took place. The simple phrase, 'the word is love', which I had not planned but seemed, rather, to have drawn from the emotion of the crowd itself, struck some deep chord of longing and need. It was as if the place exploded. It was quite a long time before I could make my speech and when I made it I knew that it was an anticlimax because I had said it all already: 'the word is love'. I knew that to the crowd this meant that the workers were to be united again, were to fight shoulder to shoulder again, were to seek some small share of justice through the assertion of their rights again. I think I learnt more about the nature of man and the levels of his loyalty in that instant than at any time throughout the rest of my life. It taught me that men will respond to the claims of institutional loyalty unswervingly. They will fight each other in the name of rival organisations without a hint of betrayal. But in the innermost parts of their beings there are other longings that are more basic, if you like more primeval, that reflect deeper impulses. The NWU, the TUC and the BITU had fought each other at different times and in different ways, each proclaiming itself the true repository of the faith; the true custodian of the holy grail of working-class progress. But deep in the heart of the workers was another understanding. It did not question the truth as it appeared to be revealed by any one union. However, it knew that there is a deeper truth and that is to do with the longing of working men to come to a new position of justice and dignity as human beings. In this understanding there is the, perhaps unexpressed, semi-conscious recognition that no one trade union can bring about that revolution in the circumstances of the working man that is so ardently desired, so incompletely understood and so terribly needed. I am not being fanciful when I say that the phrase, 'the word is love' suddenly expressed the need of every worker who had slogged away for eleven shillings, who had doubted that his wages were just, who had borne the midday sun weeding grass or cutting cane to believe that somehow the unity which made this strike possible would lead to a real step along the slow, painful road of progress.

All three strikes were completely effective. We had no intention of allowing these shutdowns to spread to the whole industry unless this became absolutely necessary. An island-wide sugar strike would be extremely difficult to handle, and granted our limited resources, impossible to finance. At the back of my mind was the conviction that we could win a wage increase and other benefits for the workers if we could only get the kind of tribunal that would not be intimidated by the claim of the manufacturers that they were unable to pay with its implied threat that this huge industry would collapse should it be required to pay a wage increase. On the one hand, we felt sure that the industry could afford to pay more. On the other, we knew that there was no way of proving this in an ordinary arbitration where there is no show of power available to compel an employer to reveal his accounts fully. We had long since realised that the employers could always stalemate the arbitration game. Arbitrators have to be mutually agreed. An employer has only to refuse to accept any person that he suspects might play rough in the matter of accounts to force a union into a stalemate. Either nothing happens or the union is driven to the acceptance of the kind of person who assumes the total honour of the employer's protestations and lacks both the scepticism and the ruthlessness to put everyone to the sword of proof! My determination was to get a commission of enquiry of the highest international calibre. A commission would have the legal power to subpoena any information if needed. An international body, properly chosen would approach a dispute of this sort with professional scepticism and would be unlikely to be intimidated by the kind of aristocratic aura that surrounded a group like the Sugar Manufacturers' Association in the Jamaica of the 1950s. As it happened, my father was the head of the Government in those days and willing to co-operate fully when I explained what I had in mind. I remember telling berg, who was a Queen's Counsel and regarded by many as commission of enquiry provided it was of a calibre that I could respect intellectually and trust morally. He immediately began a search for the kind of chairman that we would need. In due course he heard of a Canadian lawyer, H. Carl Goldenbert, who was a Queen's Counsel and regarded by many as the greatest figure in labour conciliation and arbitration in Canadian history. This was a man who had presided over a number of Commissions of Enquiry in Canada, had been Deputy Chairman of the Joint War Production Board of the United States and Canada during World War II and mediator and arbitrator in a number of major labour disputes throughout Canada. He was highly recommended by the Canadian Government. Canadian employing groups had every confidence in him. Most important from my point of view, my Canadian trade union friends told me that his reputation stood equally high amongst trade unionists. In any event, my father had decided that this was the man and although my agreement was irrelevant, I was in fact delighted. The Government eventually decided upon a five man commission with Goldenberg as chairman. The other members were to be Cleve Kidd, Research Director of the United Steelworkers of America, Canadian Division, Mr J. J. Mills a former head of the Jamaica Teachers' Association and an experienced local arbitrator, Mr John R. Church an international director of Price Waterhouse Ltd. and a man regarded as one of the most distinguished accountants in the world, and the Hon. C. H. Browne, P.C., of the firm of Manton and Hart who was a director of the Sugar Manufacturers' Association and a lawyer for the employers' group. This was and is probably the most distinguished Commission of Enquiry into a Jamaican labour dispute, in intellectual terms, in our history. By agreement, when the Commission of Enquiry into the whole sugar industry dispute was announced, the unions called off the strike and the workers of Frome, Monymusk, and New Yarmouth returned to work.

The Goldenberg Commission commenced hearing on 4 May 1959. We had a couple of months in which to prepare for the case and we decided to make a major presentation. Goldenberg had asked both sides to the dispute to prepare briefs which would set out their respective positions. The term 'brief' may have had both a technical and a descriptive relevance to the effort of the SMA. It had only a technical relevance on the union side. I made up my mind that we were going to put together a document that would not only indicate why we thought we should get a wage increase for sugar workers, but which would also put on record for all times the case of the agricultural worker of Jamaica for progress. We decided to analyse the condition of the sugar worker from a number of points of view. We set out to prove, in real terms, how little actual progress had been achieved in terms of living standards since 1938. We set out to establish, in absolute terms, the standard of living of the sugar worker in 1959. We set out to demonstrate the relationship between the sugar worker's wage and objective criteria which could be applied to the notion of a civilised standard of living. We decided to construct a 'basket of goods' based on minimum standards of nutrition as laid down by the United Nations, translated into the terms of foods available locally and related to the earning power of the sugar worker. We developed statistics that showed the capacity of the sugar worker to educate his children and provide a home. We compared the state of the sugar worker in both absolute current and historical terms to other workers in other sectors of the economy. We even carried out a statistical exercise that was new in Jamaica involving the linking of two cost of living indices. An old index of prices had been established at the start of the Second World War and had remained in vogue until about 1955. At that time it had risen to a figure well over 300 from the old 1938 base of 100. But a new index had come into effect with a base of 100 which by 1959 had shown a normal increase in the days when inflation proceeded at a stately 3 per cent or 4 per cent per annum. We linked the two indices, and traced them back to their 1939 origins while picking up the wages of 1939 and tracing them forward to their 1959 levels.

The bulk of this work was done by Carl Hall, who was then the Research Officer of the NWU, Wes Wainwright, who was the Assistant Island Supervisor, and myself. I set up a five day week working schedule in which we would meet at eight o'clock every night from Monday to Friday to work on the brief. Carl would do research along agreed lines during the day while Wes and I were negotiating for various groups in the union. We would then meet at night at eight and work at least to midnight and often till two or three in the morning. Sometimes Shearer would come in and spend an hour with us discussing aspects of the case but mostly it was Carl, Wes and myself slogging away at facts and figures, weighing and testing propositions in our search for a definitive presentation. It was one of the great intellectual experiences of my life and Carl was a tower of strength with his sharp, conceptual mind and great capacity for detailed work. Wes was the perfect activist: tough, able, loyal, cool in a crisis and blessed with inexhaustible stamina. He had a shrewd eye for the practical issue and the missing detail.

In due course the union brief was completed, running to more than a hundred typed pages. Later a group of us in the NWU were to exceed this accomplishment in another field as activists in a great moral cause. However, it was and remains the intellectual high point of my trade union career.

When the brief was completed, there remained only the question of how the task of advocacy would be shared between Shearer and myself. Protocol required that there be a division of labour. It was decided that Shearer would present the social case which we had prepared with such painstaking effort. This was the case that showed how little real increase in wages had taken place, what was the state of poverty as expressed in terms of housing, education for children, nutrition and the like. I was to present the economic case though, at that time, it was hard to know just what this case would be since all the figures available to us up till then indicated an employing group with no ability to pay. However, part of our work had involved the careful preparation of a series of demands for information which had so far been denied us. We intended to press for every kind of financial revelation. Our hope was that a commission of this distinction and impartiality would not hesitate to use its legal powers to press financial information into the service of truth. We were not disappointed in the hope. The case before the Goldenberg Commission will probably rate as one of the three great intellectual exercises in the history of labour relations in Jamaica. The other two are the bauxite case argued before the Honeyman Board of Enquiry by Norman Manley in 1954 and the JBC case argued before Mr Justice Eccleston, the sole enquirer, by Vivian Blake, Q.C., and David Coore, Q.C., in 1964. But of those more anon. In the Goldenberg case, the results of which were the most dramatic although involving issues that were less profound than in the other two cases, the high point came half-way through. We had demanded a mass of financial information hitherto denied us. The Commission ruled in our favour and for the first time in our history we began to get audited accounts of the sugar manufacturers' trading over the years. We also fought a number of major issues concerning the interpretation of profit and loss accounts and won on nearly every count. The upshot was that we got a group of figures which showed the sugar manufacturers' true performance over the five years preceding 1959.

It was an unforgettable experience, the afternoon when Shearer, Carl Hall and myself looked at the figures which we had never seen before and compared them with what we used to receive in our traditional negotiations. All this happened in the living-room of the bungalow which I used to own at 2 Washington Drive. We began the analysis in the late afternoon and our excitement was such that no one noticed when the sun set. It turned out that there had been huge discrepancies year after year between the profits that had been reported to us, as a basis for negotiation, and the actual earnings of the industry. The final five year total for the years 1954 to 1958 inclusive showed that the sugar manufacturers had made two million pounds more over the period than had been reported to us in successive negotiations.

The next day we revealed this to the Commission and it

burst like a bomb shell in Jamaica. The result was already in the bag.

The Goldenberg Commission unanimously recommended a basic wage increase of 12½ per cent, to become effective in 1960 on top of the wage increase that had been negotiated in 1957 at the time of the spectacular jump in the world price of sugar. In addition, the Commission recommended a crop bonus of 12 per cent for the 1959 crop together with certain increases in basic, minimum daily rates in 1960. In effect, the Commission had awarded to the workers nearly one and a quarter million pounds between the two years which was just over one-half of the profits which the sugar manufacturers had failed to report in the five years before. The measure of the magnitude of the triumph can be understood from the fact that the manufacturers had not been willing to offer any basic wage increase whatsoever and had insisted that they could only pay a small crop bonus.

The Goldenberg Commission may well represent the greatest single triumph of the trade union movement of Jamaica in the sense that the final achievement was so far removed from what the employers claimed they could do and having regard to the formidable intellectual and moral stature of the group who made the unanimous recommendation.

Two critical results flowed from the entire exercise. In the first place the Goldenberg Commission laid down permanent guidelines covering the reporting of industry finances to the unions which are a foundation of labour relations practice until the present time. Secondly, the findings of the Commission precipitated a break between the West Indies Sugar Company with its two huge Estates, Monymusk and Frome, and the rest of the industry insofar as industrial relations were concerned. After the findings of the Commission the WISCO group which accounted for approximately one-third of the annual sugar production of Jamaica, decided to go it alone in the field of industrial relations, clearly indicating dissatisfaction with the general performance of the industry in this area.

For our part, this represented an important vindication of our work. We had contended for five years that we thought something was wrong with the financial reporting of the industry and I had been variously accused of troublemaking, opportunism and hysteria, particularly by Bustamante himself. I regarded the outcome as important confirmation of the value of scepticism. More importantly, I felt that we had created a new standard of performance both in the preparation of the brief to the Commission and in the care with which we prepared ourselves for the arguments. Certainly, we had set a standard that others would ignore at their peril. We had also put together with that eloquence that comes from the marriage of fact and feeling a definitive statement of the tragedy of the rural proletariat of Jamaica. Would to God that there were more trade unionists who would go back to that brief, which can be found in the library of the University of the West Indies, to seek inspiration and reassurance for the task where their commitment should go beyond ordinary professionalism.

On a personal note, the whole exercise exposed me to a very great human being, full of sympathy, compassion, humour and intellectual excellence – Carl Goldenberg himself.

Much has happened in sugar since. In 1973 we were able, through the Government which I was honoured to head, to order a guaranteed price for the industry on the understanding that part of the proceeds would go towards improving the sugar workers' lot and achieving some of the elements of wage standardisation which I had championed ten years before. We were even able to finance this undertaking by persuading the British Government to grant a substantial increase in the price which Britain paid for our sugar! We have been able to play a part in the organisation of a Sugar Producers Federation which has government directors and which we hope will begin to rationalise the industry and develop new programmes involving worker participation in ownership in the industry. As I write, we are working on plans to turn some of the best sugar land into co-operative farms, which will be partly owned by the same cane cutters and grass weeders with whom I used to talk and whom I got to know twenty years before. It is a good feeling because there is less frustration now. Perhaps, political power can free the horns of the ram. However, I have not forgotten one of the dramatic high spots of the presentation before the Goldenberg

Commission of Enquiry. This came when I was able to demonstrate that all of the much vaunted progress in the wages of the workers between 1939 and 1959 could be summarised in real terms as accomplishing the equivalent in purchasing power of one additional pack of cigarettes per week. This was never refuted before the Commission for the simple reason that it was true. Between 1959 and now (1974), progress has continued to be slow and hard won. Major gains, therefore, had to await the contracts of 1974 and 1975 when high sugar prices in the world and positive government intervention continued to assist union efforts. Even now, however, there is room for further progress in the future.

6

THE BAUXITE STORY

As the long and agonising story of sugar was unfolding, another and similar story was being written: this was the story of bauxite. In the late 1940s bauxite was discovered in Jamaica and proved to exist in large quantities and to be of excellent quality. Bauxite is the raw material from which first alumina powder and subsequently, the metal aluminium is extracted. In due course two American and one Canadian corporation secured mining rights and by the early 1950s these were either established miners and exporters of bauxite or were in the process of constructing major works for the purpose of producing alumina from bauxite. The two American corporations were the Reynolds Metal Company and the Kaiser Chemical Corporation, both of which established bauxite mining facilities which extracted bauxite, dried it and shipped it to alumina plants in the USA. Alumina is a white powder representing an intermediate stage in the production of aluminium ingot. The metal itself is extracted from the white alumina dust in a process involving a massive use of electricity. The Canadian company, the Aluminium Company of Canada, decided to produce alumina locally and established an integrated operation consisting of bauxite mining and alumina processing. This involved the building of a large alumina production plant involving a much heavier investment than was required by either of the American companies who were concentrating on shipping dried bauxite.

There were interesting points of similarity between the structure of the sugar industry and the new bauxite industry which came into being between 1950 and 1954. Much of the sugar industry was foreign owned and, in the case of the two largest estates, Frome and Monymusk, which were owned by the Tate and Lyle Company of Britain, was actually in the hands of a multi-national corporation. The new bauxite industry was entirely in the hands of multinational corporations which all share the feature of carrying out different phases of a single economic operation in different countries organised with a single structure of ownership and overall management. These multinational corporations operating in Jamaica shared the further feature that they were owned, managed and controlled by the citizens of a major centre of economic power within the developed world. By contrast with the sugar industry the aluminium industry was new and consistently profitable as the demand for this metal expanded rapidly in the era following World War II; sugar, however, was subject to highly unstable conditions in which occasional short periods of high prices tended to be followed by long stretches in which the world sugar market was depressed.

At the time when the bauxite industry was established, it seemed natural to this new group of employers to take their cue in the fixing of wages and other working conditions from established industries like sugar. Consequently, to begin with, employment conditions in the bauxite industry were little different from those in the sugar industry.

It is against this background that the NWU rocked Jamaica in November 1952 by announcing a claim for one dollar (4s) an hour for unskilled labour! Union Headquarters was a-buzz. We had just learnt that the union was to claim a dollar an hour for unskilled labour in the bauxite industry as the highlight of its claims on behalf of this vital new group. By comparison, the sugar rate was just over one shilling. In late 1952, we had won our two great victories over the TUC and the BITU at the Kirkvine Works near Williamsfield where the Aluminium Company of Canada was erecting its alumina plant and at Kaiser Bauxite Company which was mining, drying and shipping raw bauxite in St Elizabeth on the south coast. This meant that we now represented well over three thousand bauxite workers, the great majority of whom were still constructing the alumina plant.

Following the poll victories, the union had faced the question of what to demand. This could have been approached conventionally by putting in the usual, careless proposal for a substantial percentage increase across the board while hoping that brute force and sentiment would somehow combine to secure a favourable outcome. However, from the outset the leaders of the NWU saw the bauxite industry as a special challenge. Here was a God-given opportunity to use a group of workers as pioneers and pace-setters for the labour movement as a whole. The bauxite group was ideally suited for this purpose since they worked in a situation that lent itself to strong organisation and a basically sound bargaining position. On the one hand, the operation as a whole depended on a work force that was highly disciplined and encompassed a wide range of skills; and on the other hand, it was obviously a highly profitable industry based upon one of the coming metals of modern industry. But there was another challenge implicit in the situation. Here was an industry geared to the needs of the powerful and highly sophisticated North American market economy but where the industry itself was based upon a Jamaican raw material. Where, then, should the standard of living of these workers be set? Should the bauxite worker be like all other Jamaican workers save, perhaps, for a small margin of difference in his standard of living and working conditions to mark his good fortune in getting into the industry? Or should he be paid the same as his American counterpart seeing that the aluminium industry is completely integrated from bauxite mining through the alumina process, along the line of reduction to ingot metal, through extrusion of metal plate and finally to fabrication which may range from frying pans to engine blocks? These were the questions that Ken Sterling, the Island Supervisor and principal architect of the great poll victories, Noel Nethersole, the PNP'S economic theorist and President of the Union and Norman Manley himself wrestled with.

In the end, a dollar an hour emerged as an approximate quantification of a theory of wages which was to guide the NWU in the bauxite industry for the next two decades. We concluded that the bauxite industry owed to its Jamaican worker a mimimum civilised standard of living conceived in Jamaican terms and having regard to Jamaican experience. In those days the bauxite industry was still on a forty-four hour work week. Bearing that in mind, the union set about trying to quantify the income that an average family would need to buy the necessities of life, with a small margin over for the creature comforts. Studies were made of average rents for modest dwellings that could hold an average family of four. Nutrition studies were made and converted to pounds, shillings and pence by observation of local food prices. Even questions like the average cost of school books were examined. In the end, it seemed that nine pounds a week based on 1953 values and prices could support a rudimentary form of 'civilised' existence. Naturally, this kind of exercise inevitably reflects an element of subjective judgment but I well remember how shocked I was to discover how little nine pounds could actually buy in a week even in 1953. Allowing for the forty-four hour work week it emerged that four shillings an hour, for that was the value of an American dollar in sterling in those days, came near enough to nine pounds a week as to supply a reasonable starting point from which to embark upon the quest for a civilised standard for bauxite workers.

What made the claim so startling, what set headquarters buzzing was not the thought of four shillings an hour but the distance between this and the existing rate of pay which was one shilling and two pence! This meant that the union was claiming over two hundred per cent wage increase. When the news broke outside it was not only union headquarters that buzzed with excitement, but the whole country. Bustamante denounced the claim as propaganda, Shearer said that we were fooling the workers and could never achieve it and the Manager of the island's newly formed Industrial Development Corporation, one Robert Lightbourne, who was later to become a Minister of Trade and Industry in the JLP Government of 1962–72, announced in stentorian tones that the claim would wreck the Jamaican economy if it succeeded and damage it gravely by the mere fact of its announcement.

In the middle of the biggest hubbub about wages and economic theory in my experience, the negotiations began. Sterling undertook the main load of the talks and in due course the one and two pence an hour was raised to one and four because of some earlier undertaking. The union dismissed this as totally irrelevant and a few weeks later the Alcan group made a 'firm and final' offer of another three pence an hour to provide a settlement figure of one and seven. The union rejected this officially when, to no one's surprise, the Alcan group decided to provoke a crisis. They suddenly announced that at the next pay day they would be putting their offer of one and seven pence an hour into effect regardless of whether the union agreed and over the union's official protest. It seemed that the Alcan group felt that their workers would grab at an offer of nearly 20 per cent. Clearly, they hoped to break the union with one quick, clean, early stroke. The company's miscalculation was as massive as it was helpful to our cause. Quite often, companies become dependent on a system of informers. What they do not realise is that informers are more concerned with the rake-off that they make on the side than with conveying the truth of things accurately. It has always surprised me that companies put trust in an inherently corrupt process, but, strangely, some of them do. The truth is that the imagination of the bauxite workers had been fired, not only by the dollar an hour itself, but by the larger concept behind it. As early as 1953 this group was developing the characteristics of an elite corps with a sense of mission. Naturally, there was a material base to this and therefore a strong element of self-interest, but it would be to sell these men short and misconceive the inner greatness of the labour movement to think that this was where their motivation began and ended. There was also a strong sense of historical mission born of those hundred and twenty years when freedom from slavery had brought little change in the material circumstance of their lives. It was born of the generations of frustration when men lived and died and saw their children following their footsteps into futility. Among the best and the most aware of the bauxite workers there was a feeling that God had put the bauxite where it was for a purpose. Perhaps, it was a national purpose but that was not for them to say since they did not have the power to explore things on that scale. They knew, only too well, the limits of possibility for a worker in a colonial society which amounted to a living wage, good working conditions and a secure job and they meant to secure these in the shortest possible time. They hoped that in doing so they would open up a path that others might follow, but this was for the time being of secondary importance.

For the present Alcan had thrown down the gauntlet and

they intended to pick it up. The great strike at Kirkvine began in late March 1953. It was to last eighty-four days. This was one of those strikes that no one involved will ever forget. There are some confrontations in labour relations that are almost routine and dull. Some are ugly; some sordid. Then, every now and again there occurs a strike that is inspiring in spite of the heat and the dust of the picket line, the terrible economic pressures, the lost production, the flaring tempers. This happens when a strike reflects a moment in history that calls for a dramatic new initiative. A Jamaican saying declares that 'nothing happen till the right time come'. There is a deep, almost philosophical truth about this in the sense that the members of a particular society tend to become aware of the need to correct particular injustices long before they possess the collective will to do anything about it. But although the gap between the admission of wrong and its subsequent adjustment may be long, it seems, nonetheless to represent the necessary period of gestation. The forces that led to the great sugar strike of 1959 were at least five years in the brewing. So too, the idea that one could apply an objective criterion of right and wrong, based upon the quantification of a concept of right had been nagging at the Jamaican conscience for a long time. Yet, when wage increases and other benefits were won they always reflected something irrational in that the settlement was considered more important than the original issue; so compromise was elevated to a self-justifying philosophy of conduct rather than being seen for the expedient that it was. To the extent that the strike at Kirkvine departed from this practice it took on a moral aspect and evoked something of the fervour of a crusade. This may sound fanciful twenty-one years later and I suppose it would be easy to dismiss it as a romanticised memory; but the fact is that the strike seemed to those who took part in it to be a definitive event and to be full of moral purpose.

After three weeks it became clear that the confrontation was headed for a stalemate. Neither side could afford to back down and neither intended to. When this became clear the Ministry of Labour moved into action and the search for a solution was on. The gap between the parties was so wide in money terms as to defy conciliation. Worse than the money gap, however, was the difference in outlook. Both Alcan and Kaiser had Jamaican lawyers as their principal representatives. Douglas Judah of the firm of Judah and Randall was and still is the principal legal adviser of Alcan in Jamaica. Leslie Ashenheim of Milholland, Ashenheim and Stone held the same position for Kaiser. Although Ashenheim is in semi-retirement he is still called upon by Kaiser in Jamaica on major issues. It is difficult to know what the real motives of the companies were. Their local legal representatives were and are men of great ability and integrity. Both honestly believed that a large increase for bauxite workers, however justified, would be disastrous for Jamaica. I have never believed that it is helpful to ascribe personal motives to the things that men do. Consequently I accepted then and believe now that the views which were held so passionately by Ashenheim and Judah reflected a sincere if conservative conviction.

With the companies it may have been another story. The aluminium industry is capital intensive and the labour content is a relatively small fraction of total costs. Clearly, then, ability to pay was not a factor in company thinking. Nor, for that matter, did they ever put ability to pay in contention in any of the labour disputes over the years. I suspect that their real motive in resisting the union claim in the harsh and uncompromising manner that they did can be traced to two factors: on the one hand the corporations that have emerged in the North American economy are predicated upon the assumption that all costs must be minimised and that human costs are no exception. Granted this basic philosophy, companies like Alcan and Kaiser would need little prompting to resist a large claim for wage increases. In fact, I suspect that they felt that it would be bad public relations to make large concessions to the union where those concessions might be used to put pressure on other employers. On the surface, however, they took the Judah-Ashenheim line that the increases sought would be bad for the economy. Whatever the reason, the fact was that there was not the slightest sign in those first conciliation meetings in 1953 that the companies had any intention of offering anything more than the one shilling and seven pence that Alcan had unilaterally sought to impose.

It soon became apparent that the only hope for a settlement lay in arbitration. But this too was full of difficulties. The union feared that the only kind of arbitrator that the companies would ever be persuaded to accept would be the sort of man who was completely steeped in the conservative prejudices and assumptions which Ashenheim and Judah shared and used with deceptive skill in argument. We were determined that our best chance lay in an arbitrator from abroad who could bring to the consideration of the case a more open mind. In the end the choice narrowed to the union preference for an arbitrator chosen in Canada and the companies' preference for one chosen in the United Kingdom. It is a fascinating commentary on the times and the situation alike that the Canadian company would have no part of a Canadian arbitrator and that a trade union operating in a British colony wanted no part of an English arbitrator. With the situation once again hopelessly deadlocked, it was decided to invite the Jamaican Government to decide which country the arbitrator should come from. The union accepted this proposal with a sinking heart because Bustamante had denounced the dollar an hour proposal and as Chief Minister would now have the deciding say in the matter of the arbitrator. It was obvious that the English arbitrator against a background of British labour experience would be far more conservative in approach. We suspected that Bustamante had no desire to facilitate a NWU triumph, particularly since the BITU still held a corner of the industry at the third bauxite operation run by Reynolds Jamaica Mines on the North coast in the parish of St Ann. There is no record to show why the Government took the decision that they did but it is a matter of record that our fears about the outcome were realised. The Government announced that the arbitrator would be sought in Britain and shortly after, George Gordon Honcyman, a British arbitrator of considerable experience, was chosen. The companies and the unions each named an assessor to sit with Honeyman though it turned out that he permitted them little part in the exercise.

It is reasonable to ask why the Union agreed to let the Government make the choice between an English and a Canadian arbitrator? The simple answer is that the strike had been going on for a long time, the workers were beginning to suffer; under pressure of those circumstances it was the sort of concession that both unions and employers are driven to make.

And so the great bauxite arbitration of 1953 was on. It still rates as one of the three great intellectual exercises of Jamaican labour history: the other two being the Goldenberg Commission in sugar and the JBC Board of Enquiry. The protagonists provided a fascinating contrast. Norman Manley argued the workers' case. Generally conceded to be the greatest Jamaican advocate of his time, some say the greatest Caribbean advocate of all time, he brought to the case an unusual mind in the sense that he combined to a rare degree the analyst's gifts of logic, simplification and incisiveness with the humanist gifts of breadth of interest and compassion. A lifetime in the courts had developed the habit of arguing on his feet. This was unusual because arbitrations were traditionally conducted sitting down. Thus throughout the case there was the visual contrast between Manley, on his feet, full of gesture and stylistic nuance and his opponents who remained decorously, almost primly, seated. Opposite Manley were the local lawyers. Douglas Judah is a company lawyer of great experience, given to painstaking preparation and capable of a kind of direct eloquence about the things in which he believes. Indeed, in defence of the basic tenets of the 'right' he can summon up a considerable degree of passion. When dealing with him I found that it was always a mistake to underrate his presentation because you disagreed with his premises. Leslie Ashenheim on the other hand is more dry and pragmatic. No less ardent in his belief in conservative causes and constructions, he is a less eloquent but more cunning adversary than Judah. Together they made a formidable pair and, of course, had everything going for them. The union's claim, on the face of it, was preposterous. Where tradition dictated they take the cherry a nibble at a time, it appeared as though they were trying to take it in one gulp. Britain has a labour relations tradition which reflects her industrial performance since the great depression of the early 1930s: industrial productivity increases imperceptibly, if at all, and labour productivity is kept consciously in check lest too great an output should put men back in the bread lines which marked that terrible period of British history. In those circumstances it is little wonder that British wage theory up to 1953 provided little that could justify a giant step forward for any group of workers however bad their situation.

On the union side, Manley was at his most effective in two areas. He established the structure and nature of the aluminium industry with great clarity. The coincidental nature of the presence of the bauxite deposits in Jamaica and the relationship between these deposits and the North American economy came across forcefully as did the moral implication that this industry owed a decent standard of living to its Jamaican workers. Even more compelling, however, was the analysis of the plight of the Jamaican worker at the levels of wages which then obtained in the island's economy. Here we saw a dazzling display of his great gifts as an advocate. Each category of household expenditure was presented with almost loving care and simplicity. As he unfolded the simple categories of domestic existence, each took on a quality of revelation. In a crowning touch, he showed that the wage claim by the union could just discharge a set of minimal responsibilities to home and children and leave spare enough for a pack of cigarettes a day. It was a moving performance.

On the company side the case was noteworthy for the repeated insistence that a dollar an hour would disrupt the Jamaican economy and set the stage for national disaster. It was as if Judah and Ashenheim were daring Honeyman to gamble with a future in which he would not personally take a part. Judah sprung one shrewd surprise having regard to the domicile of the arbitrator. With characteristic diligence, he got hold of what are known as the Fair Wages Resolutions passed by the Parliament of Britain after the First World War. These resolutions dealt with the problem of contracting out government work and provided that an employer acting under a Government contract must not pay less than the going rates of wages in the locality where the contract is being discharged. It had been common experience over the years for contractors to bid successfully for a government job only to exploit local unemployment and poverty by hiring labour at rates lower than normal for the particular area. This had two consequences. It led to bad feeling in the area concerned; and, of course, it meant in all probability that the contractor was making a greater profit than was intended for the particular contract. Judah placed great reliance on the Fair Wages Resolutions, arguing conversely that the same principles which acted to maintain wages at a floor level should equally restrain other particular wages at a ceiling level. If one is looking for an excuse to resist a strong union claim, this is a deceptively attractive argument. In the case of the Honeyman arbitration the arguments contained a subtle element of flattery since it seemed to invite Mr Honeyman to a kind of intellectual solidarity with his own Parliament.

I have often let my mind wander around the whole question of the arguments and the principles that were advanced pro and con in this case. In the end one is driven to conclude that one is involved in an intellectual tangle that cannot be satisfactorily resolved by argument. If you begin with the premise that there can be no enforceable principles in a free economy because the notion of enforcement is in itself a contradiction in the context, then you are driven to the view that ability to pay should be the sole determinant of wages. This implies, however, that companies that are losing money should have the right to reduce wages. But this is a proposition that no unionist, indeed, no social moralist can accept. If, on the other hand, you argue that wages should reflect a moral consensus among reasonable men about standards of living, you are driven to the conclusion that there should be equal pay for equal work regardless of any other circumstance. But, in a free economy where profits and the return to investment are not similarly standardised this creates one set of rules for the investor and another for the worker. It is obvious that to be consistent with social morality a nation cannot have different rules for different people and so the argument can chase its own tail indefinitely. The truth is that there is only one set of circumstances which could justify the argument that was advanced by the companies and those circumstances ironically, would be anathema to Judah, Ashenheim and every multi-national corporation that has ever sprung from the North American economy. It would only be in a completely controlled economy where profits, prices and wages were determined by a single planning authority applying moral as well as economic criteria, that one could justify in pure logic the Fair Wages principles as Judah and Ashenheim sought to apply it. Equally, the union case suffered from an internal contradiction. In the last analysis Manley had to pray 'ability to pay' in aid of the union's case even though he advanced it in a novel and attractive form. Yet the same Union was obliged, over and over in its subsequent existence to reject the faintest suggestion that wages should be reduced, even temporarily, where a company was in serious financial difficulties.

In the end, therefore, wages are determined by many things reflecting many forces in society. Most importantly, in a free economy, they are determined by bargaining power. Then again, they are influenced by political forces which lead to laws declaring minimum wages and the like. They are still profoundly influenced by competition, particularly where skills are in short supply or where there are huge surpluses of, for example, unskilled labour. And, finally, they are even influenced by individual conscience. This, of course, was never a very significant factor and is a disappearing phenomenon as the concept of *noblesse oblige* is displaced by the great collective institutions which order change and progress by the organisation of group power. The political party and the trade union are the two great instruments of this contemporary process.

Doubtless bearing all this in mind, Honeyman did three things which showed him to be mindful that discretion is the better part of valour. In the first place, he refused to discuss the case with his three assessors, Cleve Kidd of the United Steelworkers of Canada, appointed by the Union, Mr E. C. Joysey, appointed by Alumina Jamaica and Mr F. Victor Nunes, appointed by Kaiser. Secondly, he said in as many words that he did not intend to give any reasons for his award. Indeed, he set the stage for this decision in a lecture which he gave before making his award in which he argued that wage arbitration is a specific means for settling disputes between parties who have to live with each other afterwards. Therefore, he contended, 'Least said, soonest mended.' He suggested that to give reasons for a particular award would be to open up a field of continuing dispute between the parties. Finally, Honeyman contrived the timing of his own departure so as to ensure that he was safely aboard his plane before the result was known! The award was one shilling and ten pence an hour. It was a bitter blow for the unions. What he had done was to take the three pence an hour which Alcan tried to impose and added another three pence to make the total of one and ten pence. Of course, in any ordinary arbitration this award which provided an increase of 37½ per cent would have been a triumph. In the context of the dollar claim it was a major defeat.

The minute the result was known Manley called a conference in his law office. I will never forget the scene in this spare, functional room in which he had planned some of the greatest legal victories of Jamaican and Caribbean history and from which he had directed the nationalist movement for fifteen years. He was obviously hurt by the result in the sense that where the others were dazed by the defeat and its implications, he had borne the special responsibility of advocacy. I was to learn three great lessons from this experience, the first of which was taking place even as I shared the leader's hurt. It was the lesson of action. When all seems lost, act! As I watched my father I remembered how he used to love to quote Marshall Foch of the French Army in the First World War. With the Germans at the very gates of Paris, Foch remarked to his general staff that his left flank was in full retreat, his right flank in danger of encirclement and his centre smashed. His response was one of the most stirring utterances of history. He said: 'J'attaque!' As good as his word, Foch ordered a general counter-offensive, saved Paris and altered the history of the world. I was looking out through the window remembering this story and visualising the indomitable Frenchman surrounded by a group of unnerved colleagues when I heard my father saying: 'Michael, you must get to Kirkvine immediately and rally the delegates and reassure the workers. They will be bitterly disappointed and will need your presence.' I was chosen to go because

Sterling had an urgent appointment from which he could not extricate himself. We discussed what I should say for about fifteen minutes and within half an hour I was on the highway out of Kingston headed for the plant.

The second great lesson followed quickly. The workers were badly shaken by the result, as we expected, yet the mere fact that I was with them within minutes of their hearing the news on the radio seemed to make all the difference. The truth is that we consoled each other and in the course of that consolation pledged allegiance to each other, to our dream of a dollar an hour and to the road which we were to walk together. We held an impromptu meeting at the plant gate that evening and even in the atmosphere of recent defeat it was a great experience. Looking back, that meeting with its evidence of loyalty and courage in adversity was one of the turning points of my life because it served to confirm my faith in those people whom we so inappropriately describe as the masses. Up to then faith had been a function of idealism; now it was confirmed by experience.

The third lesson was learned by pure coincidence. During the arbitration, one of the arguments had turned around the question of comparative wages in other enterprises in the country. We had had great difficulty in getting information out of any company whose workers were represented by the BITU, and we suspected that orders had probably come from Bustamante himself not to divulge information which could conceivably be helpful to the NWU. The companies, on the other hand, had no such difficulty. In the course of the case they undertook to get hold of records of any wages that were higher than the one and seven pence an hour which they had offered. They had done this because they had conceded in their presentation that the bauxite industry should pay as much as the best going rate in the country for comparable categories of workers. One of the arguments concerning comparative wages had centred on the rates paid by the oil companies, Shell, Texaco and Esso, to their workers engaged in the trucking of petroleum products to various parts of the island. This involved distribution centres with fleets of truck/tankers which had to be loaded, driven and maintained. They were, obviously, a highly relevant group for purposes of a comparison since the distribution of petroleum is a lucrative element in a multi-national corporation operation and several categories of work were exactly the same as you would find in an alumina plant. In the course of the arbitration the companies had claimed that one and ten pence an hour was the highest rate paid to unskilled labour by the oil companies, and it is probably no coincidence that this figure coincided with Honeyman's award.

When I arrived at the Kirkvine plant I had to go to the office of the Head of the personnel department to ask him to release the delegates to come and see me. While I was waiting, the director of the personnel department had to leave the office briefly to answer a call. I am not normally given to reading other people's papers and am not generally speaking of a prying nature. However, as I sat across the desk making a final review of what I should say to the delegates I happened to glance to a sheet of paper in the middle of the blotter. It was headed 'Comparative Wages'. I fought the temptation to examine the document and lost the battle. At the very head of the wage column was the figure two shillings and one penny an hour as the current rate for unskilled labour in one of the oil companies. The particular company had refused to give us the information. The bauxite companies had claimed that one and ten pence was the top rate but there in front of me was the evidence which would have made an award of two and a penny an hour inevitable on the facts and arguments of their own case! I remember being enveloped in a sense of unreality. It was one of the greatest shocks I had ever had for up to then I had genuinely believed that honesty could be taken for granted at the sorts of levels that were involved in a great wage arbitration. The fact is, I was stunned. Equally, it was obviously a lesson best learned at the start rather than at the end of my career.

One of the great by-products of the union's work in bauxite was the relationship that developed with the United Steelworkers of America. The American trade union movement, like so much else in American society is a mixture that has ranged from corruption, venality, and brutality, through honourable but pathetically conservative attitudes to magnificent examples of integrity, superb organisation and liberal philosophy. Sometimes these qualities have been dominant at different stages in the life of the same union. For example, John L. Lewis of the United Mineworkers Union must surely rate as one of the great trade union figures of all time. Yet his recent successor in the post of president has been found guilty of complicity in the killing of a rival for the post who was running on a Reform ticket. The Teamsters' Union is a magnificent example of effective organisation yet one president, Dave Beck, was notoriously corrupt and his successor, Hoffa, spent several years in prison on a wire-tapping charge. This particular union has been notoriously guilty of the most brutal strong-arm tactics and is suspected of extensive underworld connections. Standing well apart from these extremes are the huge American Federation of Labour Unions, many of them old crafts organisations, which are well organised and honourable but notorious seats of resistance to opportunities for blacks and other minorities and whose typical political viewpoint is to be found somewhat to the right of the late John Foster Dulles. Then, in sharp contrast, are the great unions of the younger Congress of Industrial Organisations. The two finest of these are the United Automobile Workers which was led with such vision, courage and skill by Walter Reuther, and the United Steelworkers of America which was founded by the late Bill Murray and is now led by the redoubtable I. W. Abel. The United Steelworkers are based upon some 700,000 members employed in basic steel and allied industries in the United States and Canada. However, the union is also the traditional representative of the bauxite, alumina and aluminium industries throughout most of the continent. With the exception of Alcan's Arvida Works in Quebec, which are represented by a French-Canadian Workers' Syndicate, the workers of all the US alumina reduction plants and aluminium smelter operations supplied by Jamaican bauxite were and are represented by the United Steelworkers.

By 1952, unions such as United Steelworkers and the Automobile Workers were becoming internationally conscious. In the beginning two not altogether consistent motives were at work. On the one hand there was a growing recognition that the labour movement needed an international framework for co-operation in a world whose economy was increasingly dominated by international cartels and, more recently, by multi-national corporations. As the world shrunk its workers discovered increasingly that their nationalist isolation led to impotence and so more advanced unions everywhere were tending to commit resources to helping establish unions in foreign lands where none existed and to strengthening young institutions struggling against heavy odds. On the other hand, however, there was a growing chauvinistic concern in America about the tendency of multi-national corporations to establish plants overseas. For example, an aluminium company seeking to expand its capacity might decide to put an alumina plant in Jamaica or Guyana rather than somewhere in the United States. The unions feared that low wage rates in foreign countries were a contributing factor in this process. Resenting the potential loss of jobs to the American system and to their own membership, they were anxious to help overseas unions to push up wage rates so as to eliminate what they considered unfair competition for job opportunities.

With all this in mind the United Steelworkers despatched two remarkable men to Jamaica in late 1952. Nick Zonarich was then an important official assigned to the aluminium section of the United Steelworkers in America. He has since become the Director of the Industrial Section of the combined AFL-CIO in fitting recognition of his enormous energy and formidable organising talents. A confident, ebullient extrovert with a great gift for friendship, Zonarich was a tough, uncomplicated, uncompromising activist with a great sense of humour which he could always direct against himself in a tight spot. Charlie Millard was the director of the Canadian division of the United Steelworkers. Since retired, he was the complete contrast to Zonarich. A quiet, reflective and immensely dignified man, he gave an impression of wisdom accumulated in many battles. These two presented themselves at Palisadoes (now Norman Manley International) Airport in late 1952. They were promptly held by the immigration authorities and told that they could not enter. In fact, it took considerable effort on our part to persuade the Government to let them in. Eventually we succeeded, and we were soon in full contact explaining our plans for the industry and welcoming their offer of United Steelworkers solidarity and support. We took them to the various bauxite operations where Zonarich particularly made a tremendous impression with his hard-hitting, uncomplicated style. We were extremely happy about the contact since we were new and untried and understood only too well the multi-national characteristics of the corporate giants that we were tackling.

The thought of powerful friends with a common cause in the high places of the enemy was comforting to say the least. However, we detected early a note of self-interest in our new friends' mission and decided to lay down the ground rules at the outset. Before Zonarich and Millard left for home we had an important meeting in which we made it clear that we welcomed their presence, looked forward to working with them as allies but wished to avoid any misunderstandings. We declared our firm intention to be the sole determinants of the goals which we would set for our members as Jamaican workers. Once that was understood we assured them that we would welcome every possible assistance in the areas of research, sharing of information, assistance with organisation and worker education. It is to their lasting credit that Zonarich and Millard not only understood the critical reservation which we introduced but relayed it to their respective executives with such clarity and conviction that it became the foundation of the international policies of the United Steelworkers and remains so to this day. As a consequence there was forged in that first visit a realistic alliance that not only worked to the benefit of the Jamaican labour movement but helped to clarify principles which were to guide international unionism a generation later. What made this agreement so important was that it established a basis for an international relationship founded upon a true respect for sovereignty. It is a fascinating commentary on the world that aid programmes and international relationships generally are constantly bedevilled by the attempt of the affluent, donor nations to influence the fundamental policies of the developing, recipient countries. This has led to unending trouble to the extent that the very concept of aid is now the subject of almost universal criticism. By contrast, the union movement demonstrated a capacity to contain self-interest within boundaries dictated by idealistic commitment. It is possible to argue that the willingness of the United Steelworkers to accept our determination to be the sole judges of the goal that we would set ourselves was nothing more than a realistic appreciation of the price to be paid for having any influence at all. I think it was more than that. I think that the leaders of the great American unions are part of a movement that is founded on a commitment to ideals and I was firmly convinced that steelworker policies fully reflected this commitment. Whatever the motivation, however, the fact is that a great alliance was forged out of that visit by Zonarich and Millard: an alliance that was to prove valuable in many ways and which still endures.

After the drama of the polls, the dollar claim, the strike and the Honeyman arbitration, the industry and the union settled down to the serious business of mining bauxite efficiently and hammering out good trade union contracts. The BITU tried to capitalise upon our comparative failure in terms of the arbitration award. However, their propaganda was lost in the general excitement. Even though the workers were disappointed they knew they had been part of a historic struggle which was just beginning. In fact, with only a few though dramatic exceptions, the industry over the next fourteen years became an important success story in Jamaican development. The companies which discovered the sterling qualities of the Jamaican as a worker when he was treated decently and the workers themselves were soon involved in the exhilarating and continuing experience of ensuring that they were treated in no other way.

In 1954, just a year after the Honeyman arbitration, negotiations were resumed, again proved unsuccessful and another arbitration was arranged, this time under the chairmanship of a prominent Jamaican lawyer of liberal outlook and acknowledged integrity. Douglas Fletcher was the senior partner of the law firm of Myers, Fletcher and Gordon and was later to serve as a highly trusted member of the Cabinet in the first Government which Manley formed after Jamaica had achieved full internal self-government. More recently he was appointed as ambassador to Washington. All the arguments between the union and the industry were trotted out again and although we still failed to win our case we got an award of seven pence an hour to make a total of two shillings and five pence for unskilled labour. More importantly, this rate placed the bauxite workers clearly at the top of the wage scale in the economy and so established the principle that they should not be treated in quite the same way as other workers whose jobs made them part of the normal, internal workings of the Jamaican economy. Although we were disappointed in the amount of the Fletcher award, we were pleased with the fact that our principle had been accepted and that a local arbitrator of repute had accepted the relevance of our contention that the aluminium industry was a vertically integrated activity with part of its activities happening to be located in Jamaica. The Fletcher award, in accepting this fact, seemed to say that the bauxite worker was in a special position and should be treated accordingly. It was as if he had said that these workers were special, were entitled to a more rapid rate of progress than other groups but that this progress should not amount to a headlong dash!

During 1954 the other major excitement centred around the challenge by the NWU at Reynolds Jamaica Mines which was the one section of the industry held by the BITU. This was a difficult undertaking because the BITU had waited out the Alcan confrontation. After the Honeyman award of one and ten pence per hour, Reynolds had made a quiet deal with the BITU in which they established the rate of two shillings and a penny per hour but tied to a somewhat longer contract. This was obviously a play designed to keep the NWU out of Reynolds and so keep the workers divided. It was important to NWU strategy to bring this division to an end and so we commenced organising at Reynolds in spite of the larger increase enjoyed by that group. The first poll early in 1955 proved to be an exciting and historic event. It produced the first tied election in Jamaican labour history. The poll was conducted on 3 January, 1955, and the votes were counted at the Ministry of Labour at ten o'clock on the following day. Although I was involved in the poll I couldn't make the count, but gather that it was a wildly exciting scene with the lead swinging from one union to the other as the count wore on. Apparently, with one ballot to be counted, the BITU had a lead of one. The Ministry of Labour official, obviously enjoying every minute, took unusually long over the last ballot. It was 'NWU' and the result was a tie. A great shout went up from the NWU contingent but this soon gave way to a sad silence when it was learnt that a tied vote meant that the BITU retained exclusive bargaining rights.

In January 1955, Manley and the PNP finally came to power in Jamaica. Soon after the NWU again began to organise at Reynolds and this time won comfortably thus completing the organisation of the bauxite workers into one group. A new contract was duly negotiated at Reynolds with a rate of three shillings an hour and shortly after new deals were made at Alcan and Kaiser providing for three shillings and two pence an hour with slightly longer contracts. All companies were now standardised on the basis of eight hour work days with forty hour work weeks, grievance procedures, shift premiums and proper sick and vacation leave clauses.

The next phase of the bauxite experience I like to remember as the phase of the expanding dollar. After the three shillings and two pence contract at Alcan and Kaiser our next effort brought us to four shillings an hour and the attainment of the goal that we had set ourselves in 1952. We actually hit the target in 1958 after six years of effort. However, no sooner had we arrived at a dollar an hour than we were hit by a series of devaluations of the pound sterling. Before we knew it the four shilling dollar had disappeared and had been replaced by a seven shilling dollar. By now, the pattern of wage increases every other year was more or less established and it was more of an 'in joke' than a serious target when we set out in pursuit of seven shillings an hour. We hit this target in 1967 and had barely finished celebrating when Jamaica decided to adopt the decimal system and created a dollar of its own which was worth ten shillings. Once more we took up the challenge and set out in hot pursuit. The last bauxite contract that I negotiated, in 1971, provided for an unskilled labour rate of a Jamaican dollar hour but, by now, of course, it was worth ten shillings. In nineteen years we had moved from one shilling and two pence to just over ten shillings or some 900 per cent. During this same period of time the value of money had about halved and I figure that we had increased the real wages of the workers by about five times or 400 per cent. This meant that we had maintained an annual rate of about 20 per cent on the original basic wage.

This considerable negotiating accomplishment had been accompanied by some interesting experiments in fringe benefits. In particular we had done some good work in the fields of severance pay, sick leave and grievance procedures. Our development of severance pay as a powerful instrument of social security provided by union contract rather than state action led to some of the most fascinating arguments between the companies and the unions. All the companies came from North America and were accustomed to a pattern in which unemployment benefits and indeed sickness benefits were provided through social security systems operated by state or local governments. Next to nothing had been done on these lines in Jamaica and so the bauxite worker was left with a seriously exposed flank should his job come to an end. We determined to make severance pay work as a form of social security benefit. In the end we secured severance pay clauses which not only provided for very large payments for redundant workers but also provided coverage for loss of employment due to every imaginable cause save dismissal for disciplinary reasons. So long as a job was lost through no fault of the worker, he was entitled to severance pay and, in the end, this could amount to as much as three weeks' current wages for every completed year of service. Thus, a worker with twenty years service who became redundant would draw sixty weeks wages which was far in excess of anything obtaining by way of severance pay in North America. The key to our argument, of course, was that in the United States and Canada, legal social security systems were financed, at least in part, by company contributions. As we pointed out, the unemployment benefits which a North American worker would draw were in fact partly financed by commercial companies. We insisted that the companies undertake a similar obligation in Jamaica in the only way that this could be done in our situation. Similarly, we were able to pioneer clauses providing for maintenance of earnings during illness which were far in advance of anything obtaining in America.

However, it was in the field of grievance procedures that

we had the toughest intellectual battle outside of wages. This revolved around the question of the right to reinstatement of workers who were held to have been wrongfully dismissed. This whole issue eventually produced the greatest confrontation in the history of the Jamaican labour movement at the Jamaica Broadcasting Corporation in 1964. Indeed, it was only after that battle that we finally persuaded the bauxite companies to provide by contract that arbitrators hearing appeals against dismissal should have the right to order reinstatement in the event that a particular dismissal was held to be wrongful. Today it may seem incredible that this should ever have been an issue but this story is perhaps best told in the context of the ninety-seven day strike which it caused at the JBC.

After the first year, relations between the workers and the companies, the union and the companies and between the members and officers of the union were generally good. The union itself was well organised and able to maintain a vigorous internal democracy. In due course, a bauxite national council comprised of representatives of all the mining areas and plant operations was established and achieved a real measure of internal self-government. Negotiating claims were formulated democratically and no settlement was ever arrived at that did not rest upon the sanction of the worker's vote. By and large, the companies maintained strong personnel departments and seemed to realise that good industrial relations were an important element in efficiency. However, all this did not come about without considerable strains and periods of difficulty. In the early days, for example, there were considerable tensions about plant discipline and, in particular, about time keeping. Much of the work force came from backgrounds in which punctuality was not held to be especially important. Agricultural communities work by the sun rather than the clock and the sons of farmers do not take easily to the tyranny of time when it is measured by the minute. Hence, there were great early strains within the system as the companies struggled to establish the primacy of the time clock.

Equally understandable, but no less troublesome, were the consequences of an impersonal, non-paternalistic worker/

management relation. In all their previous working experience the bauxite workers had grown accustomed to personalised relationships in which wages might be desperately low but the boss could be touched for a loan and generally remembered to ask how the children at home were doing. The bauxite companies had already been conditioned by their North American experience to expect to define the working relationship precisely and to enshrine that relationship in a contract. Loans were out and the health of the children at home no longer seemed a relevant issue. The bauxite worker had no difficulty understanding the meaning of higher wages; nor did he fail to appreciate the advantage of job security. His problem lay in understanding the apparent lack of interest in him as a human being with a family and an existence separate from the plant. This impersonal atmosphere provoked suspicion and hostility leading to a general feeling that the 'white man' didn't care. The fact is that the modern industrial boss simply does not operate on that wavelength at all. In the early days these attitudes led to great bitterness, particularly at Alcan which was the largest and most complex operation, being an alumina plant, and which needed, but lacked a good personnel department. By 1958 feelings were running high. Before long the existing team of delegates led by a remarkable pioneer and hero of the first strike, C. T. McLean, were being accused of softness in their attitude to the management. A movement was developing under a bright but unstable young man named John Vickers which was promising to carry the fight to the management at a time when McLean was taking on the style of elder statesman. In ordinary circumstances Vickers would have spoken for a vocal minority, would have been defeated in union elections and set himself up as a sort of permanent opposition. However, even the older, more staid workers were in a state of seething discontent partly because of the profound tensions to which they were subject in this new, impersonal environment. The union election proved to be a triumph for Vickers who hurled himself into his new responsibilities with considerable energy and dash. Within months the plant was abuzz as Vickers took up cases left, right and centre, without any regard for the merits or demerits of each particular one. He won some and he lost others; but he won enough to confirm his popularity. In due course he moved from the field of industrial relations to the question of race. With a considerable, white expatriate management and supervisory staff there were inevitable tensions. Most expatriates were well trained and polite and some may even have been genuinely non-racist. However, the average supervisor in an English, Canadian or American factory tends to be a gruff disciplinarian with little skill in the niceties of polite communication and so there was always a degree of tension arising from the odd personal clash between Jamaican workers and foreign supervisors. To Vickers this must have seemed both a legitimate challenge to duty and an opportunity to pursue his burgeoning career. All of a sudden, the Kirkvine works became a hot-bed of racial tension. Then, during one fateful night a high pressure valve burst and a Jamaican worker was killed in particularly awful circumstances. In the ensuing confusion there was a clash between Vickers and a senior member of the staff and before union headquarters was even aware of what was happening, the Vickers team had shut the plant down. This triggered off one of the most difficult episodes in NWU history and one which nearly broke up the bauxite workers' movement. From the workers point of view the strike was a crusade against all the problems, real and imaginary that beset them. Racial tensions and the sense of a cold, impersonal management that did not care were hopelessly mixed up with frustrations about delayed promotions and still more commonplace worker grievances. From the union point of view, however, the strike was a disaster. First of all it was in flagrant breach of contract and had no clear focus which could lend it moral if not legal legitimacy. It was an explosion rather than a collective act further to a collective purpose and, as if that were not bad enough, it took place at a time when the market was bad and Alcan would have welcomed the excuse to shut down the plant for a few months to relieve pressure on storage space throughout the Alcan system. As a consequence, the union found itself in an impossible situation where it could not repudiate the strike, since that would have left the workers defenseless and might have led to the actual destruction of the union itself; at the same time it could not adopt the strike because this might prove the final provocation leading to a long plant shut-down.

Vickers and his group were, of course, maintaining tremendous pressure on union headquarters to have the strike made official. And Vickers, enjoying his leading role, kept the situation thoroughly inflamed in the early weeks along a general line of racial hatred. We, at the union, were in a difficult spot. I had taken charge of the situation personally on behalf of union headquarters and decided to stay close to the workers while committing myself to no line of action. I visited the strike scene regularly, letting myself be seen but maintaining a low key, non-committal line at the regular meetings which we held. It was a strange situation and the strike meetings had an eerie quality. We used to hold them in a big open field in the little town of Williamsfield near to the Kirkvine plant. The formula was always the same. Vickers would make a violent speech which I would listen to from the back of the crowd. When he was finished I would walk through the crowd which would fall silent as I passed through it. I would then speak, dealing with the efforts that the union was making through the Ministry of Labour to find a formula for the reopening of the plant and the resumption of work. I was playing for time in a situation in which the company had made it clear that it would not reopen the plant unless Vickers and the ringleaders of the strike were made to face disciplinary charges while at the same time the workers were unwilling to resume if any charges at all were pressed.

After about four weeks I was getting really worried, quite apart from the deep hurt I felt as I watched the workers grow increasingly solemn and confused in what they were beginning to recognise as a hopeless situation. Then Vickers made a fatal mistake. He began to attack the union amongst the workers and to include me personally in his attack. As long as he saved his fire for the company he had the workers on his side but when he turned his guns on me his strength began to ebb. Many workers felt that this was unfair because they knew that I had not called the strike in the first place and had never thought that it was either justified or tactically sound. By coincidence, an annual conference of the union took place when the strike was about five weeks old. Vickers seized the opportunity to attend with his group and made a speech attacking me in a most scurrilous way. He was immediately shouted down and a fight broke out. Order was quickly restored, but in no time the story spread among the strikers that Vickers had gone too far. A few days later I called a full scale meeting and secured a mandate from the workers to arrange a resumption of work with an enquiry into the circumstances of the strike and Vickers' part in it. In due course, the plant was opened and work resumed. The enquiry was held and the union fielded a top team of lawyers, but lost the case. Among other things the enquiry revealed that the strike was not a sudden explosion but had in fact been quite elaborately planned from sometime before.

I have never been sure that I completely understood Vickers' motives and have often wondered what would have happened if he had not shifted his attack from the company to the union. Many people at the time thought he did this because he had dreams of taking over the leadership of the organisation but I doubt that his motivation was that clear. In the end he paid the inevitable price of disloyalty. Having exposed himself by going far beyond the limits of legitimate union action and being guilty of a flagrant breach of contract he would have been well advised to remain loyal to his own organisation. When he cut himself off from that final bastion there was nothing left that could save him.

Although peace was eventually restored at the plant the union paid a bitter price for the whole episode. The older workers realised that we had been trapped in an impossible situation and it was obvious that their faith and loyalty were unaffected. This meant that all the big maintenance sections of the plant like the machine shop, the millwrights, the tractor mechanics and the like remained solid union groups. The leadership in these areas was drawn mainly from among the older workers because these were skills that had existed in Jamaica before, particularly in the sugar industry. However, the operators who ran the alumina plant were a much younger group who had been recruited out of the schools when the plant started, since there had been no comparable sector in the Jamaican economy before Kirkvine was built. Vickers had been a hero to this more militant and racially conscious group and the fact that he lost his case and never worked at Kirkvine again was held against the union for years. The result was that there was an uneasy situation in the plant. These were workers who would never go to any other union because they were conscious of the tremendous part that the NWU had played among the bauxite workers over the years yet they felt that the union had let them down and Vickers was the symbol of that default.

Looking back after more than fifteen years this episode remains my unhappiest union memory. I do not like ill-defined situations where it is difficult to identify specific targets and make them the focus for action. In the Vickers case I felt myself trapped in a dilemma which I never seemed quite able to resolve. Perhaps I should have ignored all the rational elements of the situation such as the fact that Vickers was wrong to call the strike; that the strike was in total breach of contract and technically indefensible; and, above all, that there was a real danger of the plant being shut down. Curiously enough, this last fear had gained credence in my mind when our United Steelworkers friends got word to me that the Alcan management in Montreal really did intend to shut the plant down for a long period of time if the situation got out of hand. In spite of all that, however, it can be argued that my duty was to commit the union to battle regardless of the circumstances. I suspect that if I were judging somebody else dealing with the situation I would find it easier to approve the course of action that was taken. My problem is that it was not some other union leader but me, hence I am not sure how far such a favourable judgment would be open to doubt because obviously self-serving. All I know is that it was a miserable experience for which we paid a heavy price.

I think the wounds are healed now because time has passed and there have been many other occasions on which the union and its members have acted in concert and harmony at Kirkvine. Memories fade and new victories heal the wounds of old defeats. And yet the Vickers case nags the memory and I keep asking: What could I have done that I didn't think to do at the time which would have solved that tragic situation?

If the Vickers case was the saddest, the least conclusive

and certainly the most frustrating of my career, the Alpart case was the most terrible. In 1967 the Labour Government under Shearer made a series of agreements with the bauxite companies that led to the building of three new alumina plants. Prior to that Jamaica had two alumina plants at Kirkvine and Williamsfield, both of which were owned and operated by Alcan. Now Kaiser and Reynolds were to form a consortium with the great copper corporation, Anaconda, to build a huge alumina plant on the old Kaiser south coast bauxite holdings. Designed with a capacity of some million tons annually the new plant was to be run by a company known as Alpart (Jamaica) Limited. Construction was planned to cover the three years from 1967 to 1970 and was expected to involve a work force of more than four thousand. Kaiser Engineers, a subsidiary of the Kaiser Corporation, had the contract to carry out the construction work. Normally speaking, the NWU would have represented the workers, bauxite wages would have been paid and a smooth construction operation could be expected. We had done this often before even though it meant that the construction workers used on a bauxite plant would receive anything up to four times the rates generally obtaining in the construction industry. In the case of Alpart we expected that the work force would exceed four thousand during the construction period and so we moved in a crack team of construction organisers. The veteran, Caswell Rodney, was in charge assisted by Derrick Rochester, Vin Foote and Headley Reynolds. Rodney had been through all the toughest battles in sugar and in the construction industry. Rochester had been a brilliant, young chief delegate at Kaiser's south coast mining operation who had joined the union staff. He is now a promising member of Parliament. Foote and Reynolds were bright young staff men who were chosen because of their proven courage and coolness under pressure. They were to need just those qualities, for any hopes of a smooth passage during construction were soon to be dispelled. The BITU, controlled the bauxite industry and felt that it was a matter of the highest priority that the BITU should secure a foothold there. Soon after the agreement to build Alpart was concluded, further agreements were made with Alcoa to build a half a million ton alumina plant and with the Revere Corporation to build a quarter million ton plant. The former was to be on the Alcoa holdings in Southern Clarendon and Revere chose a site near Appleton Sugar Estate (the home of the famous rum of the same name) in northern St Elizabeth.

The Alpart construction started first and it was soon clear that the BITU and the Jamaica Labour intended to make it a battleground for union control. The NWU had always operated a system with the bauxite companies whereby we never sought to control employment nor to interfere in the selection of workers, being content to depend on the formidable reputation of the union along with good organisation to secure our position. We imagined that Alpart would be no different and as soon as workers were taken on at the site we turned up with our usual organising force, signed up the workers doing site clearing, served a claim for bargaining rights, held a poll, secured a hundred per cent of the vote and were accorded bargaining rights. We made a temporary agreement for the site clearance workers by which their pay was increased to current bauxite rates and then waited for the main construction to begin. We soon discovered that there was going to be serious trouble.

A major construction project like the Alpart work is supervised by the contracting engineer, but the work itself is parcelled out in a series of sub-contracts which sometimes even involve sub-sub-contracts. It soon appeared that the BITU was exploiting the fact that the JLP was in power to make deals with the managers of the various sub-contracting firms involving the control of key elements in the work forces that were being built up for the project. Thus, before a subcontractor appeared on the site the management would have made an arrangement to take on certain key BITU strong arm men who would be part of the firm's 'presence' as soon as it turned up on site. Meantime, we had agreed, in the normal manner, that the bulk of the workers would be recruited through the Government's labour recruitment offices. In our innocence we assumed that this process would lead to random selection of the work force which had never presented any problems in the past when it came to organisation. However, the Ministry of Labour recruitment offices were soon under the control of hand-picked supporters of the JLP, and we began to notice that people with a firm pre-commitment to support the BITU were showing up in unprecedented numbers at the site. We were in the middle of a sizeable conspiracy to pack the work force against us as a prelude to upsetting our bargaining rights. As soon as we were aware of the danger, we hit back. I moved a major organising force into the area and began exerting counter pressure to have key people of proven political loyalty employed. I also began to maintain a strong personal presence on the work site so as to counter the considerable resources which the BITU was committing to the struggle. The BITU strategy was based on three factors. Firstly there was the control of the supply of labour; secondly, there was the technique of extravagant promises; and, thirdly, there was the introduction of a new personality. This last was important because all the old line BITU personalities were hopelessly compromised by their earlier performance when they had controlled Reynolds and the Kaiser construction work force in the early 1950s. Clearly, they needed an energetic new spokesman who could indulge, without embarrassment, in the second phase of their strategy which involved extravagant promises. A young graduate of New York City College named Pearnel Charles was chosen for the task, and set about it with commendable energy.

Within a matter of months the whole work site was smouldering with tension as the rival, hard core leaders fought for the allegiance of a work force which was thoroughly infiltrated with die-hard political activists of the JLP. It seemed to me that only my reputation as the architect of the bauxite accomplishment over the years stood between the NWU and defeat. The BITU had earlier put in a claim for bargaining rights which made it impossible for us to negotiate. The Kaiser engineers' rates were based on the industry-wide agreements which were fast coming to an end. In this respect we had been following customary practice in the industry, but naturally this opened up a tremendous propaganda opportunity for the BITU. They were able to contend that many of the construction workers had not actually been on site when this agreement was made and ought to be free to demand higher wages. We were totally opposed to this for the simple reason that the industry could quickly be reduced to chaos if the pattern of orderly contract bargaining which we had established were destroyed. The key to the bauxite workers' success lay in unity and this was exactly what the BITU sought to destroy. So the propaganda battle raged with the BITU afraid to precipitate a poll lest it should lose and the NWU nervous to force a poll before the industry contract came to an end and opened up a fresh bargaining situation.

This was a tough time. Early in the battle, in fact only a few months after I had become a Member of Parliament for the first time for the constituency of Central Kingston (1967), I had been charged with a breach of the Public Meetings Law for holding a workers' meeting during the lunch break. Obviously the police were under orders to harass me. Soon after I was caught in one of the ugliest incidents of my life. Tension was mounting on the site and there had been a number of fights between the rival factions. Right at the end of a lunch break when I had addressed yet another workers' meeting as part of a constant series on our side, I was driving along from the site of the meeting heading towards the plant where I intended to connect up with the main road back to Kingston. A couple of hundred yards along I passed a police jeep and suddenly realised, almost in a double take, that some sort of argument was taking place between Charles and three of the NWU delegates. I slammed on my brakes just ahead of the jeep and walked quickly back because I was most anxious that there should be no violence, and feared that a quarrel between Charles and the NWU delegates might spark off serious trouble. Before I could intervene I suddenly saw Charles take a swing at one of the delegates, a youngster called Clinton Cooke whose nickname was 'Big Cookie'. Cookie swayed out of reach of the punch and countered with a right cross of his own which knocked off Charles' dark glasses and staggered him. By now I was shouting 'stop it, stop it', and for a moment everyone on the scene seemed frozen except Cookie and Charles. The latter had been staggered by the punch which seemed to have thrown him against the back of the jeep. Cookie was moving towards him apparently meaning to throw another punch and it was all happening so quickly that not even the police who were standing around the jeep had moved to intervene. Suddenly Charles drew his gun and started firing and all hell broke loose. I was not more than three yards from Charles when he pulled his gun and can remember a series of impressions flashing through my mind. I was aware that a small crowd which had been walking down the road after the meeting and which must have been gathering at the prospect of a fight was now in full flight in every direction. The next thing I knew was that Charles was sprinting across the road towards a car which I subsequently learned was full of BITU organisers and minutes later tear-gas shells were going off all around me; I later learnt thirteen in all were exploded within minutes. Someone was firing from the back of the BITU car and I was aware of a gun all too visible through the right rear window just before the car did a violent turn in a cloud of red dirt on the unasphalted country road. I remember feeling tremendous pride when I realised that Cookie was throwing stones at the car from which the shots were being fired; such is the courage of the Jamaican worker when he is aroused! The car with Charles in it was soon speeding away and I still hadn't moved from where I stood because running through my mind like a refrain were the words: 'Leaders cannot take cover because there is danger.' Some people were crouching down behind the jeep which was just a few yards from me and I remember for one fleeting instant fighting down the impulse to join them. During all this I was coughing like mad from the tear gas but by now I had learnt to cope with this. Then suddenly I became conscious that the whole of Cookie's left thigh was soaked in blood. He had been throwing stones at the car after being hit high in the left thigh when Charles fired. Suddenly someone shouted: 'Oh my God, Mosewhyne dead. Dem get him, him dead.' Everything had happened so fast that none of us had noticed that a delegate named George Whynne and known as 'Mosewhyne' had been hit, apparently by the first shot. He got it in the chest where it lodged in his right lung. I hadn't noticed because although Mose had been standing close behind me when he was hit my attention had been so riveted on Charles sprinting across the road, the gun firing from the back of the BITU car, Cookie throwing stones, tear-gas shells going off and finally the car disappearing in a cloud of red bauxite dust that I did not see him go down.

Our first job was to get him to the Mandeville Hospital as fast as we could. We bundled Cookie into my car with somebody's shirt wrapped around his thigh and lifted Mose in as gently as we could. I will never forget that long drive up Spur Tree Hill round the hundred corners that now seemed like a thousand as we raced to get to medical help before it was too late. As it happened we made it and the bullet was removed from his lung, saving his life. Mose was immediately put on full salary by the NWU and he is now an organiser for the union in the area where all this happened.

For a while after the shooting things were quieter as a sense of shock seemed to bring temporary sanity to the construction site. But this did not last for long. Soon, the BITU were going full blast again with a ceaseless flow of propaganda. By now, they had moved a number of notorious Kingston gunmen on to the site with the connivance of certain of the subcontractors. Obviously, they intended to use violence as the final weapon. Then came the news that we most feared. All the radios in Jamaica were suddenly blaring the news that the BITU had called a strike and been able to shut the construction site down. Indeed, Charles had been able to work an arrangement with the television station, the Government-owned Jamaica Broadcasting Corporation. That night's television news showed striking Alpart workers being addressed by Charles in a meeting that bore all the hallmarks of a BITU triumph. All this happened on a Wednesday afternoon. By that night, however, the true story was coming in. What had really happened was that Charles had arranged to have the workers of a particular contractor who were effectively controlled by the BITU go on strike and then run amok amongst the workers in the rest of the project. Using stones and brandishing guns all the other workers had been intimidated and soon the entire place was shut down.

The NWU was in a jam. Even though many of the workers were loyal and had been intimidated, the place was in such a state of tension and uncertainty and had been so bombarded with propaganda that anything could happen. In any event, once a strike starts where there is a general atmosphere of discontent there is a strong tendency for workers to forget questions of organisational allegiance and feel that the strike is a good thing, however it started, since it may lead to the clearing up of their various grievances. Added to all this, the BITU was promising that if the workers stood firm on the strike there would be immediate, vast wage increases for everybody. To cap it all the whole episode had been captured for that night's audience, and for posterity, on television! This was particularly important because Alpart was seen as the key to a general strategy to smash the NWU in the bauxite industry, and the scene had been carefully set to make the strike appear to be a personal rejection of my leadership. The scene had been well set, the strategy well planned and the next move was clearly up to me!

I spent most of the rest of Wednesday night considering the alternatives. I could do nothing which would put the BITU in a bind since they did not have bargaining rights and could not, therefore, actually do anything for the workers. Equally, they could not hold a union election without a resumption of work and so there was much to be said for a waiting game where the long-term futility of the BITU's position might lead to the recognition by the majority of the workers that they had been used as pawns in a power game. On the other hand, this would involve maintaining the reality of the present situation where the workers were not at work as a consequence of the BITU act and where their official bargaining agent, the NWU, had not called a strike. It did not take me long to reject this strategy even though it would have been a safe way of regaining control in the long run. I remember thinking that whatever happened I would not let the BITU appear to be able to challenge the NWU even for a few weeks in a bargaining rights situation which was legitimately ours. Instead, I opted for the bold course.

I decided to announce that I was calling a meeting for the following Monday morning. I chose this in preference to Friday because I would have to make the call on Thursday and I wasn't absolutely sure that all the workers, who would have gone home because of the strike, would get the news of my meeting in time to turn up on Friday. I decided to make this a personal confrontation which, to be effective had to take place with a full work force present. My plan was risky in the extreme. I intended to make a speech and then call on the workers who were loyal to the NWU to follow me into the plant. This is the most dangerous thing that you can try to do in the union movement because workers hate to go back to work after a strike with nothing to show for it. After only two days out, nobody would be feeling the economic pinch. However, I preferred it this way because if I could pull it off then the blow to the BITU's prestige would be absolute.

As long as I live I will remember the drive down to Nain in St Elizabeth that morning. We left home at about five o'clock in the morning so that I would arrive just on seven o'clock. Since the strike had started in the presence of television I had invited the JBC to send down their cameras again. I figured that win, lose or draw, I might as well go the whole way. If I was to be humiliated let it be on TV. But if I won, then let the whole country see so that nobody could confuse the situation thereafter by lies and propaganda. The stakes were high and I do not think I have ever felt more sick, physically, brutally sick before any event in my career. There was an enormous amount at stake. Indeed that morning I felt that my career itself was waiting judgement. I would have to find words that would move and inspire the majority of an angry, confused group of men, more than two thousand strong, to go against their every instinct by crossing their own picket line. When I arrived the BITU had a meeting going and it seemed that it was made up of about five hundred men. Our microphones were set up with about five hundred of our people standing silently waiting for my arrival. The bulk of the force, about fifteen hundred strong, was standing over on a slight rise, that was not quite a hill. They were waiting.

I got out of the car and walked over to our meeting and began to speak. I don't really know what I said but as I spoke groups began to detach themselves from the uncommitted crowd and were drifting over to within earshot of our microphones. At this point I moved into high gear with an emotional account of how the bauxite workers had fought over the years, of what we had sacrificed together and the victories that we had won. Suddenly I made up my mind to move and shouted: 'Who is with me follow.' I jumped off the platform and started to walk towards the plant gate where the BITU gunmen were waiting with their strike placards. I never once looked back. There must have been a hundred yards to cover and in no time I found myself going through the picket lines and was conscious that they were falling away and that the gates were opening. I marched straight in, not looking back until I was quite a way inside, by which time I knew I had won because NWU supporters were by now dancing with joy all around me. At this point I turned and looked back and it was as if a multitude were pouring into the plant behind me. In no time even the BITU group had broken and had joined the general stampede to get back into the plant. I had won perhaps the most dramatic victory of my career.

Soon after we were involved in a long strike which established a much improved construction contract with some important new benefits such as an 'end of project bonus' for the workers. Later we were unable to fight off the combined Government, JLP and BITU combination in the construction of Revere and Alcoa. These were built under BITU control although we recaptured Alcoa soon after the plant was completed and still represent their production workers. Revere is now the only plant under BITU control with the rest of the industry once again doing great things in terms of new union initiatives and development under the leadership of that brilliant young man who succeeded me as Island Supervisor, Chief Negotiator and First Vice President of the NWU, Senator Carlyle Dunkley.

The story of bauxite would not be complete without mention of the Caribbean Bauxite Mine and Metal Workers Federation. This body was founded in 1964 as the Caribbean Bauxite and Mineworkers Federation with the bauxite workers of Jamaica, Guyana, Surinam, and the transhipment port workers of Trinidad as founding members. I was the first president, an office which I held until 1974 when I was succeeded by Dunkley. We formed the CBMF as part of a regional answer to the problem of the multi-national corporation. We were soon affiliated to the International Metalworkers Federation (IMF) with headquarters in Geneva, Switzerland. The IMF is one of the more dynamic international trade secretariats and embraces over 12.7 million workers in sixty countries on five continents. The IMF officer for Latin America and the Caribbean, Daniel Benedict, gave us great co-operation along with our traditional friends, the United Steelworkers of America, through officers like Meyer Bernstein, Dean Clowes and Larry Spitz under the sympathetic guidance of President Dave McDonald and his successor, I. W. Abel. In negotiations we felt constantly under the shadow of the threat that if we exerted too much pressure or pushed up our wages too fast the multi-national corporation might slow down its operations in Jamaica and speed up those in some other area in the world. It always seemed to us that if the corporations were capable of acting internationally so were we. All that we needed was the knowledge, the will and the contact with other groups. The first two we had in full measure and so, in due course, we applied ourselves to the last.

Our first contact was with Guyana where the workers in their bauxite industry were organised in a strong union group, the Guyana Mine Workers Union. The GMU was led by a fine officer, Winston Verbeke. Verbeke had been a bauxite worker himself with Demba, the Alcan operation. A decent and honourable man, Verbeke was quick to see the common sense behind the Jamaican suggestion for a regional federation of bauxite workers unions. He was to become the first vice-president of the organisation and has always been one of its moving spirits. In due course we were all benefiting from this association as we tackled problems of research jointly and were able to exchange information about each other's contracts and give general moral support to each other in times of stress. In many ways, what we did with the CBMMWF anticipated by ten years the International Bauxite Association which was established in Conakry, Guinea, in 1974 and for which the new Jamaica Government which I had the honour to lead after 1972 had worked so hard to establish. The IBA is the answer, for all those developing countries whose bauxite is the foundation of the world's aluminium industry, to that process of exploitation which is natural to the multi-national corporations. For decades bauxite has been mined by these corporations with little benefit to the countries where the ore is found. Just as the multi-national corporations were happy to take advantage of Jamaican labour for one shilling and two pence an hour while they paid at least ten times as much to their American counterparts, so were the multi-national corporations paying one shilling a ton to the Jamaica Government for the privilege of mining the ore. In 1952 the NWU saw the injustice of the situation but had no jurisdiction beyond the cause of the workers. We had formed the Bauxite Workers Regional Federation to assist in the development of that bargaining power which was essential to our ability to carve out a new world of opportunity and justice for the bauxite miners. Eight years later I was to be afforded the opportunity to apply the same insight and commonsense within the political situation. Determined that Jamaica itself should benefit from the presence of bauxite I launched a two year diplomatic initiative that took us to Australia, Guinea, Yugoslavia, Sierra Leone, Ghana, the Dominican Republic, Haiti, Guyana, Trinidad and Surinam in search of kindred spirits who would join with us in an international adventure involving national justice. In forming IBA and in defining its objectives the issues were more complex and the stakes far higher. However, the insight into the nature of the historical process and the reality of the dilemma facing the people of small and poor nations was the same. I have no doubt that the outcome will also be the same.

7
THE JBC STRIKE

WHILE these extended struggles were taking place in the sugar and bauxite industries, the union was expanding in many other fields, thanks to the efforts of a gallant band of field organisers and office staff. Men like Thossy Kelly, for years the President of the Union and principally responsible for leading Government workers, H. O. Thompson, a Vice-President of the Union and responsible for general agricultural workers, V. Bancroft Edwards, in printing and hotels, Irvine Jones in the field of industry, Audley Gayle in communications and Eric Harris in transport, were all leading struggles which in greater or lesser degree reflected the triumphs of bauxite or the frustrations of sugar. The ever increasing administrative demands were being met by an office staff organised and led by Miss Halcy Glasspole, for years my personal secretary and now Office Manager, Miss C. Donaldson in the Registry, Mr A. R. Bedasse in Accounts, Miss Gladys Ellington of the general staff (now a councillor of the Kingston and St Andrew Corporation), and the late J. U. Beckett who was Office Manager for most of the early, growing days.

Meantime, a completely different kind of conflict was in the making at the Government owned broadcasting station established in 1957 – the Jamaica Broadcasting Corporation. It is remarkable that the battle at the broadcasting station should have proved as basic and important, in its own way, as anything that took place in sugar and bauxite. The sugar industry was the largest single employer of labour with 50,000 workers at one point in time. The bauxite industry involved by far the most massive capital investment and was to become the largest single earner of revenue for the Government and an important source of foreign currency for the island's financial reserves. By contrast, the Jamaica Broadcasting Corporation employed less than two hundred people and had been established with capital of less than £1,000,000 sterling. It was not even the only broadcasting station in Jamaica. Yet, in 1964, the longest, most controversial, and perhaps most important single strike in Jamaica's labour history was to take place there. It lasted for ninety-seven days. It led to the longest Board of Enquiry proceedings – forty days – in our labour history. It was triggered by the dismissal of two news reporters. It took place at the Jamaica Broadcasting Corporation and was called by the National Workers Union.

To understand why an apparently simple dismissal case provoked such an intense reaction one must realise that considerable historical forces, each pursuing its own logic, met and did battle in the JBC strike. To begin with, the JBC was itself a battleground on which opposing views about the political system contended for supremacy. Even more importantly, the country was ripe for a confrontation between the trade union movement and employer groups about fundamental questions to do with workers' rights. And, finally, there was the constant and as yet unresolved tension inherent in the relationship between the political system and the trade union movement.

The Jamaica Broadcasting Corporation had been established in 1957 during the first PNP regime. It was very much my father's brainchild and reflected a clear view of the role of a broadcasting station in a democratic society. For many years previously, Jamaica had had one radio station, Radio Jamaica Limited, which was owned and managed by private British broadcasting interests. Radio Jamaica was a profit-making organisation with a clear obligation to provide dividends for its English and Jamaican shareholders. Consequently, it was a typical disc jockey type station playing popular music, importing the odd 'canned' feature and providing a rudimentary news service. One could not say that there was anything wrong with the station, on the other hand, no one would claim that it made any very positive contribution to the development of Jamaica or to the preparation of Jamaican society for the independence that clearly awaited it. I do not say this by way of criticism since Radio Jamaica was neither required to be nor pretended to be anything more than a station providing light entertainment to satisfy the lowest common denominator of discernible popular taste.

The Jamaica Broadcasting Corporation was established for a clear and well articulated purpose. It was supposed to provide an outlet for Jamaican culture, a forum for the discussion of public affairs and an additional means of public education. Naturally, it was expected to entertain and inform like its private enterprise cousin, but these were to be only a part of its total purpose. To provide the vehicle for the attainment of these objectives, a statutory corporation was created and initial finance provided by the Government. The station was modelled most closely after the Canadian Broadcasting Corporation which combines the idea of independence from political control as typified by the British Broadcasting Corporation, with the right to accept advertising as the primary source of income.

Naturally, a statutory corporation of this sort must bear some relationship to Government, however carefully circumscribed, and so, the JBC Law calls for a government minister to appoint the Board of the Corporation and to give general policy directives. However, it is not expected that the minister should interfere in the day-to-day running of the station. The other important feature of the JBC Law is the requirement that the station so manages its affairs as to equate income and expenditure over a period of time. I mention both these features, ministerial responsibility and the financial requirement, because they had a bearing on all that happened later.

Like so many institutions of this kind, the JBC was bound to depend for its success upon the kind of sensitive, political understanding which cannot be written into a law. In Manley's concept, the station was intended to be genuinely free from political interference, so that it could become an important element in the free exchange of ideas, a forum for that thrust and counter-thrust which is part of the essential ferment of democracy. To him, the thought of political manipulation of the JBC was abhorrent because his commitment to democracy rested upon a highly disciplined, intellectual comprehension of the system and what it takes to make it work. Equally, the question of the relationship between income and expenditure was never regarded by him as an immutable law of action to be followed blindly year by year regardless of circumstances. Rather, he regarded this as a long-term guideline intended to discourage inefficiency and waste. Always as good as his word and true to his beliefs, Manley helped guarantee a successful start to the corporation by attaching it to his own ministry and so protecting it from improper interference. As a result, the station got off to an inspiring start.

It became the focal point for the discussion of all the great political questions of the time. By 1961, for example, feelings were running high as to whether we should attain freedom and independence through membership in a Federation of the West Indies or whether to 'go it alone'. This was constantly and hotly debated on JBC time.

Quite apart from the political questions of the time, the station had begun to provide an outlet for local creative talent. 'Shadows of the Great House', the radio serial by Carmen Manley, was the first locally written, acted, directed and recorded soap opera in Jamaican history. It was immensely popular. Discussion programmes featuring local personalities were taking the place of similar 'canned' shows imported from the United Kingdom and the United States.

The News Room and its editorial and reporting staff were setting the pace in Jamaican journalism, incorporating stories of the kind that had previously tended to be ignored and displaying that *esprit de corps* which is the hallmark of the best news organisation. Commentators like John Maxwell and Peter Abrahams were introducing a new dimension into Jamaican journalism. Maxwell's brilliant, searching and abrasive mind was nicely contrasted with the balanced urbanity of Abraham's style.

Manley's Government was often under severe attack, particulary from Maxwell, and he was sometimes under pressure from his own colleagues to do something about it. It is to his lasting credit that he protected the station and its commentators with the shield of his own authority so that they could enjoy the freedom to explore the new possibilities which existed because the JBC had come into being.

And then in quick succession came the heavy defeat of the PNP after Federation was rejected in the referendum in September 1961, followed in April 1962 by Bustamante's return to power by the narrowest of electoral margins (less than 1 per cent of the popular vote). By August 1962 Jamaica had become an independent nation and the JBC had acquired not only a new set of political bosses but a new context of power within which to operate. In addition, within another year it had acquired a television licence and was broadcasting visually by late 1963.

In all the tragic events which were to follow it is important to understand something of the political outlook of Alexander Bustamante who had by now become Prime Minister.

At best, Bustamante's view of democracy was limited and pragmatic. It is doubtful whether he ever got much past the point of accepting the right of the Opposition to exist and of his own duty to accept the role of Opposition should it be ascribed to him by the electorate. Certainly, the notion of a radio station whose Board was appointed by a minister, the initial capital for which had been provided by Government and which was subject to governmental policy direction, being nonetheless free to attack Government, was beyond him.

Within a year of independence and the change of power, two major developments had taken place at JBC. On the positive side, it had added television broadcasting to its radio network. On the negative side, the new regime had begun to erode the foundations upon which the station rested by attacking three elements which were critical to its success. Firstly, the new Government had silenced the critical commentators and had actually driven Maxwell from the station, terminating his employment because of a commentary that was hostile to the regime. Secondly, the News Room which contained the most enterprising reporting team Jamaica had known for years had been virtually demoralised because every time a story was broadcast which did not show the Government in a favourable light, there would be the most violent reaction from the ministers and JLP Members of Parliament. In no time News Room morale began to sag and in place of the high sense of adventure which is the essence of a great news organisation, a pall of fear hung over the place.

The final blow was struck in the area of financial management. Inevitably, the station was losing money because it was running a number of entertaining but expensive shows which provided an outlet for local creative talent. Any new organisation takes time to settle down and achieve a balance between income and expenditure. In the case of the JBC this process was bound to be of more than ordinary difficulty because it involved a challenge to the accepted listening patterns of the disc-jockey type traditionally provided by Radio Jamaica. Where the station needed the encouragement to press on, creating a new audience as it went, it was suddenly subject to the appointment of a new Board which was unsympathetic to the creative ideals upon which it was based and was under the control of a minister who made it clear that the station must stop losing money at once. The particular minister was Edward Seaga and there is no way of knowing whether the financial policies upon which the new Government insisted represented his views or were really a reflection of Bustamante's own attitudes.

The consequences of these pressures were as predictable as they were unfortunate. A staff which is highly motivated and believes that it is making a significant contribution to the growth of a young country will put up with a lot in terms of salary and working conditions. The JBC staff at the time was badly paid and often worked sixteen hours a day but they did this with dedicated enthusiasm and bore their long hours with pride. When the basis of their pride was destroyed they became increasingly conscious of their inadequate pay and their long hours. Indeed, one could illustrate the mood of the station by a graph in which a steadily descending line represents the erosion of pride and *esprit de corps*, while a rapidly ascending line represents resentment and a growing demand for better pay and working conditions. By late 1963, the lines met and at the point of intersection the workers decided to seek union protection.

The union to which the JBC workers turned was the NWU. They did so for a number of reasons. To begin with the JLP Government was the immediate cause of their discontent as it was felt to be totally out of sympathy with their own ideals as a broadcasting staff. It was also natural to turn to the NWU since they already organised Radio Jamaica; and there was, in addition, the fact that the artisan and middle classes tended to be more comfortable with a PNP than a

JLP orientation. However, what was a natural response on the part of the staff in the circumstances was seen as part of a sinister political plot by the Government. Jamaica was still at the stage where people found it difficult to believe that unions could act apart from political manipulation. Hence the JLP leadership jumped to the worst conclusions about the workers' motives as soon as the NWU arrived on the scene. It apparently never occurred to them to seek the explanation for the workers' action in the most obvious cause, namely, worker dissatisfaction with their conditions of employment in a context of professional frustration.

To all of this must be added one final consideration if we are to understand what followed. This has to do with the general mood of the country at the time.

Jamaica had just become independent. This meant that all our political institutions, practices, habits of action were under critical scrutiny. The early days of independence are crucial in establishing patterns which later provide the foundations for a nation's way of life. Thus, everything takes on a larger than life significance. Those who are unusually attached to power seek openings in the new independence to perpetuate themselves in office. Equally, those of similar outlook who are not currently in power seem to press harder for power than they might otherwise do as if fearing that the opportunity may never come. Everyone is conscious of the history of newly independent nations which seem to slide early into dictatorship. It was a restless, unsettled time. The fact that the Bustamante Government seemed to have no clear idea as to where Jamaica might head in independence did nothing to improve matters but seemed, rather to add to the general disquiet. This was the state of affairs in the country when word reached us at union headquarters that the JBC staff was trying to make contact and wanted to see me in particular. One can see that two very considerable political issues were involved. To begin with there was the whole question of the relationship between a broadcasting organisation and Government, involving important considerations of political methodology. To this was added the vexed question of the relationship between an employer representing the JLP Government facing a group of workers represented by the NWU which was affiliated to the Opposition PNP, where this somewhat tangled relationship involved questions of motive and good faith.

More profound than either of these, however, was a fundamental question of workers' rights. Nineteenth century capitalism had created a fundamental change in the methods by which goods were produced. However these changes in economic methodology took place against a background of ancient relationships in society itself. Britain and Europe, which were the scene of the industrial revolution, shared common societies which were organised on the basis of a master and servant relationship. From the days of feudalism, it was fundamental to social organisation that the relationship between an employer and an employee was based upon the inherent superiority of the one to the other. This superior-inferior relationship had many practical expressions. The employer, or 'master', had the sole right to determine rates of pay, hours of service, conditions of work, and, most critically of all whether a job was available at all. The extraordinary degree of emphasis upon the rights of employer over employee was quite natural given the hierarchical nature of society and the importance which was attached to authority and discipline as the guarantors of social order. Into this framework of social relationships came the industrial revolution with its substitution of factory organisation for the more intimate productive organisations of the guilds and master craftsmen. Where production used to take place in the context of close interpersonal relationships between employer and employee there suddenly emerged large factories in which great numbers of people were herded together to tend the great new spinning and weaving machines. Inevitably, the first casualty of the new process was the close personal relationship between the 'master' and the 'servant'. However, although the basis of the relationship disappeared the authority which characterised it did not.

Employers were still regarded as possessed of the inalienable right to absolute power. However, the breakdown of interpersonal relationships coupled with the discovery of the power that is inherent in any large group of persons combining in a single project made it inevitable that absolute power and unquestioned authority would be challenged. Trade unions were the product of the dialectic of the situation and in due course established the notion of the rights of workers. However, the struggle surrounding workers' rights does not involve a single upheaval leading to some new and completely perceived ideal situation. The process by which workers' rights are defined takes place in the larger context of a society's need for order and efficiency. There is always the need for authority because there is always the need for discipline. And there is always the need for discipline because there is always the need for efficiency. However production is organised, there has to be a decision-making process together with a guarantee that decisions are enforceable. Therefore, the evolution of workers' rights is a slow and unending process which unfolds against the backdrop of a parallel redefinition of authority, discipline and the decision-making process.

Broadly speaking, there are three important stages. Firstly, there is the phase in which the workers establish the basic right to protest: it is at this stage that he establishes the right to organise, and to strike and to bargain for wages, hours and improved working conditions. One might call this a fundamentalist stage in which what is being challenged is the notion of absolute employer authority. It is interesting to note, however, that by 1963 this first phase was well developed in Jamaica but was still subject to sharp limitations. For example it was generally accepted that the worker had the right to bargain and it had even been accepted that disciplinary action by an employer was subject to quasi-judicial review. However, it had not yet been accepted that workers had a right to be safe from arbitrary employer action in relation to the holding of a job itself. Let me illustrate. If a worker had a job and was dismissed by an employer it was accepted that he had the right to complain and to have tested, if necessary by impartial arbitration, the question of whether the employer acted reasonably in terminating the employment. However, if it were found by one means or another that the employer had acted unreasonably it was not accepted that the worker had the right to recover his job. At best it was felt that the employer might owe the worker some form of compensation but there was no question of his having to reinstate him. Clearly, this attitude represented a survival of the concept of absolute authority. At the beginning of the workers' long struggle the absolute authority of the employer extended not only to whether a person could have a job but also to the terms on which it was held. The whole question of terms of employment was the first battleground and here, in due course, the notion of absolute authority yielded to the concept of mutual rights. But absolutism was not defeated, it was merely in retreat. The new line of defence was drawn at the absolute right of the employer to terminate a particular contract of employment, not because a worker was deficient, not because the job itself had ceased to exist, but for no better reason than that he wished to be rid of him.

At the time of the JBC staff's decision to seek protection in a union, Jamaica was ripe for the exploration of the second stage involving the respective rights of employers and workers. In effect, the question of whether the worker is to be free from arbitrary dismissal and whether the employer is to be denied the right to get rid of an employee arbitrarily involves what one might describe as a sophisticated democracy in the workplace. The third stage of the workers' struggle involves total democracy in which the very notion of employer and employee gives way to a completely different concept of social and economic organisation. However, it is not now our purpose to examine that development. In 1963 Jamaica was ready for the confrontation which inevitably preceded the second phase of the democratisation of working relations in our society. It was against this background that I held my first meeting with the staff of the JBC in 1963.

I will never forget them. They were as bright as they were bitter. The group included news readers, announcers, disc jockeys, operators, reporters, typists, drivers, maids, janitors, librarians, producers, TV cameramen, radio and television technicians. The pervading mood was one of determination and commitment. As a group they were argumentative and keen. They took nothing for granted. Yet they never seemed arrogant or overbearing. Rather, it was as if they were transferring the eager idealism which they had brought to the corporation to the union. Many of them were well educated and able people – some graduates of the University of the West Indies, others highly skilled technicians or people of considerable creative talent. This made them an exciting, and even memorable group to deal with. They had no desire to have the union play the role of the godfather who makes everything come right by mysterious and obscure processes. For me this was a particular joy because of my own deep commitment to the idea of a trade union as a living, democratic organism.

From the outset, the group wished to be assured that there would be nothing political in either the act of joining the union or in any subsequent action which the union might undertake on their behalf. It was clear that for most of them this was a pre-condition of joining. I was happy to be able to assure them that they need have no fears on that score. As it happened, my own professional integrity joined with my tactical sense made it easy to give the guarantee that they sought. It had always been fundamental to my concept of unionism that it should act purely in terms of the workers' interests which should never be tampered with in the interests of partisan politics. Here I draw a sharp distinction between politics in the wider sense of the system of government and the processes by which laws are made, on the one hand, and party politics, in the sense of those activities which are aimed at securing power for a particular organisation, on the other. The distinction is not always easy to draw or maintain since both the politics of a nation and the party political interest of a particular organisation are interwoven. However, a considerable step forward is taken when it is admitted that the two are not necessarily the same and that the workers' legitimate aspirations must never be compromised by purely partisan political interests. However, quite apart from the principles which are involved, there was also the matter of practical reality. I did not need anyone to tell me that the Bustamante Government would be extremely suspicious of a situation in which the NWU represented a group of workers in as sensitive an area as a broadcasting station. I had no illusions about the economic importance of a radio station to the country and so began with a realistic appreciation of the true extent of the bargaining power of the JBC group in any confrontation with the sovereign Government of independent Jamaica.

In due course, we had organised a substantial majority of the staff of the station which had some one hundred and fifty employees including managerial staff. The categories on whose behalf we sought bargaining rights totalled about one hundred and twenty. When everything was set and the union properly established with a chairman, an executive, departmental delegates, shop stewards and the like, we served a claim for bargaining rights. After the usual hassle we established the validity of our claim and were duly recognised as the bargaining agent. Already, a sensitive ear could detect an unusual degree of tension at the station, particularly on the management side. Obviously, there was more than the usual concern that attaches to the first advent of a union in any enterprise. Pressures were undoubtedly mounting behind the scenes from the political bosses who had been increasingly evident at the JBC since the change of Government. For our part we did everything possible to keep things calm. Our main concern was to negotiate a good contract without getting into a fight. Certainly, we had a very strong case. Comparisons which were made with concerns like Radio Jamaica, the Telephone Company and the Cable and Wireless Organisation which handles Jamaica's external telephone and cable communications showed that the JBC salaries and working conditions were well out of line.

Perhaps because the facts were so clearly on our side, the negotiations went surprisingly well and in due course the union proposed a final package of wage increases and reduced working hours, leave and pension facilities and the like which would have cost the station about $20,000 a year. We put forward this proposal in January 1964 and later the same month a meeting took place in which the management indicated that this latest union proposal seemed reasonable and would enjoy their support. They pointed out that the matter would have to be referred to the Minister, Mr Seaga, since they were actually losing money but this was little more than a formality – or so we thought. About a week later we were invited by the corporation to come back to another meeting.

We actually thought that we were going to formalise the new contract and were aghast when we heard that the corporation was not prepared to accept our proposals. It emerged that the management had referred the matter to the board of directors who had, in turn, referred the matter to the Minister. The Minister had refused to sanction the increases proposed and so we had been called to be told that our extremely modest package had been totally rejected. I called a meeting that same day in the canteen of the corporation at about five p.m. when the normal work day for the office staff comes to an end. I made a full and accurate report of what had happened and got the staff to agree that, bitter as the blow was, we should remain calm and report the matter to the Conciliation Department of the Ministry of Labour as a dispute. It was clear that the staff were angry and frustrated but the meeting was orderly and ended on a completely disciplined note.

The next day I was out in the country negotiating with the Reynolds bauxite group when I got an urgent phone call to say that there was an extremely serious situation at JBC where two members of the News Room staff had been fired. One was Adrian Rodway, a Guyanese and UWI graduate who had been on the staff for about a year, and the other George Lee, the union delegate for the News Room staff. Lee was a Jamaican who came from the parish of St Thomas, had learnt his trade as a newsman at the *Daily Gleaner* and was an avowed member of the Jamaica Labour Party. In spite of this he had been elected delegate for the section and had, up to then (and since) proved to be a loyal union member and a vigorous delegate. My enquiries over the phone revealed that Lee and Rodway had been fired for the part they had played in the publication of a news story which had been broadcast in a late night news bulletin over JBC following the union meeting which I had held. This item had been repeated in the early morning news the next day. The news story had simply stated that the Minister had turned down the proposed wage increase and that as a result a dispute now existed between the union and corporation and that the Ministry of Labour was to be asked to intervene. I heard this in a state half way between shock and disbelief. How, I asked, could Lee and

Rodway be fired for putting out a news story which was an exact, uncontroversial account of the truth? Union headquarters could throw no light on the matter and I set out for Kingston convinced that something else must have happened which headquarters had not heard as yet.

Before leaving Reynolds, I got union headquarters to set up a meeting with the management for that very afternoon and broke a number of speed records between Reynolds' Lydford plant near the north coast and the Odeon Avenue offices of the corporation in the heart of greater Kingston. In the course of the meeting with the management it transpired that George Lee had written the story of the union management meeting, doing so right after the worker meeting which I had addressed. He had filed this story, which was accurate in every detail and had gone home. Adrian Rodway was in a somewhat different position. He had been at the union meeting where he had heard my report and then taken up duty on the late shift in a post known as 'man in the slot'. The 'man in the slot' is the name given to a reporter whose duty for a particular shift is to check all the material which is prepared for broadcast. Certain categories of news were, by standing order, to be checked with a senior news editor for clearance. Otherwise the 'man in the slot' was supposed to exercise a general discretion to see that nothing libellous, ridiculous or obviously inaccurate got through. When in doubt on any matter he was supposed to double check with a senior news editor.

It appears that there was a standing order requiring that all stories to do with politics or trade union matters were to be cleared with the news editor automatically. Rodway had not done this, explaining that he knew the story to be true because he had been present at the union meeting which I had addressed. However, even allowing for this explanation, it was obvious that he had been guilty of a technical default.

It was clear to me that Lee was guilty of nothing, and I proposed his immediate reinstatement along with the withdrawal of all charges against him. In the case of Rodway, I pointed out that he had been guilty of a technical mistake but with strong extenuating circumstances arising out of the fact that he had been present at the union meeting and therefore could vouch from his own knowledge for the accuracy of the story which was being published. Accordingly I suggested that he too be reinstated but with a reprimand and warning because of the element of technical guilt. The management heard these arguments and promised to relay them faithfully to the board. In the course of the next couple of days I heard through the grapevine that the board had rejected my proposals and intended to confirm the dismissal of both men.

Acting entirely on my own initiative and because I could feel that disaster was imminent, I relayed to the General Manager, Mr Mickie Hendricks, and the Chairman of the Board, Mr K. H. Ivan Levy, certain strong views about the dispute. I went over the grounds of the dismissal very carefully and I tried to explain why the corporation was wrong on every possible count on the facts of the case. Then I went further. I tried to explain how much JBC had meant to my father and how much it meant to me and could come to mean to Jamaica. I hoped this would help them understand that I did not want to be involved in anything that would hurt the station. At the same time I warned them that the union could not sit by and see two people victimised in the savage and unreasonable way that they had proposed and that they would force me to fight with every weapon at my command if they held to their present course. I implored them not to force me to do this and tried to indicate that I was not the sort of person who would put up a half-hearted battle for the sake of appearances, but that if it came to a fight it would be a fight to the finish. With more foresight than I was then aware of I urged them to understand that the only casualty in a fight of this sort would be the JBC itself which would inevitably be dragged into a bitter, partisan struggle in which it would be compromised both politically and as an employer. Once again I was told that my views would be considered but I had the feeling that I was up against a brick wall compounded as much of stupidity as suspiciousness. I had a sense of impending doom. Sure enough, the news came the next day that the board had officially and finally rejected the union's submissions and confirmed the dismissal of Lee and Rodway.

I was due to fly to Trinidad the next day to attend an important meeting of the Caribbean Bauxite Mine and Metal Workers Federation of which I had recently become co-founder and president. I held another meeting with the staff on the day before I left. Before I spoke the group of delegates urged me to see them privately and unanimously informed me that the workers had come to an irrevocable decision to strike. We spent some time considering the possibility of reporting the matter to the Ministry of Labour and seeing what might happen. However, their view was that the decision to fire Lee and Rodway was politically directed and that it would be a waste of time to go through the motions of a Ministry of Labour intervention. They felt that if we went straight to the ministry the morale of the group would not stand up before the pressure of long drawn-out discussions with the management who could only employ delaying tactics, having regard to the orders under which they were presumed to be acting.

With these warnings fresh in my mind I proceeded to the general workers' meeting where I found ample confirmation of the delegates' analysis. Thereupon I made up my own mind that the right course of action was to take a strike vote, having first indicated the possible options. The vote was unanimous and vociferous. Indeed the strike decision was by acclamation. Thereupon I informed the management, and made arrangements for picket lines and headquarters liaison, informed the Ministry of Labour and, asking everyone to be calm until I could return in four days time, set off for Port-of-Spain.

On 1 February 1964 the strike started quietly enough. In due course I returned from Trinidad to begin the battle in earnest. In the course of the long flight to and from Trinidad I had ample opportunity to weigh the tactical situation. As I had rightly forecast, the management intended to fight to the finish. They had offered the entire managerial and supervisory staff who were outside the bargaining unit double salary to keep the station on the air. They clearly intended to spend any amount of money to break the union and before long had entered into a contract with a luxurious neighbouring restaurant to supply expensive meals throughout the day and night as a supplement to the double salary to which they were committed. The delegates had predicted that the management would not be able to keep the station going for more than a week but this proved to be one of those frequent occasions when the judgement of a group of delegates succumbed to their optimism. In fact, apart from two hours on one memorable morning, the station was never off the air once during the ninety-seven days. However, I was not affected by the question of whether the delegates' judgement was going to prove right or wrong.

I have always believed that tactics are best developed on the assumption that the worst will probably happen and so during the long hours alone with my thoughts on the plane I planned everything on the basis that we would never be able to shut the station down. I was by then a seasoned veteran of twelve years and had developed a certain skill in estimating the reality of bargaining power in different situations. I had begun by admitting to myself that the very last place I would have chosen to join battle with a government headed by Bustamante was a broadcasting station. The JBC was not vital to the dissemination of news because there was *Radio Jamaica* also the *Daily Gleaner* and its evening cousin, *The Star*. The JLP had its own newspaper, *The Voice,* and the Government Printing Office was there to publish the new laws, the official *Gazette* in which government announcements are made as well as a record of parliamentary proceedings. The JBC produced no food, mined no bauxite, shipped no sugar, provided no revenue, could cut off no trade, despatched no telegrams, posted no letters, supplied no power, and transmitted no phone calls, local or international. The fact of the matter was that if the JBC vanished without trace nothing in Jamaican life would have been dislocated for as long as a single hour. Obviously, this fight could not be won in the arena of power. Where then to fight? It seemed that this battle had to be fought out on the uncertain seas of public opinion and would finally rest on an appeal to popular understanding. This meant that the union's position would have, at all times, to be carefully chosen, well prepared and amply explained. Our battle cry would have to be 'injustice' and our appeal would be to the public's innate sense of fair play.

At a deeper level, we would have to make the dismissal of Lee and Rodway a test case for worker security and the right of the trade union movement to security from arbitrary management action.

If our position was weak in terms of power, our case was enormously strong in natural justice and it was clear to me that nothing must be done to prejudice the public's perception of this. Clearly, the biggest danger which we faced lay in the political ambiguity of our situation. To begin with, Bustamante was not a man to weigh natural justice in the same scales as political danger. To him, the NWU was not a union with a case, but a political enemy to be exterminated if possible and contained at the very least. Equally, there was the danger that a politically indoctrinated and cynical population might fail to understand the issue because of its preoccupation with the apparent politics of the situation. In short, I did not delude myself that we were heading into any ordinary contest. In fact, my own mood was a curious mixture of detachment and passion. I was detached in the face of the tactical problems of the case but felt a passionate conviction that we were right. In common with a lot of other people who have found themselves going into battle outgunned and outmanned, I could also detect in myself an almost irrational refusal to consider the possibility of defeat.

Throughout the entire period of the dispute, the strike was very much the workers' own struggle. A strike council was established involving all the regular delegates along with other activists specially elected by the strikers. Every day the council would meet, sometimes with me or with other union officials, sometimes alone. Full meetings with the strikers were held every week and sometimes several times in a week. Every aspect of tactics and strategy would be assessed and then the form of recommendations put to the full worker body. Among other things, it was a fine example of democracy in action and proved, during the long days to come, what men and women will endure when they believe in a cause, understand what is happening and feel themselves to be crucially involved in the decision-making process.

Our first task was to set out a clear platform upon which to take our stand. We proposed to the corporation either that

Lee and Rodway be reinstated or that the matter be put to arbitration. We proposed that an arbitrator be mutually agreed and asked to say whether the dismissal of either or both men was unjustified and if so, whether either or both men should be reinstated or paid compensation, and if the latter, in what amount? And so, after some early skirmishing, we took up an irrevocable position which could be described thus: we were not claiming to be the final judges of the guilt or innocence of the two men. We were prepared to have this decided by an impartial third party. The corporation was invited to do likewise. Then again, provided either or both men were found to be innocent we were not setting up ourselves as the final arbiter of whether they should get their jobs back or whether there existed special circumstances to warrant their being paid compensation in place of the jobs which they had held. We would accept the impartial determination of this question as well. Again we invited the corporation to do the same. And finally, even if compensation was decided on, in either or both cases, we were not claiming to be the final arbiters of how much should be paid, but were willing to have this also determined by an impartial third party. Fundamentally, our position was that the only reasonable position which the parties to an industrial dispute can take is to agree that everything be subject to the test of reason. We contended that it was obvious, from the positions adopted on both sides, that force could not settle this particular matter. The union had no intention of bowing and it was equally clear that the corporation was not going to succumb to pressure.

The response of the corporation to this was interesting. In due course they accepted the idea of arbitration but in the event of a finding of wrongful dismissal they proposed that the arbitrators' powers be limited to adjudicating on the question of compensation only. In other words, the corporation invoked the old concept of absolute authority to say that even if an impartial third party held that they acted wrongly in dismissing the men, there could be no question of them ever working at the station again. At most the corporation would pay compensation for wrongful dismissal. Within two weeks of the commencement of the strike, all the forces of history had crystallised in this single, sharp and absolute confrontation: were there any circumstances in which the men could get their jobs back? It was obvious that from the Government's point of view the question of their right to rule in an independent country which had elected them was fundamentally at issue. Equally there was the question of whether an 'Opposition Union' could force them to do anything. From the corporation's point of view the issue was seen as a straight test of its right to absolute employer authority. From the union's point of view the issue was whether Bustamante's political mandate gave him the right to impose a wrong decision by arbitrary methods at the expense of the workers' human rights. The dispute also involved the question of the employer's right to act in an arbitrary and unjust manner, more particularly in a case where the union's right to existence was threatened because a delegate was involved.

During the first four weeks we concentrated both on the battle for the public support and on the maintenance of worker morale. We did a number of broadcasts on Radio Jamaica, wrote a spate of letters to the *Daily Gleaner* and the weekly and sympathetic journal, *Public Opinion*. There was a stretch of open land immediately opposite the station and there we pitched two tents which we had borrowed from the Boy Scouts' movement, from which we organised the picket line, prepared and served hot meals and generally maintained morale while directing operations. This camp became the scene of one of the most memorable episodes in the history of the union movement. The camaraderie, the good nature, the cheerful courage in the face of pressure and adversity, the sense of mission had to be experienced to be believed. Virtually the whole staff of the NWU played a part at one time or another. Of particular significance, however, was the involvement of a young officer who had just joined the union fresh from the University of the West Indies. This was baptism by fire for Carlyle Dunkley who was to go on from there to such a distinguished career in the union. In the common cause, class ceased to matter as men and women from every walk of life, some from prosperous homes in Barbican, others from the slums of Trench Town, came together.

We launched a public fund to help feed the strikers and

for the first time in Jamaican history, set up a strike fund as well as daily meals for pickets. Applying a rough means test, we paid about $8 a week to married staff and $6 a week to the rest. All of those who did picket duty got a good meal with every shift spent on the picket line. The response to the appeal for funds was remarkable. Indeed, when it was all over, more than $16,000 had been contributed. Even more remarkable were the widespread sources of these contributions which even included branches of the BITU who took up regular weekly collections and brought them late on Friday evening to the strike camp.

Within the first fortnight we won our first great victory when all the commentators and many of the freelancers working with JBC held a meeting and announced that they would not cross the picket line. From the very start, that great figure in unionism and journalism, Frank Hill, had said that he was discontinuing his commentaries on JBC because it was a matter of principle with him never to cross a picket line regardless of circumstances. Other journalists, such as the distinguished black South African author, Peter Abrahams, made it clear that they would not cross this particular picket line because they felt that the corporation was denying the fundamental human rights of two members of the staff. In the event, the commentator boycott was complete and was the first great moral blow to the corporation's position.

Meantime, we were holding regular public meetings and drawing larger and larger crowds. Coming into the fourth week of the strike we held a protest meeting in the Half Way Tree Square, less than quarter of a mile from the station, which was attended by more than 10,000 people. By then the strike slogan had emerged 'We Shall Never Bow' was at once a battle cry and the recognition of a moral imperative. By now the public was beginning to take serious notice of the case as our positions hardened. It was becoming clear that the union was making an effective appeal to all except the most dyed-in-the-wool employers and partisan supporters of the Jamaica Labour Party. To an extraordinary degree the middle classes and the working classes were making common cause in what appeared to them to be a breach of natural justice. We were hammering the simple thesis that the two young men had been victimised for telling the truth and then invited to take part in a 'heads I win, tails you lose' game where the one thing that they could not get back was the jobs which had been unfairly taken from them. During the fourth week it became clear that the Government was getting worried and conferences were arranged with both Seaga and Bustamante successively, though nothing came of them.

As we entered the month of March it appeared that the Government may have been concerned about the effectiveness of the battle but was still prepared to see it out. At that stage a momentous decision was taken which I believe to have had a real bearing on subsequent Jamaican history. By now, there were voices counselling violence. The contention was that the Government had no intention of budging and that, as a consequence, the union had no choice but to shut the station down by violent means. It was pointed out that the uninterrupted flow of daily broadcasts made a mockery of the workers' courage and the justice of our cause. The debate in the strike council was extremely serious and sincere. I examined my own mind and soul long and hard and in the end was guided by my deep and instinctive distrust of violence. By temperament and outlook I believe that the non-violent methods of Gandhi and Martin Luther King are both morally right and effective unless faced with the kind of absolute intransigence of situations like that in Southern Africa. It is not that I do not understand that violence will sometimes be the only midwife capable of delivering historical change. It is just that I see it as an absolute last resort and not a path to be taken because the moral courage is lacking to try other ways. I think the majority of strikers felt as I did. Certainly, the council was virtually unanimous in the end. And so after much soul searching we settled the debate in favour of civil disobedience.

On the afternoon of March 5 a group of young men and women worked feverishly to get their placards ready. The camp was tense. In a visceral way everyone knew that history was about to be made. At four-thirty p.m. they began to file out of the strike camp and by four forty-five they were in position. Arms locked, this gallant, romantic and implacable group of youngsters blocked Half Way Tree Square, one of

Kingston's main crossroads, during the great afternoon exodus to the suburbs. While some lay down across the street, others proclaimed their cause with placards. For half an hour traffic came to a complete halt while a big and obviously sympathetic crowd began to gather. Then the police arrived and the tear gas was released – the first major mistake committed by the Government. The strikers were lifted bodily into waiting police wagons and taken off to jail. In due course the traffic was flowing again, but the workers had made their point. The JBC strike was now a *cause celebre*. The Government which up to then had remained in the background like a still and silent shadow now seemed to have acted with disproportionate harshness.

Two days later we struck again when, on a Saturday morning at eleven a.m., we blocked the intersection of Kingston's main shopping thoroughfare, King Street, with Barry Street. In no time a crowd estimated at over 3,000 had gathered. I remember noticing, while lying on the hot asphalt, what a rich mixture of so-called working-class and middle-class support there was. There were a few tense moments when the police considered using tear gas but they were talked out of it by the famous local impresario, Stephen Hill, who delivered himself of an impassioned harangue at the expense of a bewildered superintendent of police. Shortly thereafter an officer of even higher rank tried to persuade a constable driving a police wagon to bear down on the line. I watched in fascinated horror as he shouted at the young man who was obviously torn between conscience and duty. In the end he seemed to engage the gears reluctantly with the officer beating a tattoo on the side of the vehicle with his cane. The wagon inched forward, straight at me and I was overcome with an odd sensation, part detached, part scared, part rooted to the spot by an animal determination which I had not suspected I possessed. Mercifully a crowd of people swept past the line where I lay and hurled themselves upon the vehicle which came to an immediate stop. In fact I was beginning to wonder whether I had condemned myself to an indefinite confinement to a bed of asphalt. Too late I realised that I had not figured out how to disengage should the police decide, or be persuaded, to leave us alone.

Thereafter, the position developed into a stalemate. Then the ever resourceful John Maxwell, by now the editor of *Public Opinion*, got into the act and negotiated a truce in which it was agreed that I would be lifted aloft and carried away from the scene so that the workers could unblock the road with honour and without further loss of face to the police.

By now the strike had begun to assume epic proportions. It had already produced its heroes like the chief delegate Jeremy Verity who was the sort of intellectual young man it is difficult to associate with civil disobedience. Yet he had now tasted tear gas for the first time. There was Hu Gentles who had earned the nickname 'Jail Bird' because he had managed to make the police wagons and jail at both Half Way Tree and on King Street. To his comrades, this put him in a category not unlike that of an airforce fighter ace who had achieved so many 'kills'. Then there were the girls like Jean Barnes and Monica White who had crossed the barriers of sex as well as class to block public highways. And still the Government would not budge.

Five weeks had now elapsed and public support was growing daily, but it was obvious that we would have to push the conflict further. I still had the weapon of sympathy strikes up my sleeve but this is a tricky card to play and I was determined to hold it as a last resort. If you set up sympathy strikes and they get out of hand there is no knowing where they may lead. If you fail you may find that you have lost everything. So we opted for further civil disobedience.

At the start of the sixth week I applied for permission to stage a march. As I expected, the police turned us down. We then applied for permission to hold a public meeting at Coronation Market in Western Kingston so that we could protest publicly against the refusal to grant permission for the march. I deliberately chose the site in the heart of Seaga's constituency in the hope that I would provoke some kind of response. The ruse worked and the police took the quite unprecedented step of refusing permission for the public meeting. We were now approaching the Sunday that would mark the end of the sixth week of the strike. And then I set in motion the most daring plan that I had tried so far: I decided to stage a protest motorcade. However, a number of difficulties had to be overcome. For example, a motorcade is very easy to break up so it was imperative to keep the police in the dark as to what I really intended. This implied making no application for permission. It also implied maximum secrecy since the security forces were working overtime to find out our plans now that civil disobedience had begun. For the first and only time in the strike, I got the permission of the council to plan the whole of the next phase by myself. Next, I hit on the idea of simply passing by word of mouth the message that all sympathisers with the strike who had access to a car should foregather on the Sunday morning outside the JBC's main entrance. This, I calculated, would help keep the police in a state of uncertainty.

I remember discussing the plan with my father and a number of other distinguished PNP loyalists late on the Saturday night. They tried to warn me that a motorcade was the same as a march and that marches without police permission are illegal. I told them that I did not want to hear about it because I was committed to action, convinced that action was necessary and being told that the particular action was illegal would not stop me but might affect my confidence. At that point we all laughed and talked about something else.

The next morning I drove to JBC and found a large group of cars waiting for me. I figured that the police would expect me to head for the west which was the area from which they had banned our meeting. I led the motorcade down Maxfield Avenue in that direction but kept a motor cycle rider near to me. As I had hoped, within a quarter of a mile we ran into a huge detachment of policemen with rifles blocking the road. Thereupon, I sent the rider back down the line of the motorcade to tell everybody to disperse and take any route they liked provided they regrouped in the eastern part of the city near a movie house called the Palace. In no time there was the reassuring sound of screaming tyres as excited motorists gunned their cars in various directions. In due course the whole motorcade had regrouped in the east where I prepared to set the second part of the plan in motion. This consisted of blocking Rockfort Road, the main highway connecting the city to the eastern part of the island and, most importantly, to the International Airport at Palisadoes. By pre-arrangement, four cars severally owned by Anthony Spaulding, now Minister of Housing, Ken Sterling, former Island Supervisor of the NWU, Hopeton Caven, General Secretary of the Trade Union Congress, and me were strategically parked across the Rockfort Road making it impossible for anything bigger than a bicycle to pass. All four cars were locked and I had the keys to each in my pocket. We then withdrew to a nearby gas station to await developments. In no time there was a fantastic traffic jam stretching back for more than a mile. The traffic coming from both east and west had piled up indiscriminately across the road in both directions making it almost impossible to disentangle. One mile westwards, firmly anchored in the area to which they had been drawn by our feint, was the police force.

And so the crowd began to gather. In the meantime, Radio Jamaica was carrying bulletins about the events at Rockfort every quarter of an hour. The enthusiasm of their news reporting was not untouched by amusement at the discomfiture of their competitor, the JBC. After about an hour the police arrived in the charge of that great police officer, Mr Basil Robinson, who is now the Commissioner of Police, together with Mr Owen Stephenson, head of the mobile reserve. They arrived on foot, needless to say. In no time Robinson sized up the situation and realised that the cars had been placed in a position where to use tear gas would have involved the danger of blowing up the entire area since they were parked right alongside the storage tanks of the gas station. Nor was there any chance of getting a bulldozer to clear the road because there was no way in which a bulldozer could get to the spot. Once again it was a stalemate.

Negotiations commenced and I laid down simple terms. Firstly, in view of the fact that I had been denied permission to hold a public meeting, I demanded the right to address the crowd which had gathered at the scene and which was estimated at around 12,000. Secondly, I demanded the right to lead the cars with which I had embarked from JBC in a motorcade and with the clear understanding that this was carried out with permission. In retrospect these may seem a bit like 'grand standing' but then one had to understand both the passion of the moment and its tactical requirements. One cannot bring about a confrontation of that sort without having ready some formula which will permit disengagement with honour. This much had been learned on King Street the week before! The two conditions which I had imposed seemed the best at the time. Certainly it would have been pointless to say that I would not move until Rodway and Lee were reinstated since there was no way in which Bustamante could have bowed to that kind of pressure. In the event, my claims were met, I addressed the crowd, led the motorcade to a neighbouring suburban area named Harbour View and back and we then dispersed. That evening I visited the strike camp to attend a council meeting. There was a single light burning at the entrance to a tent. The scene was half in shadow with strikers huddled in groups, tired after the day's excitement. But through the fatigue one could sense the almost exalted sense of purpose which enveloped this entire group of extraordinary young people. And still the Government would not budge.

By now the Leader of the Opposition, Norman Manley, had moved a resolution in Parliament calling for a board of enquiry. We had accepted that the Government did not intend to permit an arbitration that included the question of reinstatement in its terms of reference. In fact, after the blocking of the Rockfort Road, there had been a meeting with the JBC management at the Ministry of Labour and an agreement to arbitrate, including the question of reinstatement had been reached subject only to ministerial approval. Once again the Minister intervened personally and refused to allow the agreement even though it had the full backing of the Ministry of Labour. There was nothing left therefore but to turn to a sympathy strike.

In the course of the third week of March, I had the whole union organisation out across rural Jamaica organising a first, token shut down which was to take place for two hours on a Monday morning. The morning arrived and on schedule stoppages began across the bauxite and hotel industries, in the public utilities like the light, power and telephone companies and even on some of the sugar estates. There is no doubt that the call met with a considerable response although one could not claim to have achieved anything like a hundred per cent shut down. But it was enough. By midday the news came that the Hon. L. G. Newland, the Minister of Labour, had proposed a board of enquiry into all aspects of the dispute and the Prime Minister had agreed.

And so phase two ended with a partial victory secured through civil disobedience. At least it was open to a board of enquiry to find for reinstatement. Until then the JBC's position had been that it would only agree to an arbitration if reinstatement were specifically excluded from the arbitrator's authority. In other words, they had taken the view that we had to accept that Lee and Rodway would never work at the JBC again as a pre-condition for having an enquiry into their dismissal. Now the board of enquiry was set up on a basis where the issue of reinstatement was to be considered alongside the question of whether the young men were innocent or guilty.

Mr Justice Eccleston was appointed the sole Enquirer, and the third phase of the battle was joined. The Enquiry was to last forty days. It brought together on the union side David Coore, who is now the Deputy Prime Minister of Jamaica and then a Queen's Counsel of rare brilliance, and Vivian Blake who is also a minister of the present Cabinet and who was then the Dean of the Jamaican Bar and an advocate of formidable powers. On the other side was Queen's Counsel, Raymond Alberga, together with the distinguished solicitor and company lawyer, Mr Deryck Stone. The case fell into two distinct parts. Firstly, there was the question of what really happened leading up to the news story and, having regard to the duties and function of Lee and Rodway together with the part they played in the publication of the story, whether their dismissal was justified. The other aspect of the case centred on the question of whether an employer ought to have the right to refuse reinstatement either in the particular case or as a matter of general principle.

In the first part of the case the Chairman of the Board was battered by Coore for seven consecutive days and was forced to admit that his minister had taken all the major decisions which had led to the trouble. The General Manager, Hendricks, was cross-examined for six days by Blake and at the end of that time it was perfectly obvious that Lee had done absolutely nothing that could constitute an offence. In Rodway's case everything that emerged confirmed the view which I had expressed to the management at the very start, that Rodway had been guilty of a technical offence since as 'man in the slot' he had not cleared the story with a senior news editor. However, it was equally obvious that the story he had allowed to be published was true and that it had been peculiarly within his province to know this as he had been at the meeting where I had reported the facts to the workers.

In the matter of reinstatement, one of the great intellectual confrontations of union history in Jamaica took place. We called witnesses from all over the world, relying on our friendship with bodies like the Trade Union Congress of Britain, the United Automobile Workers of America and the United Steel Workers of America to provide us with evidence of international practices. The two American unions sent experts of the greatest distinction. The British sent a stack of relevant material. It was a remarkable display of international solidarity and inter-union generosity. It became obvious from the local evidence that this issue had not been fully clarified one way or the other in Jamaican industrial relations. No contracts dealt clearly with the point and an examination of the history of actual practice was inconclusive.

British evidence seemed to suggest that no clear rules or precedents existed. Under British common law you cannot enforce specific performance of a contract of personal service. In spite of the passage of nearly two centuries since the invention of the spinning jenny and the steam engine, it seemed that it had not yet occurred to the British that there is a distinction between the personal relationship between a man in his home and his domestic help, on the one hand, and between management and worker, under modern economic conditions and where a trade union establishes the nature of the employer-employee relationship by collective bargaining, on the other. It seemed that the British still accepted the right of an employer to get rid of an innocent worker. The most they could say was that the workers might respond to that kind of arbitrary behaviour by striking. This took the question of principle no further.

The American evidence was as conclusive as the British was vague. In America it has long since been established that a job is a species of property and that a man cannot be separated from his property except for a just and proper cause. The Americans have gone even further to recognise that compensation in cash cannot ordinarily be substituted for the full value of a job itself. Hence, the reinstatement of wrongfully dismissed workers is completely automatic in American practice. These issues were to come into even sharper focus later in the context of a reconsideration of Jamaica's labour laws nearly ten years later. At the time, however, the issues were brilliantly adumbrated in the JBC enquiry including one argument of Coore's which was never rebutted. He contended that the right to reinstatement by arbitration flowed logically from the right to strike. An arbitration, he pointed out, is a means of settling, by the route of reason, any dispute between an employer and employee which could be the subject of a strike. Since the reinstatement of a wrongfully dismissed worker can be the subject of a strike, then equally, it must be capable of determination by arbitration. Otherwise, arbitration cannot be the means by which the rule of reason is substituted for the rule of force.

On both the question of the dispute and on the principles of arbitration, reinstatement and the rest, I spent seven days in the witness box, six of which were under cross-examination by Alberga. It was a stimulating experience.

Towards the end of the enquiry pressure began to mount on the JBC to bring the strike to an end. It came from an unexpected quarter. The management staff who by then had kept the station going for some twelve weeks were getting fed up. There were threats to quit if the corporation would not agree to some formula which would permit the resumption of work. Thus began the fourth and final phase of the strike – the search for a formula for resumption. Arguing that they had lost too much money ever to be able to operate as they had prior to the strike, the corporation announced that it had worked out a reorganisation plan and would only need about thirty of the one hundred and twenty workers who had gone on strike. As far as the rest were concerned, it was announced that their services had been terminated and that no question of notice or compensation for loss of employment would arise. When questioned they also made it clear that they intended to retain the right to hire new people to fill some of the jobs of the workers who were to be fired. Needless to say, the union rejected this out of hand.

The strike continued and so did the efforts of the Ministry of Labour to find a formula which could bring to an end this bitter, stalemated and exhausting conflict. We decided that the only course open to us was once again to make proposals that were based on clear principles. Just as we had said from the start that we would accept some process of quasi judicial enquiry as the means of determining the quarrel about Lee and Rodway, so too did we propose a formula for the resumption of work that was rooted in logic and practice. Accepting the right of an employer to reorganise his business in such a manner as to bring a particular job to an end, we insisted that we must be shown a clear, new organisational chart indicating what jobs would exist in the reorganised corporation. We then insisted that the rule of seniority must apply in determining which of the old staff would occupy the new jobs and which would be made redundant. Thirdly, we insisted that those who were declared redundant should be paid severance pay in accordance with a reasonable severance pay formula. And, finally, we insisted that no new members of staff could be engaged while old members of staff were available and willing to be re-engaged. It took another fortnight of talks for these simple principles to be accepted, but in the end reason prevailed. The final settlement accepted the union's conditions along with a proviso that delegates should be specially protected insofar as the new jobs were concerned. And so, ninety-seven days after it began the strike ended. First the council and then a large but sad general meeting approved the terms of the settlement. On the ninety-eighth day the picket line was withdrawn and the next morning I led about eighty survivors of the original force back to work. About a dozen of the original strikers had migrated or got jobs elsewhere. Some thirty had been declared redundant and received $16,000 in severance pay. The rest tried to pick up the pieces in the wreckage which was all that remained of the great democratic dream which the station represented in its early years. In retrospect, the JBC strike is a fascinating example of the price that can be paid when obstinacy and suspicion influence decisions.

At the time when Lee and Rodway were fired the corporation had rejected a wage settlement that would have cost $20,000 a year. On the day that the workers resumed, the corporation had lost $60,000 in revenue, had spent $16,000 to finance the extra payments and food for the group who kept the station going and had paid $16,000 in severance pay. All told it is estimated that the corporation spent $100,000 in three months because they fired two young men who published the fact that it had turned down a claim worth $20,000 a year. In the meantime, the union had spent $24,000 on the strike in addition to the $16,000 which the public had subscribed. All told $140,000 was lost. Far worse, the station lost its credibility. This is being written ten years later and it is only now that the first signs of renewed public trust seem to be emerging.

In due course the forty day enquiry came to a close and we awaited Eccleston's findings. Thereupon, we embarked upon the fifth phase of this epic struggle. It is sad that the end should have been as ignoble as the first four phases had been dramatic. Eccleston had a rare opportunity to pronounce upon matters of great social significance in the sphere of industrial relations. Arguments of great force had been marshalled on either side and his findings were eagerly awaited. Incredibly, it took Mr Justice Eccleston and the Government that appointed him fourteen months to make and publish his award. Not until mid-June of 1965 did we discover that Mr Eccleston found George Lee innocent of all charges, Adrian Rodway justifiably dismissed and Lee entitled to compensation but not reinstatement. It is difficult to know which was the more unworthy: the time that was spent in promulgating the report or the findings themselves. There was no comment on the great issue of reinstatement except the almost irrelevant assertion that Lee was entitled to compensation. There was not a word of comment on the extraordinary blend of arrogance and mulishness with which the corporation behaved. Naturally, lacking the courage to chastise the corporation, the goodly Justice would hardly have dared to comment upon the union's civil disobedience; this presumably, was the price for silence elsewhere.

The management of the JBC was, naturally, jubilant. Deciding to rub salt in the union's wound, they offered Lee $150 compensation and virtually dared us to do anything about it. They well knew that the staff was in no position to face another strike. Then when all seemed lost, my father came to our rescue. We were all fuming about Eccleston's findings and the corporation's offensive offer of compensation when he suddenly summoned me and told me that he wanted to look at one of the advertisements which the corporation had published in the early stages of the strike. Not for nothing did he have the reputation of being the greatest lawyer that the Caribbean ever produced. Although seventy-two years old at the time and despite the fact that more than a year had elapsed, he remembered that the corporation had published in a newspaper advertisement that Lee and Rodway were guilty of incompetence and dereliction of duty. In the light of Eccleston's finding in relation to Lee, this clearly constituted libel! He really was an astounding man. We promptly sued for libel and the corporation's directors found themselves over a barrel. After a brief negotiation they capitulated and agreed to pay Lee $4,000 as compensation for libel. At least in that regard the last laugh was ours.

In the end, we lost the JBC strike in the sense of the immediate issues that were involved. However, I believe that we can claim to have changed Jamaica even as we were contesting a battle which we could not win. We could not win because, short of revolution, you cannot make an elected government do what it does not want to do unless you are able to bring tremendous economic pressure to bear on them. Of course there are those who contend that we should have continued the civil disobedience and sympathy strikes and there are those too who have criticised me for not resorting to violence. It is not for me to say whether they are right or wrong. At the time it was my judgement that the great public support which the strike commanded in a country which had recently elected Bustamante to power, although by a narrow majority, was due to the iron discipline with which it was conducted. I felt that if the activist side were pushed too far along the route of civil disobedience one might provoke the repolarisation of society into its politic components and so make things worse than ever. As it is, the JBC strike was a watershed in Jamaican history. The right of reinstatement of wrongfully dismissed workers came increasingly to be accepted in industrial relations and in due course a number of contracts were made which provided specifically for reinstatement powers in cases of dismissal arbitrations or, failing this, conceded the right to strike.

Besides, we might well have started a tradition of violence if we had adopted that course when we had our backs to the wall. It may be that our conscious choice of the non-violent, disciplined route of civil disobedience may have helped to set a newly independent nation on a peaceful course. It is noteworthy that ten years later there is no sign of public violence becoming a part of the labour or other traditions of Jamaican society. Again, the scrupulous care with which the union kept politics out of the dispute helped, I believe, to establish a trend in Jamaica in which the unions, though politically affiliated, act with less and less partisan political intent.

Most importantly, however, the strike marked the end of the first phase of the struggle for the democratisation of the workplace. By 1963 the right to an equal voice in determining what a job was worth had been established. But the job itself was still held by the owning class to be exclusively in the gift of the employer. After the strike, Jamaica embarked upon the second phase of the process where the right to continue in a job was no longer regarded as being subject to arbitrary unilateral employer decision. If nothing else, the strike guaranteed a favourable outcome of the struggle.

What is equally certain is that the strike was a unique experience for all Jamaicans, provoking intense controversy, idealistic involvement and contributing to the evolving self-image of a young nation.

For those who lived through it, it fashioned a bond that will endure as long as life lasts. Never before or since has a labour dispute turned so completely on questions of human rights and the place of principles and ideals in our society.

8

UNIONS AND THE LAW

THE JBC strike had revealed deep, unresolved differences between the labour movement and the employer groups. The argument over George Lee and Adrian Rodway went far deeper than the particular case and really had to do with fundamental rights in society. The concept of equality before the law was at least theoretically true in criminal cases or in civil disputes about property. It is true that some were more equal than others to the extent that they could afford the best legal representation but this was not a fault of the law so much as of the relationship between economic power and the whole administration of justice. At least the law itself was unequivocal in its avowed purposes. The law as it related to the respective rights of employers and employees was, however, quite another matter. First of all, throughout the entire period, 1952 to 1974, the Master and Servants Law remained on the statute books although it was first enacted in 1838. Its very name betrayed its historical antiquity no less than its elitist purpose. Ostensibly providing for the right to notice, or pay in lieu thereof, of a servant about to be dismissed by a master, the law really served to confirm the power of the employer to dismiss arbitrarily without legal let or hindrance. This law was finally repealed in 1974 and replaced by the Termination of Employment Act which is a comparatively sophisticated and progressive document.

It is an interesting commentary on Jamaican society that it took thirty years of popular, representative government and twelve years of independence to remove from the statute books this iniquitous piece of legislation, conceived in the shadow of the slave system. However, it is not our purpose to discuss that law here since it had no effect on the relations between workers and employers in any area of the economy which had been organised by the trade union movement. The unions established their own system of worker rights and protection by collective bargaining which led to labour contracts. These contracts made the Master and Servants Law redundant so far as the unionised workers were concerned. Comment upon the Master and Servants Law belongs more properly to the political than the trade union dialogue.

There was a law, however, which reflected oppressive class attitudes and their effect upon the employer/employee relationship with which the trade unions had to deal constantly. This law survived thirty years of representative government and twelve years of independence. This was the *Essential Services Law*.

All societies which recognise the right of the worker to organise in unions and to withhold labour in support of particular claims face the problem of what to do about their essential services. They cannot take lightly the prospect that those who operate the water, fire or the light and power services might suddenly withhold their labour. Obviously, the question of essential services bristles with difficulties. To begin with, there is the question: when is a service genuinely essential and when is it merely convenient? But assuming that one can isolate such a group the question arises: how do you reconcile the workers' right to achieve reasonable wages and working conditions with society's need to be assured of the continuity of indispensable services? Obviously, the traditional method which recognises the workers' right to organise and strike is inappropriate in the context of an essential service. Therefore, an alternative means must be found which will secure the workers' rights without threatening society with intolerable disruption.

Prior to 1938, the question did not really arise in Jamaica because workers were not organised and were therefore unlikely to cause shut downs but by 1939 two events combined to aggravate the problem: organised labour was now a fact of life; and the Second World War had broken out. As the fight against labour action in Jamaica intensified the British came up with an answer in the form of the Public Utility Undertakings and Public Service Arbitration Law, Chapter 329 of the Laws of Jamaica. Actually the law, with very little regional variation, was introduced in parts of the

British Empire, although we are only here concerned with its outcome in Jamaica.

The Essential Services Law, as it was commonly known, had five major elements. First of all, it served to define what types of activities would be classed as 'essential' for the purpose of the law. The governor-in-council, later the minister responsible, had the power to decide these matters. Secondly, the law laid down a procedure for the reporting of disputes between workers and their employers and, where a dispute had been reported, required the minister to take action within twenty-one days. In this section 'disputes', for the purpose of the law, were defined. The action which the governor-in-council, later the minister, was to take was the subject of the third section dealing with the arbitration of disputes. If a dispute existed or was apprehended, then the law required the appointment of a tribunal with the power to hear the case. The fourth section dealt with the question of obedience. Once a dispute was referred to an arbitration tribunal, the parties were required to attend the arbitration proceedings and to put their case to the tribunal. When an award was made this was final and binding with no appeal possible save on grounds of misconduct or if it were contended that the arbitrators acted outside their authority. This section made it clear that there could be no strike by workers or lock-out by employers provided the governor-in-council or minister acted within twenty-one days of notification of a dispute and this proscription applied before, during and after arbitration proceedings. It was clear, however, that if the minister did not appoint a tribunal within twenty-one days of the report of a dispute, then both parties, worker and employer, were free to take such normal industrial action as they saw fit. The final section dealt with sanctions. If workers went on strike or if an employer locked out his staff in contravention of the provisions of the law, both could be tried in a resident magistrate's court. If found guilty, the resident magistrate could impose a fine of $20 upon each worker in the case of an illegal strike; the same fine could be levied upon the employer in the case of an illegal lock-out. Both were subject to prison sentences of up to a maximum of thirty days hard labour.

In my early union days we tended to take this law for

granted. We accepted, as a matter of social logic, that there were certain services that really were essential and were consoled by the fact that disputes were subject to arbitration. The fact that the arbitration was compulsory did not disturb us as much as it might other Union leaders in other societies. The fact of the matter was that the pattern of Jamaican industrial relations had always shown a tendency towards the acceptance of arbitration as a means of determining difficult disputes. On a number of occasions where wage negotiations broke down, we had agreed to go to arbitration and had benefited from awards which were sometimes reasonable, at other times not. When unreasonable, we protested, but we noticed that all the awards that we thought were reasonable were the subject of equally vigorous protest by the employer concerned. By the early 1960s the list of essential services included light and power, city bus transport and the waterfront, all of which involved privately owned companies. Other essential services like the railway were operated by public statutory corporations and yet others, such as the fire services, by local government authorities. The rest were operated directly by the Government. By the time of the JBC strike in 1964, it was clear that the Essential Services Law, far from guaranteeing an alternative to the workers, was in fact an insurmountable obstacle to progress.

As might be expected of a young, popular movement in a poor country, the unions had no elaborate research apparatus at their disposal. There was no legal department whose duty it was to study laws like the Essential Services Law and come up with a thorough analysis of its implications. We proceeded by trial and error having in view a consistent set of objectives but dealing with problems as they arose. The first serious difficulty we had involving this law occurred in 1961. City bus transport had been provided since 1953 by an organisation known as the Jamaica Omnibus Services Limited which was to be nationalised in 1974. A British organisation, they had come to Jamaica under a monopoly franchise and taken over a hopelessly incompetent bus system. An efficient group, they achieved a marked improvement in the quality of the service but were better at organising bus schedules than handling industrial relations in a situation where management and top supervision were white expatriates and the rest of the workers local and black.

The NWU had captured this outfit from the BITU in 1955 and thereupon embarked on an uneasy relationship. By around 1959, the workers elected a chief delegate called Samuel Watson. He was a maintenance man, energetic, articulate, racially conscious and quick to spot a grievance. In no time he was a thorn in the side of a management trying to walk the kind of operational chalk line which provides a cheap, efficient service to the public at the same time as a regular dividend to the shareholder. In due course Watson and the management were locked in a collision course which might have been programmed by fate: Watson in his search for justice, the management wholly preoccupied with matters of efficiency. At nine o'clock one night – I am told that it was a hot night – another in a series of wildcat strikes took place. There was nothing new about the strike but much that was new in its cause and outcome.

Watson and a group of workers claimed that a maintenance supervisor from Britain got into a quarrel with a group of maintenance men on the late shift. During the fracas which followed he was alleged to have boasted that he had once hunted niggers in South Africa for a shilling a head. The anger which this provoked can well be imagined. All hell broke loose and it was several days before the buses rolled again. By then the Government had appointed a board of enquiry to examine the allegations and the supervisor was off the job, suspended at our insistence, but on full pay at the management's. The enquiry itself was quite an affair. It was just like a full scale legal battle in a criminal case with Vivian Blake once again leading for the union and that brilliant solicitor advocate, H. O. A. Dayes, representing the company. In the end the union won and the board held that the supervisor had indeed boasted of hunting niggers for a shilling a head. He caught the next boat back to England but the company never forgave Watson. In due course there was another row and this time Watson was fired. His dismissal case led to another tremendous battle with witnesses galore on both sides. Diligent cross-examination pressed hard upon carefully led evidence-in-chief. Once again Dayes appeared for the

Company and this time I did the honours for the union. Once again the union won.

When we won the case, we moved for Watson's reinstatement assuming that this was a mere formality. To our consternation, the company refused to reinstate him and pointed out that we could not compel them to do so under the Essential Services Law nor, indeed, before any legal tribunal available in Jamaica. I had the law ransacked by everyone from Manley himself through Blake and Coore to various solicitors that I happened to know. It transpired that the company was right. Arbitrators acting under the Essential Services Law could not have powers beyond those possessed by a judge in a high court unless those powers were conferred by the terms of reference under which they sat. The terms of reference, however, had to be agreed by the parties. Therefore, if an employer who was a party to a dispute refused to agree to put a particular question into the terms of reference, the arbitrator could not make a finding upon that question unless a judge in a high court would have the power to determine a similar matter.

An examination of the common law revealed that no judge in court could order any employer in any circumstances to re-engage a dismissed worker. A judge could find that a dismissal was wrongful and in certain very special cases could award damages for wrongful dismissal but he could not compel the employer to take the worker back. This paralysis within the judicial process apparently arose from a general doctrine in common law. According to this doctrine you cannot enforce specific performance of a contract of personal service. We were to hear this principle invoked time and again during the JBC case. But we first discovered it at JOS. The argument of the company was that since the bus transport business had been declared essential and fell under the Essential Services Law, the relations between the workers and the management should be determined in accordance with the law itself. They made it clear that they would not agree to take Watson back and that they did not intend to give up the right to decide whether a dismissed worker, subsequently held to be wrongfully dismissed, should be actually reinstated in his or her job. They claimed that they might be willing to reinstate wrongfully dismissed workers in the future but they would not do so in Watson's case, nor would they guarantee that they would do so in future cases. The company's attitude was bad enough but what was worse was that the Essential Services Law made their position legal.

At the time, it seemed to us that we were the victims of a peculiarity of the law which restricted the powers of arbitrators to those powers possessed by a judge in court. It was obvious that we could not do anything about Watson's case without a deliberate confrontation with the law itself. This we were not prepared for at that time. Instead, we set about agitating for the repeal of the law. Clearly, all that was needed was a simple amendment creating for arbitrators a specific power to order reinstatement where the case seemed to merit it. Preliminary conversations with the PNP Government, then in its last year in office, were hopeful and Manley himself agreed that the existing law was monstrously unjust. He prepared a memorandum as a guide to his Minister of Labour, indicating a number of amendments which he felt ought to be made in the law. However, his good intentions were overtaken by events and the law was to remain unchanged on the statute books for another thirteen years.

In 1963 we had another run-in with the Essential Services Law. Once again it involved the Jamaica Omnibus Services. On this occasion we had been negotiating wages and fringe benefits in an attempt to set up a new contract with the company. As usual we broke down and all the efforts of the Conciliation Department of the Ministry of Labour were to no avail. It was agreed to report the matter as a dispute under the Essential Services Law and in due course the minister announced a tribunal. However, this tribunal involved the appointment of a Mr F. St Hill as chairman. As it happened Mr Hill was the father of a minister of the JLP Government, the Honourable Wilton Hill, Minister of Housing. At the time the BITU was agitating to unseat the NWU and one of their main arguments was that a JLP Government would name people who were sympathetic to the workers' cause to any essential services tribunal that might be appointed. They cunningly sought to suggest that the NWU could expect no favours from the Government and that NWU representation would make unfriendly tribunals inevitable. In the face of this propaganda it seemed to us intolerable to be asked to submit our wage claim to the father of a minister of the very Government which the BITU claimed would assist them but not us in the search for worker justice. We protested vigorously and asked for a new chairman. The Government refused.

We were in serious difficulty. I felt that the time had come when we would have to strike because not only was the law unjust but it was being unjustly manipulated. Having decided that a strike was inevitable, I felt it my duty to report this to the Executive of the PNP since a strike in the city bus transport system would obviously seriously affect the public and so had political implications. I had no intention of allowing anybody to dissuade me because we had reached a clear decision with the delegates and that was final. I explained the whole issue to the PNP Executive who were, as usual, extremely sympathetic. However, once again it was my father who came up with a brilliant solution to the problem of the strike in itself being illegal and the consequent exposure of the workers to certain prosecution. He held up the business of the Executive while they fetched him a copy of the laws of Jamaica. Within a few minutes he found what he was looking for and announced with a mischievous smile that a strike was very carefully defined in the law and stood in a very special relationship to the law as a whole. As we followed him through the relevant sections we came to see that a mere cessation of work was not a strike. Before a strike, within the meaning of the law, could take place there had to be a dispute. Only after a dispute could a cessation of work be legally classified as a strike. It emerged that if the workers simply stopped working one day and, when questioned, said that they had no dispute with their employer, they would not be guilty of a strike and could not be prosecuted. Hence, all we had to do was to withdraw the claim before going on strike to be immune from prosecution. At this point, the strike would be a stoppage of work in protest against the action of the Government in appointing an unacceptable authority. Such an eventuality was not contemplated by the law-makers and therefore outside the scope of the law.

The next morning I despatched a letter to the company withdrawing the claim and to the Ministry of Labour asking for a new arbitrator. That night the buses rolled in one by one and were stowed away in long grey lines. I remember looking at them early the next morning and thinking how pathetic they looked by comparison with the silver monsters that normally hurtled through Kingston's streets, intimidating everyone by the sheer disproportion between their size and the narrow often winding streets and lanes which they navigated.

The 'stoppage of work' lasted six weeks and although it never attained the height of romance and excitement of the JBC episode a year later, it was not without its own character and personality. In due course the Government gave in and appointed a new arbitrator, Mr N. J. Fraser, a city solicitor and arbitrator of experience and repute. We immediately called off the strike and reinstated the claim. We won a very big wage settlement but paid the price of our stratagem since Fraser held that we were not entitled to retroactivity beyond the date when the claim was withdrawn. Still, this seemed a small price to pay for the blow struck at the law itself and at the politicians who had used it so carelessly.

After the '63 strike the JLP Government virtually gave up on the Essential Services Law.

All attempts to enforce the 'no strike' provisions of the law were abandoned and strikes in essential services became as common as those elsewhere in the economy. Indeed, at one stage, it seemed that they had become more common because the employers in the group continued to act as if they enjoyed the protection of the law which meant that they were slow to make reasonable offers in collective bargaining. This led to restlessness followed by strikes. When the strikes occurred the companies would sit back expectantly waiting for the Government to see to the prosecution of the workers. However, the Government clearly had no such intention so no prosecutions were ever attempted.

In 1967, shortly after Shearer became Prime Minister, the Government presented a set of amendments to the law through the Minister of Labour, the Honourable L. G. Newland. In spite of the fact that Newland had been General Secretary of the BITU and Shearer its Island Supervisor and effective leader for years, the '67 amendments served mainly to entrench the implied employer authority which the original act enshrined with such care. There was no attempt to empower arbitrators to order reinstatement nor to make it clear that arbitrators' powers were to extend to cover any kind of dispute between workers and employers. In the new formulation arbitrators would still be limited to those powers which a judge would enjoy in a court of law with the sole exception of a provision which would have permitted an arbitrator to award compensation to a worker who had been held to be wrongfully dismissed. The only other change in the law was an increase in its penalties from the old $20 to $100 maximum fine.

I had just been elected to Parliament for Central Kingston and these amendments provided me with the occasion for my maiden speech. I spoke for an hour and tore the measure to shreds pointing out all the deficiencies in the situation ranging from arbitrators' powers to the manifest injustice of providing an equal fine for workers in cases of strikes and employers in cases of lock-outs. As I pointed out, you could have a situation where a thousand workers went on strike. They would be subject to a maximum fine of $100 each and so could be called upon to pay $100,000 as a punishment for a deterrent against illegal strike action. But if the employer locked them out he, probably representing a multi-million dollar enterprise, would be subject to $100 fine. Clearly this was as ludicrous as it was unjust. By that night I received a phone call from a highly placed member of the Government in which I was informed that the bill would be withdrawn and referred to a select committee. The next day, Newland announced as much and the bill duly found itself before the select committee where it slept undisturbed for the next five years.

In 1972, the PNP was returned to power and I was asked to undertake the responsibility of Prime Minister. Among the many things that I would clearly have to face was this question of the essential services. We worked on the matter for some two years consulting with trade union leaders, employers, groups and the like. The preparation of the bill which we finally tabled in Parliament in early 1974 went through many stages involving a number of adjustments and changes. In the outcome, however, we decided to make the new law a companion piece to the progressive Termination of Employment Act which we had introduced and passed late in 1973. Called the Labour Relations and Arbitration Act, it established a clear platform for trade union rights by introducing for the first time into Jamaica a law guaranteeing workers the right to union representation. By this act, we were extending the original right of the worker to join unions and to withhold labour. In the old arrangement the workers' right was recognised but was not matched by a parallel responsibility on the part of the employer to recognise a chosen union and bargain honourably with it. The new law provided that workers should have the right to join unions and to request unions to bargain on their behalf. If the employer questions whether the majority of his work force wish to be so represented, the Law provides for the compulsory taking of a poll. If a majority of the work force vote in favour of a union or unions the employer is required to accept this democratic verdict and bargain in good faith with the organisations that the workers choose. Against this background the law goes on to define essential services and to provide a procedure for the reporting of disputes. Thereafter, three vital changes occur. In the first place it is made clear that the powers of arbitrators are not limited to those enjoyed by judges in court. On the contrary, arbitrators are empowered to resolve any dispute that may arise between the worker and the employer. It is further provided that arbitrators have the specific power to order reinstatement in cases of wrongful dismissal. To ensure that arbitration procedures are not unreasonably protracted, the new law provides stricter time limits within which verdicts must be handed down or specific permission for extension sought. It also provides that workers may be fined up to a maximum of $200 for taking part in illegal strikes but it extends the sanction to employers who may be fined the same amount for each worker they illegally lock out. By this simple formula, justice is done. Finally, in the event of illegal strikes or lock-outs, a judge would no longer have the power to impose a prison sentence instead of a fine as he was able to under the old law. The new act removes the latter power and makes the fines that might be imposed civil debts recoverable in accordance with normal civil procedures. What this means, in effect, is that a worker who has genuine difficulty in meeting a fine can put his problem before the court and secure more time to pay, a change in the amount of the fine itself or whatever the judge deems reasonable. Only in the event of open defiance of the court's verdict could further action be taken. In this event a judge could conceivably find that a worker or employer was guilty of contempt of court which would have to be dealt with as he thought best.

One interesting new feature of the law which provoked considerable comment in union circles was a clause according the Attorney General the right to appear in disputes to represent the public interest. The fact that the unions regarded this with deep suspicion is an interesting indication of how brainwashed we have all been by the colonial experience. In the old days of the colonial power, and even more recently than that, it would have been natural to assume that Government could only favour the employer and oppose the worker in any dispute. Not only did this seem to be so but, having regard to the structure of colonial society and its economic interests, this was in fact the case. Hence, when we proposed this clause in the 1974 Act the union leaders instinctively assumed that this was part of the old colonial pattern. It did not occur to them that in a progressive society with a progressive government, there would be innumerable occasions on which the government favoured the workers' side and where the presence of the Attorney General would be a help. In any event, even where an Attorney General might speak for an unfriendly government, his arguments could never be more than one point of view to be considered, albeit an important one. More fundamentally, however, the question of the Attorney General's presence in an arbitration goes to the very root of the rights of groups in society. In terms of one possible view of social organisation, it is quite natural to assume that a government has no right interfering in or even making a comment upon a dispute between workers and employers. However, a moment's reflection will serve to show that such a view is as naïve as it is out of date. No group in organised society has the right to act without regard to the interest of the whole of that society. Hence, no employer locked in battle with his workers is entitled to contend that they represent a private enclave complete in themselves and bearing no relation to the rest of the social group. It is my view that employers and unions are going to have to learn that the economy is not a private cake into which they are entitled to cut as they wish without regard to the general sharing of that cake between all members of society. The rights of all groups are ultimately subject to the overall interests of society as a whole.

The reaction of the unions is a classic one of responding to a proposal in terms of ancient reflexes. The notion that a government would inevitably oppose workers could only be true if it is assumed that all governments are the prisoners of employer as distinct from worker interests. Furthermore, the notion that disputes between employers and workers are private affairs not properly of concern to the society at large is an unconscious reflection of the very philosophy that produced the kinds of experience that led to the fear of government bias in the first place. The kind of *laissez-faire* thinking that underlies the interpretation of a labour dispute as a private matter was part of the intellectual apparatus of nineteenth century capitalism. The governments of the nineteenth century were certainly opposed to workers' causes as a general rule. The political systems that favour workers' causes are those that have produced the notion of society as a total organism from which each individual part derives its rights and to which each individual part owes commensurate responsibilities. In that view, governments may favour either a worker's or an employer's case from time to time according to circumstances. But that judgement will always be based upon an attempt to interpret the general needs of society as a whole. In any event, the new Industrial Relations Act of 1974 may have marked the beginning of the end of the second phase in the struggle for worker democracy. Certainly it took us a long way from the events of 1963 and 1964.

9
UNIONS AND POLITICS

My years as a Union leader with strong political attachments and a certain degree of activist political involvement and later as a political leader with a deep commitment to worker causes has put me in a position where I have been peculiarly well placed to observe the interaction between unionism and politics. This relationship is always important in understanding the dynamics of modern society. In Jamaica's case, however, the relationship is critical. This is one of the reasons why the small nations of the English-speaking Caribbean area occupy an interesting place in modern political history. Almost without exception these islands, along with mainland Guyana, have tended to produce political movements that are closely bound up with trade unions. With the possible exception of Trinidad, every island has produced at least one major political party which was based historically on a mass trade union. Some islands, like Jamaica and Antigua, have actually produced two-party systems where both parties are affiliated to powerful trade unions. In Guyana the two major political parties, the People's National Congress and the People's Progressive Party, both maintain strong links with a number of affiliated unions. What makes this phenomenon unusual is not the existence of political parties that are related to trade unions for this kind of polarisation is common throughout the democratic world but the extent to which the entire political apparatus is linked with unions of one sort or another and the fact that opposing political organisations have each had strong links with opposing trade unions.

I cannot pretend to speak for the Caribbean in this matter. However, there are important parallels between the historical experience of Jamaica and that of the English-speaking Caribbean. Hence analyses of Jamaican institutions has considerable relevance in the understanding of the wider region. Certainly, Jamaica represents an interesting case study in which it is possible to observe certain tendencies and offer some tentative explanations. It is interesting to observe the striking difference between the popular movements during and after the Second World War which led to independence in Jamaica and to contrast them with similar forces which led to the same result in India and in Black Africa. All of the early popular resistance to imperialism in India and Africa was essentially nationalist and political in character. One has only to whisper the great names of the drive for freedom, Gandhi, Nehru, Nkrumah, Nyerere, Kaunda, Lumumba, and to remember the political parties which they founded, ranging from the Congress Party in India to TANU in Tanzania, to conjure up a picture of intense nationalism. In fact, it would be fair to say that nationalism and the drive for political independence dominated both the emotions and the practical actions of the heroes of the struggle against colonialism. Until political independence was attained all tactics and strategy centred around freedom. In these countries the union movement played a significant part but was never more than a secondary contributor to events while freedom remained to be won.

By contrast, the Jamaican situation was quite different. In 1938 there were simultaneous expressions of popular discontent. Manley formed the People's National Party and declared for freedom. Bustamante formed his trade union and dismissed Manley's nationalism as irrelevant. In India and throughout Africa the result, in such a situation, would have been a foregone conclusion. The nationalist movement would have become the focus for all the significant mass emotion and preoccupation. In Jamaica, the reverse happened. Bustamante's union became the great rallying point for the masses and Bustamante himself the Messianic leader. The nationalist movement seemed, by comparison, to be concerned about an institutional adjustment to which the people could attend in due course. In the meantime, however, the main preoccupation was the union. What one can observe here is an almost complete reversal of mass response. In the other parts of the colonial empire it was the union movement that was viewed in terms of institutional adjustment. The nationalist movement dealt with fundamental change.

What can possibly explain this paradox? I suspect it is to do with the nature of Caribbean history and the effect of slavery. When the British conquered India they were as an intrusion in the broad sweep of Indian history. They had no intention of settling a major element of the population there: on the contrary, they meant to rule India from Britain and had no thought of integrating into Indian life. They even went out of their way to make it clear that this was an inferior place to be and only brave souls, willing to undertake the 'white man's burden', would deign to live there at all. Therefore, the process of conquest and the later structure of colonialism served to underline the separate superiority of the conqueror from the 'native' population. The same was true in Africa. It must also be borne in mind that in both India and Africa a degree of cultural continuity was maintained. The imperialist master was a visitor and interloper. The host population remained at home continuing to live in terms of their own cultural experience. Here then, were all the emotional elements of nationalist resistance. The question of who was the visitor and who was the host was never in doubt. Exploitation, therefore, could be readily seen as a process involving foreigner against local. Equally, the arrogance of the imperialist could be viewed from within the comparative self-confidence of an unbroken cultural experience. When discontent approached the flashpoint of revolution, it was logical for the spirit of resistance to be channelled in nationalist directions.

By contrast, Jamaica presents an entirely different picture in which one must consider exploiter and exploited in terms of their own peculiar history. The objects of colonialist exploitation were not a local population interrupted in a common history and enjoying a continuing cultural experience nor were the exploiters, the beneficiaries of the system, expatriate visitors living in Jamaica temporarily as part of a visible process of external exploitation. On the contrary, the beneficiaries of the system were mainly white British settlers who came to Jamaica to live and put down permanent roots. Britain benefited from the colonial process just as much in Jamaica as elsewhere but the process of exploitation was less visible because there was a settled white plantocracy which could claim to be Jamaican. The transfer of resources as between Jamaica and Britain, therefore, was less obvious to an unsophisticated observer, than would have been the case say, in India. Thus, we begin with a group of white settlers.

Next, one must consider the situation of the slave. The bulk of the Jamaican population came to Jamaica as a consequence of the slave trade. A crucial objective of the slave system had been the destruction of cultural recollection. Every effort was made through the destruction of family patterns, the separation of children from parents, the banning and punishment of the practice of ancient rites, to break the cultural continuum in the mind of the slave. Hence, by 1938, when Jamaican discontent reached its flashpoint, the Jamaican masses conceived of their plight in terms of exploitation as did their African and Indian brethren. But whereas the African and the Indian saw British imperialism as the source of their troubles, the Jamaican reacted against the local employer group. Thus where Indians and Africans saw their problems in political terms involving, of necessity, a political solution, Jamaicans saw their problem in economic terms and involving an economic solution.

In the early days the name Bustamante was evocative of imminent salvation and provoked the same mass response in Jamaica as did the name Nkrumah in Ghana. In 1944 the political party which Bustamante formed as an extension of the Bustamante Industrial Trade Union swept the first elections under adult suffrage just as completely as did the great nationalist parties of black Africa and India. In other parts of the crumbling empire no political party could face the electorate if it was not passionately and avowedly nationalist. In Jamaica, no party could face the electorate if it was not passionately and avowedly concerned with higher wages and it would be well advised to support a strong trade union as visible evidence of its sincerity.

As it happens, the PNP was a socialist party. As such, it had always been concerned with the workers' lot, had always supported unionism, and in fact had encouraged the unions to affiliate to the party. This undoubtedly helped the PNP to survive the early setback of 1944. Its early difficulties sprung from the fact that it did not make the struggle for better wages with its simple, implied challenge to the local economic power structure, the central thesis of its appeal to the masses. It was trying to teach the masses that colonialism was the general enemy and that the local power structure was only a part of a total system of exploitation. While it argued in favour of unions, higher wages and workers' rights it sought to set these activities in a wider context. By contrast, Bustamante had one appeal: higher wages and one protest: exploitation by the local employers. Where the colonialist process had been as complex as in the Jamaican experience it was difficult for the masses to understand the PNP's interpretation of history. What they knew was that they were getting a shilling a day and that it was a local, Jamaican born white man who was paying them that. In fact, for some of the peasantry, British royalty was seen as a fount of justice to which one could turn in extreme difficulty. This quaint illusion could be traced back to a complete misunderstanding of the events which led to the hanging of Paul Bogle and William Gordon after the abortive rebellion of 1865. Many Jamaicans blamed the local plantocracy alone for the bad conditions that created the Morant Bay uprising and for the brutality with which it was crushed. The rebellion was followed by the abrogation of the Jamaican constitution and the downgrading of Jamaica to the status of a crown colony. As a consequence Jamaica had been ruled exclusively by the Queen's representative since 1865 and, there having been no further rebellions, it had been concluded that the Queen's rule was kinder than that of the local plantocracy!

Being neither an anthropologist nor a historian, I can only guess at the causes which make Jamaican, and indeed Caribbean, history so different from that of others who shared the colonial experience. But whatever the true cause may be, it is a fact of Jamaican life that the only parties that have ever made a significant impression on the Jamaican electorate have been the two which maintained close ties with powerful, mass trade unions. Certainly, it is impossible to understand either contemporary politics or contemporary unionism in Jamaica without some understanding of the effects upon both of the close relationship that exists.

To begin with, the form which unionism has taken in

Jamaica has, I suspect, been profoundly influenced by the process which I have just sought to analyse. All Jamaican unions tend towards the blanket form of organisation in which one organisational structure tends to spread out to cover the workers in a number of different occupations. The Bustamante union began with this avowed intention and has never departed from it. The trade union council group began as separate unions, but by 1950 had succumbed to the centrifugal forces which were at work and formed the blanket organisation, the Trade Union Congress. The National Workers Union started out as an avowed blanket union and has remained so. A number of small unions which have been launched since the 1960s have all tended to coalesce into blanket unions, although small in size and scope. This can be partly explained by the economic realities of operating in a small country, however, I suspect that there is a deeper reason than that. Even thirty-six years after the events of 1938, there is an intensity to worker feeling that imparts to the union movement some of the emotional quality of a crusade. One would expect that by now the better paid Jamaican worker groups enjoying advanced contract protection would enter their periodic negotiations with something of the detachment of professional adversaries preparing for an essentially technical contest. Not so. To this day there is a heat and intensity about the engagement that suggests the smouldering emotions of unresolved class tension. The battle, therefore, is as much about property as about status. It is contested not as if shares were at stake, but the right to existence. Here I believe we see continuing the same underlying hostilities which made Bustamanteism seem to be the answer to the deepest needs of the masses. Inevitably, in this context the rational niceties concerning forms of union organisation tend to disappear in the fires of deep emotion.

One consequence has been the legitimate criticism of the Jamaican union movement as insensitive to the particular needs of specialist groups. Like all blanket unions, the tendency is to formulate broad categories of response like 'across the board' percentages of wage increase and generalised proposals for sick and vacation leave. This blunt-edged quality to Jamaican bargaining technique is characteristic and has led to less than adequate representation for specialist groups whose needs are too individual and complex to be satisfied by a single global claim. Aware of the criticism, the unions have constantly tried to improve their bargaining techniques within the blanket structure and have met with a measure of success. However, the basic weakness remains and has led to sporadic attempts to form little craft and occupational unions which are 'fine tuned' to the special needs of particular groups. By and large, however, the blanket unions can still show a better record of performance even for the specialist groups because of the sheer power that they can bring to bear on any employer.

Another point of speculation concerns the question of the extent to which the politically affiliated unions are manipulated by the parties. The charge has always been levelled, and is inevitable in the circumstances, that the Jamaican worker is used as a political football by the political parties acting through their agents, the unions. When pressed for details, one set of critics argues that the Jamaican worker is kept from aggressive action by both the political parties, in or out of power, so as not to alienate middle-class opinion and big business financial support. Another set of critics argues that the party in power restrains its affiliated union so as not to 'rock the boat' while the opposition party provokes its affiliated union to extravagant claims for that precise purpose. Yet a third group of critics contend that whether in power or out the political parties provoke their affiliated unions with extravagant claims in an unending search for working class support. The internal inconsistencies that separate the three analyses have never disturbed their respective protaganists who continue over the years to chant these views in season and out.

The truth is that political considerations have little more than a marginal effect upon union action. Against the background of the attitudes which I have sought to describe, it is very difficult for a union to 'slow down' its members even if it wants to. Workers' claims are partly a response to economic pressure and partly an expression of class hostility. In a poor country the economic pressure is not easy to remove and within our present capitalist economic structure class hostilities are bound to continue. Thus, the unions tend to be the creatures of larger social forces rather than themselves the manipulators of history. Naturally, I cannot say that no situation ever occurs in which a government may ask a union to respect the national interest nor can I say that Oppositions have not sometimes suggested that a little labour disturbance might be politically useful. By and large, however, these are rare occurrences which have at best a marginal impact on the total course of events. A much more serious problem for the Jamaican union movement is the effect of the political dichotomy on the prospects of labour unity. As the years have passed unions have become more and more conventional in their response to worker needs. There is a steady decline in table-thumping and the exploitation of pure emotion in spite of the lingering class tensions which I have described. More and more the unions seek to examine specific causes of complaint and difficulty with a view to hammering out professional solutions.

A remarkable feature of Jamaican unionism has been the extent to which, in response to professional necessity, unions belonging to opposing political camps have learnt to co-operate with each other within industries where both hold bargaining rights. In large areas of the economy, such as the sugar industry, the nation's ports, many of the public utilities, throughout the government service and so on, more than one union is firmly established and here the tradition of joint bargaining and genuine co-operation thrives. However, in spite of logic, history and institutional practice which all point towards the structural unification of the labour movement, the political division continues to make this impossible. Somehow, the unions seem unable to break free of the political trap to the point where they can form some sort of general national body which can co-ordinate labour strategy, reduce union conflict and provide a self-administered means of adjudicating differences. As a result, the union movement continues to maintain parallel organisations which duplicate personnel and administrative overheads and generally lead to a squandering of scarce resources. Inevitably, the movement remains incapable of putting together really effective initiatives in vital areas such as worker education, the mobilisation of worker savings for housing and other urgent needs of the masses. A lot of time and effort are wasted in trivial and essentially irrelevant attempts to capture sections from each other rather than in concentrating upon the organisation of those sections of the working population which are unorganised because this is more difficult. In fact, statistics show that all the effort now spent on trying to 'capture' sections result only in marginal gains for either side. Quite apart from the effect of this tragic duplication of effort in missed opportunities, there is the deeper question of its effect upon the development of worker attitudes.

No matter how legitimate workers' grievances may be, no matter how real the injustices that are endured, the process by which these disadvantages are overcome must be accompanied by the development of positive work attitudes. Workers who resist authority and discipline because it is exercised unfairly and because no one seeks to engage their intelligent understanding of the economic process, do not need any apologist. The negativity with which they respond is guaranteed by the process itself. On the other hand, no society can succeed without efficient production and no society will in fact be happy if its workers do not get genuine satisfaction out of working hard. After all, nearly a third of most people's lives is spent at work and if most people are unhappy at work then it is safe to assume that most people are unhappy most of the time. It must, therefore, be a fundamental objective of social organisation to achieve an attitude towards the productive process which is constructive and positive. This involves a relationship between the worker and the productive process which satisfies the emotional as well as the material needs of the human being. There are some aspects of this challenge, faced by all of mankind, which are extremely complex and involve an analysis of the very foundations of social and economic existence.

Other aspects of this problem are quite simple. It is not difficult to explain why particular productive processes depend upon human efficiency nor what kinds of human behaviour lead to efficiency and which do not. On the assumption that a union is controlled by its members and is the vehicle through which its members seek to attain satisfaction, union negotiations which increase worker satisfaction should have their counterpart in a process of education which increases the workers' understanding of their role in the productive process and the importance of their conforming to certain standards of conduct. For this to succeed the worker must feel confident that the union is in fact achieving reasonable progress. At the same time, the union must be willing and have the authority to try to play its part in the parallel educational process. In Jamaica, the divisions in the union movement make it almost impossible to meet the educational need. The constant rivalry between the unions maintains a mood of agitation amongst the workers in which the union is constantly suspected of not doing enough because there is another union spreading propaganda in the wings. As a consequence, the union is often too busy defending itself to have time for simple but vitally needed worker education. Furthermore, the union is often so undermined by the propaganda that it lacks the authority to get the workers to listen. There is no question that the development of responsible worker attitudes has been frustrated by the artificial split within the union movement that is perpetuated by the political connection.

What, then, of the effect of unions upon politics? Casual observers of the Jamaican scene are tempted to conclude that the close relationship between unions and political parties has led to a series of governments committed to the cause of the workers and tending to govern with the workers' interests predominantly in mind. The irony is that the exact reverse is true. The very fact that both political parties are allied to unions and that the unions have tended to maintain a chronic and ideologically irrelevant state of combat amongst themselves has tended to blunt any political impact which the unions might have had on the system. Historically, the unions have been far too busy fighting each other to spare the time and energy to form a strong ideological wing committed to certain kinds of political action within the political parties. On the other hand, the governments concerned have tended to ignore that whole area of political and legislative action which could make such a dramatic impact on the quality of workers' lives and upon their status in the community. It is as if successive political parties in power have tended to assume that the union movement can look after the workers so that the government can be free to concentrate on the condition of the farmer, economic development, education, and so on. As a result there have been incredible examples of neglect such as the generation which passed before the Master and Servants Law was repealed and the similar failures to deal with the Essential Services Law and a number of other matters of urgent concern to workers.

When one considers this comparative bankruptcy of policy in the field of labour legislation between 1944 and 1972, it makes the comment about unions dominating government almost incomprehensible. Equally incredible is the suggestion that usually accompanies that particular criticism to the effect that the unions should have no political ties at all. This comment is remarkable because it is always advanced as a corollary to the suggestion that Jamaican governments have promoted the interests of the workers at the expense of all other groups. The reverse has been the case although we are now trying to remedy that deficiency with all the vigour at our command. The truth is that where the union movement has split and attached itself to the different elements of the political movement, it is not the mere fact of a connection that is bad but the whole process. Since the union divisions have been about nothing that is real and have flowed from no differences in ideology or policy, the very fact of the division has tended to create an atmosphere of petty squabbling rather than the pursuit of fundamental objectives. To this extent unionism has tended, however marginally, to infect the political system with its own lack of fundamental purpose. I do not say this by way of excusing the political system and would be the first to concede that a seriously focused political system must, by definition, be proof against irrelevant infection. On the other hand, granted a lack of fundamental purpose which has sometimes characterised the Jamaican political parties, the unions have done nothing to supply that purpose because they themselves have lacked an ideological rudder.

In any serious view of social development it bcomes nonsense to suggest that unions should not be concerned with and involved in politics. Obviously, politics is the means by which society organises its major decision-making processes. The goals which society pursues and the means by which it pursues them are articulated and organised within the political system. The nature and thrust of our laws are fashioned within that system. In a society like Jamaica's, the workers are an identifiable group in the sense that a certain type of wage earner recognises himself and herself as belonging to the working class. One day we hope class divisions and, hence, class-consciousness will disappear. Until that time comes, however, the working class is by far the largest single group in society and has therefore the largest single vested interest in the laws that we pass and the way that we govern ourselves – in politics. The union movement as the major institution within which the working classes organise themselves, must therefore be permanently concerned with politics and constantly involved in the workings of the system. As I remarked, the tragedy of the Jamaican situation is that the workers' institutions are split and have as yet shown little capacity for the formulation and articulation of clear goals about the kind of society in which all people would regard themselves as workers and true worker happiness might be successfully pursued. So far from becoming less concerned with and interested in politics, what we need is a political movement that is more concerned with and more involved in serious purposes. It is clear that we still suffer from the effects of those historical and social forces that made the masses gravitate to the 'bread and butter' appeal of a union movement rather than the nationalist appeal of a political movement that was seeking to challenge the total framework of colonialist oppression. What we need is a total movement which sees both traditional unionism and nationalist politics as preludes to the basic task of building a new kind of society in which equality and social justice are consciously organised.

10

A VOICE AT THE WORKPLACE

THE JBC strike was a turning point in my life. However great its impact on Jamaica may actually have been, there is no question that it brought to a head a number of moral and political issues that were of growing concern to me. For many years I had been so engrossed in the day to day business of running the union, organising workers, trying to ensure the democratic involvement of our membership and, above all, in the unending round of negotiations, that I seemed to have had little time left for fundamental thinking. After the JBC strike I began to take serious stock of the way in which Jamaica was developing and found myself increasingly concerned at the lack of clear purpose at all levels of society. It did not surprise me that the government of the day was headed in no particular direction because its leaders were notoriously unencumbered by philosophy and unconcerned about the fundamental relationships which existed in Jamaica between classes, between employer and worker and between the individual and the society as a whole. This did not worry me as I was confident that the day would come when the PNP would return to power and challenge society to change once again. What did worry me deeply, however, was the danger that the union movement was coming unconsciously to assist in the perpetuation of the system.

One has to remember always that the union movement is a product of the capitalist system, and more often than not, represents no more than an attempt by the workers to mitigate its worst effects. Unions, therefore, do not necessarily challenge the system itself. While they may secure an increasing share of national wealth for their members they often act as fundamental props to capitalism because, accepting capitalist values, they divert attention from the fundamental shortcomings and inequities of what is, for all practical purposes, a morally bankrupt way of life.

I am often asked, and often ask myself, where do I think the union movement should go; along what lines should it develop?

By 1974 the union movement had grown into a major economic institution. Total paid membership between all registered groups was well over 150,000 and some 200,000 workers, about one-third of the work force, were covered by union contracts. In the twenty years of my own active involvement the movement had roughly trebled in actual size and quadrupled in its range of influence.

The future of the union movement has to be considered from two points of view. First of all, regardless of any questions of social philosophy, it is obvious that the Jamaican union movement is weak in five areas. Firstly, it has failed to meet the organising challenge in extensive areas of the economy. One has only to consider the size of the work force compared with the size of the union movement to see that much remains to be done. Because of the intense rivalries which have been imported into the union movement as an entirely artificial consequence of political forces, too much time and energy is spent in raiding membership that is already organised. This energy would be far better directed to the more difficult task of bringing the unorganised within the fold. Part of the problem lies in the fact that the unorganised sections of the work force are to be found in the distributive trades, the smaller manufacturing establishments and medium-sized farms. Developing effective unionism among these groups is a back-breaking task requiring great skill and patience. By comparison, the act of raiding a large establishment in which the foundations of an organisation have already been laid represents an easy, indeed a tempting choice. Furthermore, one can rationalise this effort by pretending that a political cause will be furthered by the theft. Real progress would, however, be better served if the effort were reserved for some group suffering the effects of exploitation with no immediate hope of relief.

The second great area calling out for action is worker housing. Jamaica suffers from an acute shortage of housing and a matching scarcity of resources with which to tackle the problem. To the extent that decent housing is the foundation upon which so much else in human development depends, we need to mobilise every possible source of finance for this objective. In fairness, it must be said that a start has been made. However, future bargaining should place great emphasis on schemes that invest workers' savings with matching employers' funds, in co-operative housing developments. This can become a practical and useful extension of the principle of group action which is the foundation of trade union method. Instead of harnessing the will of the group exclusively for benefits at the workplace, this will can be directed towards improving the quality of life outside.

Thirdly, the movement has got to come to grips with the problem of wage differentials. As I write, the minimum wage for a sugar worker, or unskilled labour in government for that matter, is seventy cents an hour. In the premium industries such as bauxite, cement and petroleum, it is anywhere from two to three times as much for exactly the same kind of work. There are sections of the agricultural economy in which rates are still one-half those obtaining in sugar. Hence, wages for similar types of basic, unskilled labour vary by as much as a multiple of six. Clearly, this is unreasonable and unjust. The unions must, sooner or later, accept their responsibility towards the development of national standards. Their ability to respond to this challenge, however, will be to some extent conditioned by the political environment in which they operate. If that environment is unplanned and continues to reflect the worst features of 'laissez-faire' capitalism, the unions will have neither the ability nor the duty to tackle the problem. On the other hand, attempts by the Government to develop the economy along orderly socialist lines which seek to tackle the gross inequalities of wealth which now exist, will deserve the support of the trade union movement. In fact, without that support, policies aimed at the equitable distribution of wealth and broad access to social justice may prove difficult if not impossible to achieve.

Fourthly, the movement has substantially failed to recognise the special problems of women in employment. To give just one example, the Government only fully recognised the principle of equal pay in 1973 but the unions have not made it a standard practice yet.

Finally, the movement must commit far more of its resources to worker education. Again, a significant start has been made. A trade union education institute under the brilliant direction of Rex Nettleford has been providing a fine service. The institute is located on the Mona Campus of the University of the West Indies. There, groups of delegates from various unions undergo training courses which give them a broad grasp of union history and techniques of union representation. They are also exposed to the first principles of business organisation and labour economics. This type of operation could be greatly expanded if the unions were willing to commit the necessary resources to the effort. Far too little is done to organise classes and seminars among workers at the workplace and in the various population centres. As a result, the educated leadership of the movement is spread dangerously thin. Often the gap in understanding between the delegate who has been through a course of training at the institute and the working group with which the delegate must deal, is dangerously wide. The work of the institute should be the springboard for extensive programmes of mass worker education which should be pursued constantly throughout the length and breadth of the union movement.

However one approaches the five current shortcomings of the Jamaican union movement, one is driven to an inescapable conclusion: at the root of the problem lies the split. The unorganised are ignored partly because the unions compete with each other for the same membership. Initiatives in areas like co-operative housing are uncertain and belated because union competition places a premium on those results achieved at the bargaining table which are visible, immediate and of obvious popularity. When all of the results of collective bargaining go into wage increases and vacation leave, the benefits are felt immediately and are, therefore, easy to sell to the membership. If part of a wage increase is diverted from ready cash into a savings scheme for housing, the benefit will take longer to mature and depends upon a deliberate act of short-term self-denial. This is less obvious, less immediate and less popular. Under the competitive pressure of the situation, the unions tend to take the easy rather than the more challenging route. The development of a national wages policy aimed at closing the present gap which yawns like a chasm between the standards of living of different categories of workers, is almost impossible to undertake where each union is scared of its rivals every time it sits at the bargaining table. Where the competitive scramble is so fierce, little time is left for the more fundamental enterprises like worker education.

I suggest that, for all its great achievements, the movement cannot fulfil its basic task under the present conditions of rivalry. And I have defined the task in minimal terms. On any definition, the union movement must exist for the purpose of securing for all the workers of a country the basic conditions of a civilised existence which must include security of employment, adequate wages, basic protection in sickness and old age, reasonable social amenities on the job and sufficient leisure. At present, the union movement tends to accomplish these things for those who come within the scope of its own operations. The rest of the working classes are either untouched by, or the victims of the process. To the extent that the union movement acts for its own members alone, it has little or no effect on those outside its boundaries. Far worse, the achievements of the union movement for the members of its own group often take place at the expense of unorganised labour. If large contract settlements are accompanied by increased prices of goods which unorganised workers must buy, the result of the process is to depress the standard of living of the unorganised to finance the progress of the organised. In the absence of concern for the whole working group, unions sometimes contradict the wider purposes which the movement should exist to serve. In a unified trade union movement capable of developing coherent national policies, these unintentional consequences could be dealt with. Where there is a constant scramble to survive, these negative by-products are barely noticed, much less tackled.

The present shortcomings of the movement are even more acute if one takes a more fundamental view of its historical mission. In his search for progress, man has distilled from the idea of the fundamental equality of human beings, the political concept of democracy. This implies that each individual has a right of access to the decision-making process in a nation. Consequently as my own attitudes developed in response to the protracted union experience, I found my concept of the task increasingly defining itself in terms of the democratisation of the workplace. By the time of the JBC strike, I had become convinced that we were dealing with three great phases of a general and protracted struggle. To begin with, there was capitalist society. With its overwhelming emphasis on the rights of property, capitalism had entrenched, and was well served by, the concept of master and servant. The possession of wealth led to the control of the means of production and conferred absolute authority upon its possessor. Those who had only their labour to sell had no rights at the workplace. Naturally enough, the first phase in the struggle was concerned with the right to determine the price of labour. This led to the formation of unions and the acceptance of the right to collective bargaining. However, the right to bargain about the price of labour was still subject to areas in which the authority of the employer was unquestioned. Although the price of the job might be subject to contractual agreement, the availability of the job to a particular worker was under the exclusive control of the employer.

The second great phase of the struggle was associated with the right of the workers to continue to hold their jobs so long as they measured up to a basic standard of performance. Once again fundamental issues concerning ultimate authority were at stake and the struggle in the second phase was waged as intensely as before. Eventually, victory was won and the principle established that no person could be removed from a job arbitrarily. This phase was completed when it was finally accepted that an employer did not possess the right of arbitrary dismissal at all, compensation notwithstanding. In short, if as a consequence of economic necessity, a job ceased to exist, then it was understood that a worker could no longer enjoy it and would have to accept severance pay for the loss. If, however, a job continued to exist, a worker who was not guilty of a proven offence, would be entitled to continue in the enjoyment of that job unless voluntarily entering into an agreement with the employer to terminate the relationship. Viewed historically, the workers' search, has been for a voice in their own affairs: first to fix the price of their labour and later to determine the extent of their security.

In a capitalist view of society, the working class struggle may be said to come to an end upon the completion of the second phase. In this concept all that would remain to be done by the union movement would be to ensure that all workers benefited from the struggle and enjoyed the rights which were its outcome. The five immediate challenges which I have suggested that the Jamaican union movement faces, can all be pursued consistent with the objectives of a capitalist system. Phases one and two represented important challenges to the operation of the system and have culminated in substantial restraints upon its workings. They leave untouched, however, the most fundamental questions of all. These are: the workers' position in relation to the ownership of the means of production; and the part workers are to play in the decision-making process.

Unquestionably, the first two stages of the struggle have achieved a massive change in the original nature of the master and servant relationship. However, when all is said and done, the worker remains a servant. True, he is a servant who can bargain and who may not lightly be removed from his job. He is a servant who can bring up his children in a comfortable home and enjoy the material benefits of life, security in sickness and old age and adequate leisure but at the workplace he remains a servant where his existence is defined by the boundaries of an authority that he cannot penetrate and whose workings he cannot influence.

If the union movement is to be true to what I have suggested is its fundamental historical mission, it must be concerned with the third phase of the struggle which is the extension of the principle of equality to human relations at the workplace. Complete rights for workers are inseparable from this question. Only when it has been achieved will we be able to claim that full democratisation of human relationships in the productive process has been accomplished. As we shall show, this cannot be separated from larger questions about whether the society is organised along capitalistic or socialistic lines.

Capitalism is both a method for the organisation and distribution of goods and a social philosophy. It has to be understood in historical context. In Europe it emerged in the eighteenth and nineteenth centuries and was shaped by the political and social environment of the time which it was later to change. Of particular concern to us in Jamaica is the form of capitalist organisation exported to Jamaica from Britain by the colonial process. Britain itself was an elitist society whose history showed feudalism brought under control by a strong central monarchy which in turn created an aristocracy in recognition of past favours and as a guarantee of future security. The Cromwellian intervention may have brought the monarchy within the bounds of constitutional and financial restraint, but it made no impression whatsoever on the elitist quality of English social organisation. The people who colonised Jamaica were, in every sense, the products of a highly class-stratified social system. Their journey across the waters had no more effect on those attitudes than the defeat of the Cavaliers by the Roundheads. Thereupon the African slave was introduced into this elitist social milieu. Slavery is, of course, the last stage and the final product of elitist stratification. As if to ensure that the system would be supported by a constant visual reminder of social differences, the elitist colonisers were white and their slaves black.

It is against this background that one has to examine the effect of the capitalist system upon the Jamaican worker. It is in the light of the attitudes and social relationships created by this history that we must consider the last and most important stage of the workers' search for equality at the workplace.

The capitalist system rested originally upon the notion that goods and services were best produced and distributed by private persons seeking profit. The system turns on two fundamental propositions: that the means of production should be privately owned; and that the ownership of the means of production confers exclusive authority in the decision-making process. The sale of labour involves denial of access to that process. Therefore, the system creates a basic inequality of status between those who own enterprises and those who work for them. Implicit in the system are owners who make decisions and workers who owe obedience in return for a wage. The superiority of the owner and the inferiority of the worker are assumed. This involves a fundamental denial of the principle of equality and is, therefore, morally unacceptable to those who take equality as their starting point in the search for justice in human affairs. Furthermore, the whole history of man reflects the application of creative intelligence to the control and mastery of the human environment. This involves making choices between possible courses of action. Yet, under this system, human beings are denied access to the decision-making process in their work experience, denying them the opportunity for creative self-expression in this critical area of their lives.

The power of decision-making is the vital factor which separates the two participants in the productive process. Jamaican capitalism did not, however, stop there. A system founded on the notion of superior and inferior beings assumed a permanent hereditary division of classes along these lines. In other words, the owner of an enterprise did not feel superior to his workers only to the extent that he was a decision-maker and they his obedient workers. He came to the economic relationship long since confirmed in the view that his superiority was more deeply, indeed divinely ordained. He was a member of a superior class, of which the members could refer to centuries of entrenched advantage as confirmation of God's manifest purpose. Finally, as if to underline the difference in status to which the employer was born, he was white, or nearly so, and his worker black. Hence, a social force of long standing collaborated with a contemporary requirement of the economic system to confirm owners and workers in an unequal relationship. In truth, Jamaican industry was, until very recently, not populated by bosses and workers; in a profound, psychological sense, it was populated by masters and servants.

Leaving aside for the moment the social and historical problem of elitism, one is left with an immediate contradiction that must be resolved. On the one hand there is the capitalist system which rests upon private ownership of the means of production and reserves decision-making to that ownership. On the other hand, there is the workers' claim for the full recognition of their intrinsic equality. On the face of it, the basic tenets of capitalism are incompatible with the principle of equality. But the principle of equality is the foundation of the democratic system. Democracy is founded in the belief that people are the best judges of their own needs and must have a means of influencing the decisions which affect their lives. Sooner or later, therefore, those who believe in equality and see democracy as a logical extension of that belief, must tackle the problem of capitalist economic organisation which begins by separating its participants into unequal categories.

Lest one assumes that the argument is fanciful, it might be well to take a closer look at the workers' experience in a privately owned enterprise organised along capitalist lines. It is true that workers will have a voice in fixing all the conditions under which they serve. Unionism has seen to that. However, one must remember that approximately one-third of a human being's waking life is spent at work. Work is, perhaps, the most fundamental aspect of human experience. In the average enterprise, in industry, commerce, services or agriculture, a person comes to work in the morning and carries out a series of tasks throughout the day. They will have had no part in determining how or why those tasks are performed nor are they consulted as to whether the tasks could be better performed. No means will exist whereby they can express an opinion about the course that the business is taking and it is unlikely that they will understand either the great or the small decisions that affect the present and the future of the enterprise. They are, literally, blind ciphers in the total operation. It is true that, in common with other animals, human beings are concerned with the organisation of security and are willing to surrender considerable freedom of action to guarantee it. However, it is the quality of creativity that distinguishes human beings from the other animals. This expresses itself in both the urge and the need to experiment with one's environment and to seek new and different ways of increasing the chances of personal happiness by modifying the nature of social organisation. Of all creat-tures, therefore, human beings seek self-fulfilment through the sense of participating in the decisions that affect their lives. Man seeks a voice in the determination of his affairs and it is precisely this voice that is denied at the workplace.

Older workers, conditioned by history and experience to the acceptance of an inferior status in life, may have been content to wage a personal and collective war against poverty. In the main, older workers are satisfied with a successful outcome to that encounter. The political system, however, reverberates with the rhetoric of equality. Democratic politics lead naturally to the spread of education. Political democracy, therefore, breeds workers increasingly educated to appreciate the contradiction between the expectations aroused by the political system and the reality that is their experience at the workplace. This new breed of worker takes victory in the war against poverty for granted. Their concern is with their exclusion from any meaningful participation in the industry; they know that they are capable of a meaningful contribution to decision-making and resent exclusion from the process. Increasingly, therefore, the status of obedient cipher breeds frustration and hostility. Hence, those who claim that equality is the foundation of their social and political beliefs cannot accept the present exclusion of workers from decision-making. Equally, those who repudiate idealism and stick to the lower ground of so-called 'common sense' are well advised to ponder the fact that higher wages will not head off the hostility which is bred by the frustration of the new educated worker who demands a voice and who is trained to use that voice effectively. In due course this new worker is going to be every worker. Clearly, the system as presently organised, cannot contain this new force.

As the idea of equality gave birth to democracy as a concept and method for the government of people, so did it spawn socialism as a concept and method of social and economic organisation. As is the case with democracy, there are many views of how the principles of socialism may best be applied. Common to all forms of socialism, however, are two basic propositions. Firstly: that all economic activity must be organised to serve the needs of the people as a whole. Secondly: that all social institutions exist to promote both individual and collective well being. Both ideas require that individual and group needs must be in harmony. Socialists do not accept the view that the private pursuit of individual happiness without full regard being paid to the needs of the whole group can lead to a set of social relationships that are either just or viable. Hence, socialists are concerned with organising social activity so that every member of the group has a secure base from which to explore opportunities that are equally available to all. By these means all have the opportunity to seek personal fulfilment within the society of which they are a part.

This search for fulfilment must begin with the chance to influence all the decisions which affect a person's life. Without this right human beings can neither change their present condition nor shape the world which they would like to occupy. Hence, a decision-making role for the individual at all levels of activity is fundamental to socialism. Herein lies a crucial difference between capitalist and socialist philosophy which is highly relevant to the workers' search for equality at the workplace. It is also a consideration which must be kept in mind when looking at socialist alternatives.

Since the superior status accorded to private ownership in the capitalist system is the first cause of our problem, one might be tempted to feel that public ownership would resolve it and that nationalisation would remove the difficulty since workers would no longer be working for individual owners, but for the state. Certainly, public ownership removes one immediate cause of difficulty which is the psychological effect upon workers of the superior status of the owner. However, the difficulty does not stop there. To begin with, modern industry is often so large and complex as to require the development of a management which may be quite separate from the ownership and where owners exercise their decision-making powers through an agent. The nationalisation of an industry, therefore, may merely substitute the state for the shareholder while leaving the structure of management unchanged in personnel and attitude. If the management continues to reflect the authoritarian attitudes of the former owners, the workers could well derive no benefit from the change in terms of their daily experience. Even if the old management were removed and some new controlling bureaucracy interposed, the workers' experience would continue to be determined by the quality and sensitivity of the bureaucracy which now exercised the management function. The workers might still find themselves as effectively excluded from decision-making as they were before. One must therefore beware of the notion that nationalisation is any panacea in itself.

Many people concerned with this question have fallen into the trap of assuming that ownership provides a solution. This is because they define equality in terms of the sharing of wealth. Since owners are the beneficiaries of the residual wealth of an industry, that is to say the profits that are left after all expenses, it is assumed that once the workers share in the ownership they will become residual beneficiaries of profits and will enter into the final kingdom of equality. However, wealth is not really our problem. The share of the proceeds of an industry which each contributor enjoys can be determined in many ways. Trade union action, Government taxation policies, and, indeed, enlightened managerial recommendations, can all contribute to a situation where the shareholders and workers of a privately owned business may feel comparatively content with their lot insofar as monetary benefits are concerned. The worker might still, however, feel frustrated by his exclusion from decision-making. Therefore, insofar as ownership is seen only as a means of creating access to residual wealth through profits, it would contribute nothing to the solution of the problem which could not be achieved by other means. Furthermore, if ownership is tied to the ability to put up cash, the workers will be at a distinct disadvantage. In most enterprises it would be highly unlikely that, even acting collectively, they could raise the sums of money that would give them a meaningful level of participation in ownership. As long, therefore, as ownership confers power and money defines ownership, workers will be excluded from significant participation in decision-making.

Clearly, our solutions cannot be sought within the traditional framework of the capitalist system. Our task must begin with a reordering of fundamental rights and relationships in the economy. We have seen that our problem is not merely the sharing of wealth and that it cannot be solved by state ownership nor by seeking to include workers in private ownership. Our problem is to find a means for the inclusion of the worker in the decision-making process as a full and equal partner. It is the creation of a society in which the workers feel themselves to be equal partners at the workplace that must be our primary objective. Therefore, we must begin by changing society itself.

The first enemy is to be found deep within the class responses of the social order. Indeed, it is the very notion of class that must first be attacked. Our aim must be the creation of a society in which no persons are felt to be intrinsically superior. The goal must be a nation where all work is intrinsically understood as necessary and important. The intention must be the development of a society in which all members feel that they are part of a family, performing different functions, yet all themselves functionaries. In such a society workers will no longer feel themselves a group apart, since all able bodied, adult persons will be regarded as workers. There must be so strong a sense of unity that the group would automatically face sacrifices to ensure that no member falls below an agreed standard. It must be as a family which permits differentials in reward, but forbids extravagant benefits secured at the expense of others. Such a society would forbid extremes because of its belief in the intrinsic equality of each member. A nation which is bound together by a sense of shared experience and loyalty based upon the equality of its members will have no difficulty in organising its economy in terms of equal access to decision-making. I am convinced that capitalism, as a philosophy of social and economic behaviour, is incapable of this task. It must be the aim of socialism to create such a society.

Our search must be for techniques through which the workers will come to possess a real voice at the workplace because their equality and right to participate in the making of decisions are assumed. Insofar as privately owned industry is concerned, the basic assumption which must be changed is that which governs the relationship between labour and capital. Labour must be seen to be equal to capital. Instead of requiring workers to meet the terms and conditions of capitalist ownership which are normally defined by money, the workers' rights to participation must be accepted as a consequence of the contribution which they make through their labour. In fact, many European nations have evolved a relationship between owners and workers which is called 'co-determination'. Here, bodies like the board of directors are comprised of equal numbers of representatives of shareholders and workers. Both groups act through the process of democratic selection and meet in the boardroom as equals. Similar experimentation is beginning at the level of management where committees representing workers sit with the traditional management to consider the plans which are necessary to carry out the policies previously determined at the level of the board of directors.

Different countries will have to experiment with different techniques. Jamaica will prove to be no exception. In considering techniques, however, one distinction is clear. Public ownership does not in itself confer equality of status through participation in decision-making. However, it does provide a bridge for it is far easier to involve workers in the making of decisions at the top levels of policy, the middle levels of planning and the shop floor levels of implementation in an industry which exists only to serve the public. Where the interest of the private shareholder must be met, and properly so, it is more difficult to share policy making and planning between owners and workers. Often marginal decisions will tend to suit the interest of the shareholder at the expense of the worker and *vice versa.* This creates inevitable difficulties. However, these problems are by no means insurmountable. To the extent that the workers' interest is fully represented in decision-making, the cause of justice is advanced and sources of tension reduced.

The difficulties which we are analysing arise because the ownership of wealth in the productive process was accorded a privileged status in the mythology of capitalism. This mythology was invented by those whose wealth and power gave them control of the apparatus of the state. They pre-empted not only control over the security forces through which the state exerts its immediate power, but over the most subtle and pervasive instruments of propaganda including the educational system. Emerging in an elitist social climate, capitalism entrenched elitism in the workings of the economy. It is the whole system of values which must be changed before we can hope to complete the revolution in the workers' experience at the workplace.

The trade union movement must, therefore, begin by understanding the environment of power within which it operates in any economic system which has experienced some continuous history of capitalist organisation. Without that understanding, unions will find that they get as far as the second phase of the struggle, where workers' rights are defined in terms of bargaining about the price of labour and security of job tenure as long as the job exists, but they never have any say in the third and final question which may be concerned with whether the job exists at all. These last questions of ultimate importance will remain forever in the hands of powers that are foreign, remote and lost in the impenetrable mysteries of a system which workers can neither understand nor control. Nor will they ever experience that sense of fulfilment which comes from knowing you have a voice in the control of your own affairs.

Unfortunately, many unions become so enmeshed in the workings of the system that they lose both the ardour and the thrust for revolutionary change. Confusing shadow for substance, they assume that the politician will manage society in such a way as to take care of the ultimate question – whether a job should exist at all. Furthermore, being themselves the products of a system, the union functionaries fail to appreciate the extent to which self-expression is denied and equality of status precluded when the worker remains a servant at the workplace. Many union leaders seem to believe that their own existence depends upon this servant status and see the union as having no function beyond that of the protector of a person who would otherwise be helpless. The prospect of a set of relationships within the society and the economy in which workers would be full, democratic participants rather than objects of exploitation, makes some union leaders feel insecure. They seem to feel that in such a society their own purpose in life would disappear. Consequently, the union movement often ends up as a bulwark of an exploitative, capitalist system.

If the future of the worker is to evolve into the kind of full democratic status which we are envisaging, it is the political environment which must first be changed. Obviously, no view of society which rests upon the foundation of capitalist philosophy will permit this development. Socialism presupposes a human community which organises its laws, its institutions and its productive processes in the interests of the total community and in which the ownership of property or the means of production cannot be seen as conferring any superior or even special status. A productive enterprise, under socialism, can only be owned privately if the community is satisfied that its interests are promoted by the resulting activity. Indeed it could be said that under capitalism, the people are servants in the national house of the capitalist. Under socialism, the capitalist is a guest in the national house of the people. It is for all these reasons that the world will, I suggest, increasingly explore its future in terms of socialist possibilities under democratic political management.

What then of the democratic system itself? Can the changes that we seek be achieved within this political framework? In the course of my twenty years as a trade unionist, I have become absolutely satisfied that the principles of democracy, as we understand them in Jamaica, are not only correct but indispensable to an egalitarian strategy. But we must understand that these principles lead us far beyond the mere existence of political parties. In fact, they lead us to questions of how political parties are organised within themselves; how governments maintain the flow of communication with their people in between elections; and, most fundamentally, how democracy can be organised at the workplace itself.

It is the realisation that democracy must finally come to the workplace which has led me to the conclusion that ultimately democracy and capitalism cannot co-exist. As a matter of fact, their association in the nineteenth and twentieth centuries is misleading. Neither is necessary to the other and the fact that they have co-existed in certain societies is the result of an historical accident. There can only be true democracy when each person has access to the decision-making process at the basic levels of his or her life. It is a participatory concept. The capitalist process vests economic decision-making in the hands of those who own capital and is incapable of making ownership available to all who are affected by decisions within the productive process. It is authoritarian in method, intention and outcome and excludes the democratic process from the workings of the economy. Consequently, an effective democratic process must eventually destroy capitalism. As we have observed, popular control over the choice of governments leads inevitably to mass education; our educated youth detect the difference between the egalitarian promise of the political system and the elitist reality of the workplace, and so the contradiction within the system will eventually become intolerable. Already signs of this conflict are clearly evident in the capitalist based democracies like the U.S. and U.K. Confrontation between unions and employers, between the union movement and governments and between young people and the establishment occur constantly despite the growing affluence.

Finally, I have been confirmed in the belief that the true objectives of socialism can only be achieved in terms of the most careful development of democratic processes for the management of both the political and the economic system.

In practical terms, since the accessibility of the decision-making process is crucial to our argument, we may summarise what this implies in alternative situations and for the trade union movement itself. To begin with, we saw that it implied that nationalisation is not an end in itself but only a convenient opportunity for developing the institutions through which worker participation in management and decision-making can be organised. Secondly, it implied that if parts of the productive process are left in private hands, means must be devised for involving workers, not only in the equitable sharing of wealth, not only in job security, but most fundamentally, in decision-making. This is going to require a surrender of traditional rights by shareholders which they would do well to anticipate willingly by an imaginative grasp of the directions to which we are impelled by the democratic process itself.

The most fundamental challenge is to the union movement

itself. If it is to be true to its roots and its historical purpose, its first task now is one of intellectual disengagement. Union thinkers need to analyse the economic and political system within which they are operating. If they do so honestly. I am confident that they will share my belief that this third phase remains to be tackled and that we are reproached by every extra day during which we avoid the challenge. A moment's reflection will show that the exercise of participatory rights in a system of worker democracy within the economy will need expert organisation. The managerial class was created to give thrust and purpose to the interests of those who own the means of production. It permitted the owners of the productive process to adjust to the increasingly sophisticated pressures and demands of the modern economic system. So complex have these demands grown that some now contend that the managerial class wields more real power than those who own shares or otherwise exercise ownership. The union movement is an example of an equally powerful agent. Acting within the terms of the first two phases of the struggle, the movement has evolved an expert management of its own, dedicated to the fullest protection of the worker. However, this has operated within the clear definition of worker as servant. The workers will evolve, in the future, into the status of full democratic participants in the productive process in the economy and they will need expert agencies through which their new-found decision-making powers can be exercised. The new need for expert agents will be just as great as was the need in earlier aspects of the struggle. The challenge, therefore, is to the union movement to respond to the workers' need for a redefinition of status and to prepare itself to undertake the new type of agency which this status will require.

At this time the union movement should be preparing its best young minds in the disciplines of economics, statistics, cost accountancy and business administration. The movement should be challenging the political system to accept the full implications of the democratic ideal. It should be insisting that this ideal leads us away from the sterile divisions of the capitalist mythology and into the creative adventure of the socialist view of society. A huge programme of worker education is needed, both within the trade union movement and in society at large. Our educational process, our political institutions and our unions should all be engaged in devising mass education schemes aimed at releasing the public from its present sense of class inferiority. The workers should be challenged to claim freedom within the economy. Still without a voice at the workplace, they should now be organised to claim it. Simultaneously, they should be taught to recognise that no society can work without discipline and the capacity to accept restraints in the interests of larger purposes. This implies a new kind of worker who will accept the responsibility that is the other half of the freedom which we all long to experience in our lives. In both the public and the private sectors of the economy, experiments in worker participation in shop floor decisions should be commenced so that a foundation of experience in the processes of responsible worker democracy can begin.

Once again, one must consider the implications of the split in the union movement. I am convinced that the worker will never achieve a full voice at the workplace in a society dominated by capitalist philosophy and forms of economic organisation. Hence my conclusion that the mission of the union movement cannot be completed without parallel political action involving a complete, if peaceful, revolution in social attitudes and relationships. This, I suggest, cannot be accomplished until the union movement recognises that its primary responsibility is to the working class as a whole, and that the movement's divisiveness is contrary to their interests. One prays that the movement will come to understand its final responsibility to those processes which alone can liberate the human spirit.

In the last analysis the transformation which we envisage and which is aimed at a re-definition of democracy to include the economic as well as the political process is a challenge to the whole of society. If the union movement is unable to respond, it can become a major constraint, both upon the workers' search for freedom and self-expression, and upon the capacity of the society at large to reorder its internal relationships. It would be a pity if this should happen because although the union movement can obstruct progress, it is my belief that the forces of history, however much they may seem to meander, tend in an inevitable direction. However catastrophic the occasional setbacks, the direction is inexorably towards freedom because such is the creative, innovative spirit of man. As I have suggested man, like all animals, needs and must organise security. Unlike other animals he is capable of infinite experimentation and is driven by a creative need for self-expression. However they contrive their security, people seek always to express themselves by experimenting with their own social arrangements. This is why I believe so passionately that each society must draw from the concepts of social responsibility which are suggested by socialism, the ideas of participation in decision-making to which we are invited by democracy and the insistence upon equality which is fundamental to the thinking of both. Those sections of the union movement which are incapable of thinking in these terms will find themselves swept aside. It is my faith that at least the part of the union movement with which I was associated for over twenty years, if not the whole movement, will prove equal to the challenge that was implicit on the first day of the first strike at Frome Estate in 1938. It is my confident expectation that the movement will once again emerge from its present somewhat uncertain conservatism to the repossession of its rightful place in the vanguard of Jamaican progress.

Human progress is often defined in terms of the workers' experience because throughout history it is the worker who has been at the bottom of the pile. In the Jamaican experience they have come a long way, but the rest of the journey remains to be travelled. In its present state of internal division and competitive pre-occupation, the union movement is in no state to attempt the final assault. Therefore, unification may have to precede its fullest participation in the adventure to which it is invited by history. One thing is certain. Jamaica will never be a true society of equality until the journey is undertaken.

AFTERWORD

By 1974 the government which we formed in 1972 had passed the Termination of Employment Act which replaced the Master and Servants Act of 1838. The new law conferred a measure of job security upon workers who did not enjoy the protection of union contracts. In the same year the Labour Relations Act made the recognition of trade unions compulsory and required employers to bargain in good faith.

History has since favoured us with five new opportunities to further the causes which are adumbrated in the final chapter of this book.

Firstly, we have passed a new national minimum wage law which establishes an advisory commission on wages. This body sets minimum wages and maximum hours which govern all contracts of employment and reviews these national standards from time to time. This provides a measure of protection and enforcement of social justice in areas that the unions have never been able to touch.

Secondly, we are introducing a law guaranteeing year round employment to the forty thousand sugar and cane farm workers. For one hundred and thirty-seven years some half of this group have only been able to work for half of each year, hustling to survive for the rest of the time. The new law enables the 'crop workers' as the seasonal groups are called, to register when the reaping periods ends in mid-year. They are guaranteed employment or a portion of their regular wages throughout the rest of the year.

Thirdly, we are setting aside part of the proceeds from the sale of sugar to finance housing for sugar workers. This is organised under the Sugar Industry Authority which governs the industry and which is planning the operation in co-operation with the unions. This is a good example of co-operative action, putting the earnings of industry to work through savings for the benefit of the workers in the industry.

If the sums involved, running to millions of dollars, had been paid out as part of direct wage increases, the workers would have been unlikely to achieve the same results since each would have had to act individually.

Fourthly, having reacquired considerable areas of sugar lands from the British Tate and Lyle and American United Fruit Company groups, we are organising worker co-operatives to own and farm these lands. The new owners are the regular workers who used to cut and load the cane, weed the grass and spread the fertiliser. They work the land and share the proceeds communally. Meantime, they co-operate in building themselves houses with government help so that their new-found economic status can be reflected in that most basic of all human needs: a home.

Finally, we are conducting our first national experiments in worker participation in ownership and decision-making. We have nationalised our major public utility companies. Acting through the National Bauxite Commission, we now own 51% of Kaiser Bauxite Company and Reynolds Mines in Jamaica. Similar action will follow with the other companies. These are providing the major opportunities, and we are grateful that history gave us the chance.

INDEX